GUARDING
HITLER

To Fang Fang,

with love

GUARDING HITLER

The Secret World of the Führer

MARK FELTON

Pen & Sword
MILITARY

First published in Great Britain in 2014 by
PEN & SWORD MILITARY
an imprint of
Pen & Sword Books Ltd
47 Church Street
Barnsley
South Yorkshire
S70 2AS

Copyright © Mark Felton, 2014

ISBN 978-1-78159-305-9

Typeset by Concept, Huddersfield, West Yorkshire, HD4 5JL.
Printed and bound in England by CPI Group (UK) Ltd, Croydon CR0 4YY.

Pen & Sword Books Ltd incorporates the imprints of Pen & Sword Archaeology,
Atlas, Aviation, Battleground, Discovery, Family History, History, Maritime,
Military, Naval, Politics, Railways, Select, Social History, Transport, True Crime,
and Claymore Press, Frontline Books, Leo Cooper, Praetorian Press,
Remember When, Seaforth Publishing and Wharncliffe.

For a complete list of Pen & Sword titles please contact
PEN & SWORD BOOKS LIMITED
47 Church Street, Barnsley, South Yorkshire, S70 2AS, England
E-mail: enquiries@pen-and-sword.co.uk
Website: www.pen-and-sword.co.uk

Contents

List of Plates

Acknowledgements

I would like to acknowledge the kind assistance of the staff at the following institutions and individuals who were of invaluable assistance during the researching and the writing of this book: The British Library, London; Bundesarchiv, Abteilung Militärarchiv, Freiburg; The Imperial War Museum, London; The National Archives (Public Record Office) Kew; The National Army Museum, London; Shirley Felton; Brigadier Henry Wilson, Matt Jones and the staff at Pen & Sword Books; my editor Barnaby Blacker, and a special thank you to my wife Fang Fang.

Introduction

Hitler's body lay inside a shallow shell crater in the Reich Chancellery garden. It was wrapped in a grey army blanket. Only the *Führer*'s black trousers and black lace-up shoes protruded from the blanket. Beside his body was that of his wife of just forty hours, Eva. A group of SS officers, their field grey uniforms dusty and stained, stood close by, sheltering inside the *Führerbunker*'s emergency exit, a single thick green steel blast door. The garden was a churned up mess of fire blackened trees, broken statuary and craters, the once elegant Reich Chancellery buildings behind windowless and smoke blackened, with great gaping holes in its roof from Allied bombs and Soviet shells. In the distance the crump of artillery rumbled like thunder, while closer by the sudden burp of machine gun fire or the bark of rifles echoed off the surrounding buildings. The men standing by the bunker exit hardly noticed.

Around the crater were several empty army petrol cans. The stench of gasoline was very strong, the bodies both soaked with petrol and lying in a small puddle of fuel. One man stepped forward from the group, a short, heavyset man in a grey nondescript uniform, his receding black hair slicked back from his thuggish face. Martin Bormann, Hitler's secretary and one of the most powerful men in Nazi Germany, quickly lit the thick twist of papers that had been fashioned into an impromptu torch and flung it into the hole. The petrol ignited with a loud whoosh, orange and yellow flames shooting skyward before they died back a little and began to consume the blankets and the corpses beneath. The small group of Nazis came swiftly to attention, their right arms shooting out one last time in the 'German salute'. Hitler's loyal valet Heinz Linge stood beside the club-footed Dr. Goebbels, Hitler's brilliant propaganda minister, while the *Führer*'s tall SS adjutant Otto Günsche betrayed no emotion, his face like granite beneath his field grey cap with its death's head badge. Erich Kempka, Hitler's driver since the mid-1930s, stood with them – he and his men had brought the petrol to consume 'the Boss'.

For three men present, the Viking funeral for their leader was their final act. They were men who had devoted their lives to protecting Hitler, his senior bodyguards. Now they would ensure that the Soviets would not find Hitler's body. For the rest of the day these most loyal men of all, whose own fates had been so inextricably interwoven with the fate of the man they guarded, would tend to the task of reducing their leader's mortal remains to a tangled mass of burnt flesh and bone. Where once they had guarded the world's most famous man, travelling the length and breadth of Europe as Hitler's power bestrode the continent like some great octopus, now they stood silent beside a muddy hole in the ground beside the shattered remains of the Thousand Year Reich. Their futures looked grim. Berlin was surrounded and they were marked men. Suddenly the air was rent by the whistle of incoming shells – quickly the little group of mourners piled through the open bunker exit door, which was slammed firmly shut behind them by more of the *Führer*'s elite bodyguards who were in full battle kit with steel helmets and MP44 assault rifles. The group descended once more beneath the earth, into the damp and fetid underworld of the *Führerbunker*, the last funk hole of Nazism.

Hitler's end was remarkable for one fact: his bodyguards remained absolutely loyal to him during the final days of his life, when his power was at an end, and even long enough after his death to ensure that his body was disposed of properly. This loyalty was borne not from financial gain but of professionalism and adoration. The men who staffed Hitler's bodyguard units were pioneers in the field of personal protection. The senior officers who founded and commanded Hitler's close protection details effectively wrote the book on modern VIP body guarding techniques. And this was because Hitler himself evolved a completely new type of leadership style.

He was the first politician to combine different forms of travel, using aircraft, trains and cars, and the first world leader to use multiple homes and headquarters complexes, all requiring differing types of protection to match particular circumstances. He was unusual among twentieth century leaders in actually going to war fronts and placing himself in harm's way on several occasions. In fact, Hitler's security needs, and the needs of his inner circle of Nazi paladins, required multiple bodyguard units drawn not only from the SS but also from the army and the police.

The *Führer*'s bodyguards were probably the first such units to conduct threat assessments, keep complex files on suspects, and carefully guard routes and venues. They were the first to use modern tech-nology to protect their asset, including X-ray machines and 'bomb-proof' materials. Hitler was easily the world's most carefully guarded man, particularly during the latter half of the war, and in this regard we can see a lot of the methods pioneered by the *Führer*'s close pro-tection details in the techniques used by today's US Secret Service in its guarding of American presidents and Congressional leaders. Armoured limousines, guarded routes, high-tech gadgets, the mon-itoring of potential threats, and special VIP aircraft all originated with Hitler's protection. But no American president has ever been the subject of so many assassination attempts. The figures vary, but it is believed that during his lifetime over forty separate attempts were made to kill Hitler by both individuals and groups. Some, like the 1944 July Bomb Plot, came very close to succeeding. But Hitler's security was virtually impenetrable and extremely professional, and through a combination of his bodyguards' vigilance and his own almost unearthly luck, the *Führer* survived every single attempt on his life.

As the bodyguards stood before the shell crater and watched the man they had guarded for almost twenty years slowly burn on 30 May 1945 their duty was at an end. They had shielded Hitler from his enemies so successfully that in the end the person that killed Hitler was himself. Much of the misery inflicted by the Nazis upon humanity was caused by Hitler's elite bodyguards, for on countless occasions the *Führer* was destined to be struck down by bomb or bullet but had miraculously survived every attempt. Now these selfsame body-guards who had kept the tyrant alive long enough to destroy Germany and much of Europe would themselves face their own judgment, trapped in a burning city that was about to be conquered.

Chapter 1

Time of Struggle

*'Like a nursery gardener trying to reproduce a good old strain which has
been adulterated and debased, we started from the principles of plant
selection and then proceeded quite unashamedly to weed out the men
whom we did not think we could use for the build-up of the SS.'*
(Reichsführer-SS Heinrich Himmler, 1933)

The long column of chanting men slowly wound its way through
Munich's Odeonsplatz during the afternoon of 9 November 1923.
Hundreds were dressed in the drab brown uniforms of the *Sturmabteilung* (SA), the Nazis' quasi-military bullyboys, while others wore
a motley collection of First World War steel helmets or uniforms. Red
party armbands were worn by virtually everyone, while large swastika flags were carried by standard bearers, adding an almost festive
splash of colour to the drab grey streets through which the angry
young marchers tramped. A few open trucks and cars joined the
throng while hundreds of Bavarians watched the procession. It was a
revolution, a *putsch*, and an attempt by the National Socialist German
Worker's Party, formed four years before by a group of disgruntled
right-wingers, to overthrow the city government and take control of
Bavaria. It was supposed to be the first stage in the Nazis' seizure of
power, the beginning of a grand march on Berlin aping Benito Mussolini's March on Rome the year before. But it was all going wrong.

Marching at the head of the column, flanked by his lieutenants and
bodyguards, was 34-year-old Adolf Hitler, the controversial leader
of the NSDAP and the man who had started the revolution. Earlier, at
the Burgerbraukeller beer hall, Hitler had interrupted a meeting of
the local city leaders and had taken the civil leader, army commander
and police commissioner hostage. After whipping up the huge crowd,
orders had been sent out for his Nazi supporters to seize important
buildings in the city. But mistakes had been made and the plot had
begun to unravel. In a last desperate gamble to prevent the putsch
from failing Hitler had led his followers in a march … but to where
no-one really knew.

Hitler was counting on a last show of strength and unity to over-throw the elected government, but the march was a desperate move. Blocking his path were 100 *Reichswehr* soldiers and policeman. Many in the Nazi column were openly carrying rifles and pistols. Faced with the order to halt, Hitler encouraged his followers on, marching straight for the line of grey uniformed troops who were kneeling on the ground, their Mauser rifles pointed directly at the head of the column. Hitler did not believe that German soldiers would fire on him. But he was wrong. The officer in command shouted one word above the Nazis' chanting: 'Fire!' In a few murderous minutes of mayhem four policemen fell dead while sixteen Nazis were killed. The man next to Hitler was killed instantly while others in the front row fell wounded onto the pavement, screaming in agony. It seemed as if Hitler, the other leaders and the Nazi movement were finished. Not for the first time during his inexorable rise from beer hall agitator to political leader was Hitler in the gun sights of his enemies and not for the first time was he saved from almost certain death by his bodyguards.

Hitler was a target for assassins long before he became German chan-cellor in January 1933. Mired in rough street politics, his extreme views made him a target for assassination from the earliest days of the National Socialist movement. Hitler therefore required protection virtually from the first. In the beginning his bodyguards were no more than enthusiastic thugs, but Hitler's personal protection would slowly evolve through the 1920s and early 1930s from its street fighting origins into the prototype multi-layered security that is so familiar to any-one who has seen an American president interacting with his public. In the same way that Nazi propaganda chief Dr. Josef Goebbels invented the mass political rally, Hitler's extreme security needs created modern presidential and VIP protection.

Guarding Hitler was to prove a challenge, not only because so many people wanted to kill or harm him, but also because Hitler held bizarre views about his protection. Although people took occasional potshots at him during the years of struggle, Hitler remained remarkably unfazed by this potentially lethal attention. This apparent insouciance in the face of mortal peril ran deeper than his being a grizzled veteran of the horrific trench warfare of the First World War. Hitler was notori-ously difficult to guard because he held a very contradictory view of his own life. He believed himself to be a great 'man of destiny' yet at the same time thought that his time on earth was limited.

Hitler was not particularly fazed by dangerous situations – he had proved his physical bravery during four years service in the front lines between 1914 and 1918. Hitler was a regimental runner, a position that held him back from the very worst of the trench fighting, but still exposed him to artillery barrages and occasionally to machine gun and rifle fire. During the Battle of the Somme in October 1916 shrapnel wounded him in his left thigh when a British shell exploded inside the runners' dugout. Hospitalised for two months, Hitler was decorated with the Wound Badge in Black. He had already been awarded the Iron Cross 2nd Class for bravery in 1914. In 1918 Hitler, only a lance corporal, received the prestigious Iron Cross 1st Class, rarely awarded to the lower ranks. He was gassed during a British attack at the end of the war and hospitalised again.[1] There was an element of the reckless in Hitler, and sometimes he would deliberately place himself in danger.

His first association with what would become the Nazi Party was not as a supporter but as an army intelligence agent sent by the *Reichswehr*, Germany's postwar military, to monitor its activities. But Hitler joined the party, left the army when he found the party's message to be genuinely appealing, and was soon elected its leader. Hitler became part of the violent political world of postwar Germany, representing one of many competing ideologies and groups seeking power in the weak Weimar Republic. His style of politics, his ideology and his desire to take power by means of direct action against the state meant that Hitler was often in physical danger. He had to be tough, and the younger *Führer* had no compunction about taking matters into his own hands. At a rowdy meeting in Munich in 1922 'he stormed the speaker's platform and physically attacked the speaker, surrounded by an unfriendly crowd; he was sentenced to three months in jail for this.'[2] This was but one of several occasions when Hitler got violent with his enemies. 'Once, in the Black Forest city of Freiburg, when his car was pelted with stones, he jumped down from the vehicle waving his whip, forcing his astonished attackers to scatter.'[3]

Germany had a long history of political assassinations, a fact that Hitler was fully aware of. During the nineteenth century the 'Iron Chancellor', Prince Otto von Bismarck, had escaped two murderous plots. During the unsettled Weimar Republic era after the First World War German leaders were particularly prone to assassination. One of the most notorious examples was the fate of Matthias Erzberger, the head of the German Armistice Commission charged with signing the hated Treaty of Versailles in 1919. Erzberger argued forcefully that Germany had to accept the humiliation of Versailles or face occupation by Allied forces. But ideological elements on both the Left and the Right were almost pathologically incapable of accepting this position and vented their anger through the medium of political assassination. The first attempt to kill Erzberger was made by the regular German Army in Weimar, but failed. A few days later someone fired shots through Erzberger's office window in Berlin. A grenade was also flung into the hapless negotiator's bedroom. Erzberger was finally killed while hiking in the Black Forest in August 1921.

Foreign Minister Walther Rathenau was shot to death whilst sitting in an open-topped car in Berlin in 1922. Rathenau, wartime chairman of the giant industrial concern AEG, had been given the task of getting the Allied Powers' huge reparation demands modified or reduced. He failed and was killed for it. It didn't help that Rathenau was also a Jew, invoking the hatred of many on the Far Right where anti-Semitism was already on the advance.[4] Hitler and his ilk were already accusing the Jews, particularly those in international finance and business, of being in league with the generals and politicians who had 'stabbed Germany in the back' in 1918 when they surrendered to the Allies. In the search for answers as to why Germany had lost the war, the Jews were becoming convenient scapegoats.

In 1922 a Dresden merchant named Willi Schulze was arrested with two pistols on his person – under police interrogation he stated that he had intended to assassinate Chancellor Joseph Wirth at the Old Reich Chancellery in Berlin. In 1931 someone sent a homemade bomb to Chancellor Heinrich Bruning but his staff intercepted it before it exploded. The following year a woman armed with a large knife managed to infiltrate to the second floor of the Old Reich Chancellery, the main Berlin office and home of the German head of state, before being arrested, a significant and embarrassing security failure.

Altogether, in the particularly tumultuous period of 1919–22, there were 376 political assassinations in Germany. It was almost politics by the gun, grenade and knife, and it was into this milieu that Hitler strode. Between 1919 and Hitler's rise to become Chancellor in 1933, a total of 228 Nazi Party members were killed. The *Führer*'s ascendency was truly a bloody and vicious rise.[5]

Hitler's complex psychology meant that he could be both reckless and a hypochondriac, suffering from a variety of real and imaginary health issues that added greatly to his deeply held feeling that he did not have enough time to achieve his grandiose goals.[6] He was obsessed by assassination and took an almost perverse interest in the finest details of his security apparatus, yet conversely stated that if someone wanted to kill him, there was nothing that could change his ultimate 'fate'. Hitler believed that he would achieve great things before his life ended, and this overweening self-belief made him careless about his physical life. Of course, each time he managed to dodge an assassination attempt, his sense of destiny was further reinforced – he thought it was not his time, and that he was being preserved for a higher purpose.

Roger Moorhouse notes in *Killing Hitler* that the *Führer* 'was fundamentally unconvinced that his bodyguards would actually serve any practical purpose. His belief in 'fate' and 'destiny' caused him to ascribe his continual survival not to the police, but to pure chance.'[7] What to most people appeared to be chance or luck was to Hitler affirmation of his own greatness. And it is indeed remarkable that Hitler managed to survive for so long as he was the target of plot after plot both before and after he assumed the mantle of *Führer*. Few leaders in modern history have attracted so many people bent on killing them – and survived.

It is small wonder that, given the extremely violent times that he inhabited, Hitler realised early on that if he was not to fall victim to assassination, and therefore be prevented from achieving his goals, he needed protection. Hitler said that he required bodyguards who were 'men who would even march against their own brothers.' He was not to be disappointed.

Hitler's first protection detail was a small collection of trusted heavies appointed in 1920. At this time the Nazi Party was simply the German Worker's Party (DAP), and its name was changed in April 1920 by the addition of the words 'National Socialist'. Political meetings in Munich were extremely rowdy and the heavies would violently eject hecklers from mass gatherings when Hitler spoke. Their basic function was to protect Hitler from getting beaten up during his early and often very dangerous public appearances. Their weapons were fists, boots and truncheons. They were known informally as the *Saalschütz Abteilung* (Hall Defence Detachment) under the command of

Emil Maurice, a former watchmaker and *Freikorps* soldier. Maurice, aged 23, had been a personal friend of Hitler's since the year before. The new unit's proper name was *Ordnertruppen* (Order Troop). On 3 August 1921 Hitler refined the unit, now that he had been confirmed as supreme leader of the Nazi Party. In order not to antagonise the Bavarian government Hitler chose the rather innocent sounding title *NSDAP Turn-und Sportabteilung* (Party Gymnastics and Sports Division). It was well-organised, particularly after command was handed to an ex-naval officer, Hans Ulrich Klintzsche, and consisted mainly of ex-soldiers and street fighters.[8] In September 1921 the unit became the *Sturmabteilung* (Storm Division – the SA), but was quickly dubbed the 'Brownshirts' after the colour of their uniforms. Maurice was appointed *Oberster SA-Führer* (Supreme SA Leader).

Throughout the 1920s Hitler's inner circle of bodyguards consisted of only five trusted men: Ulrich Graf, a former wrestler built like a nightclub bouncer who was Hitler's personal protection officer; Emil Maurice, his driver, a job that often necessitated violent evasive manoeuvers; Christian Weber, a rather unsavoury part-time pimp and horse dealer who acted as the *Führer's* private secretary; Julius Schaub who was Hitler's valet; and *SA-Obergruppenführer* (an explanation of SS ranks is found in Appendix 1) Wilhelm Brückner who acted as his adjutant. Brückner was well liked, a former Bavarian army officer and *Freikorps* man who was affable and straightforward.

These men were kept busy. For example, in November 1921 Hitler spoke at a beer hall in Munich to an audience of around 300 heavy drinking supporters and enemies. The audience began arguing among themselves and then throwing beer steins, followed by chairs and eventually fists. During the resulting melee unknown assailants fired several shots at Hitler. His bodyguards, and possibly Hitler himself (who was routinely armed), returned fire with their pistols. No-one was killed but it was a lucky escape for Hitler.[9]

Meanwhile the SA grew in size and influence. Now under the decorated war hero and secret homosexual SA Chief of Staff Ernst Röhm, Hitler's personal security detail was augmented and expanded. In 1923 the SA *Stosstrupp* (Assault Squad) was formed around Hitler's five-man protection team and it would eventually number 100 trusted men.

Another assassination attempt took place in 1923 when Hitler spoke in Thuringia. Shots were fired at him from the crowd. And later when he was driving through Leipzig more shots were fired at his car.

Five *Stosstruppen* were killed during the abortive Beer Hall Putsch in Munich in November 1923 when Hitler disastrously attempted to seize power in Bavaria by force from the Weimar government. This was the moment when Hitler had come closest to being killed – ironically not by political opponents but by professional soldiers, a situation that was to be repeated several times during the Second World War. The Beer Hall Putsch was a defining moment in the history of the Nazi Party and also of Hitler's personal security. Marching at the head of 2,000 SA and other Nazi supporters, Hitler was in the front row along-side First World War hero *General der Infanterie* Erich Ludendorff when 100 *Reichswehr* and police opened fire outside the Feldherrnhalle (Field Marshal's Hall), a monumental loggia in the Odeonsplatz. The Feldherrnhalle was built in 1841–44 at the behest of King Ludwig I as a symbol of the honours of the Bavarian Army. The initial volley cut down several top Nazis, including Hermann Göring who was shot through the thigh. Hitler's bodyguard Ulrich Graf actually dislocated the *Führer*'s shoulder as he tried to protect him from the gunfire, dragging him violently down to the pavement. In total, sixteen Nazis died, including five of Hitler's protection team. Hitler fled the scene by car and was arrested two days later.

Hitler was jailed for his role in the Putsch, imprisoned alongside Rudolf Hess and Emil Maurice, both men helping him to prepare his famous book *Mein Kampf*. When Hitler was released from Landsberg Prison in 1925 both the Nazi Party and the SA, dissolved in 1923, were rapidly recreated. Maurice was appointed commander of the newly formed *Stabswache*. From the rebirth of Nazism emerged an entirely new and sinister organisation that was charged with protecting Hitler. The *Stabswache* was renamed the *Schutzstaffel* (Protection Squad), and this was the moment the infamous SS was born. Eventually the SS would entirely supplant the power of the SA.

Its first commander was 28-year-old Julius Schreck, a close friend of Hitler and a fellow First World War and *Freikorps* veteran. Schreck had also been imprisoned at Landsberg alongside Hitler and the other Nazi leaders in 1923–25. Emil Maurice, holding SS membership No. 2, was appointed Hitler's full-time driver, but only until he was abruptly sacked by the *Führer* for having an affair with Hitler's niece, Geli Raubal.

The SS would remain part of the SA for a long time. When formed in 1925, the SS consisted of a single, thirty-man company of bodyguards.

In September 1925 all local Nazi Party offices were ordered to create ten-man bodyguard units from among their most promising SA storm troopers. The next year six *SS-Gaus* were established, supporting all such units. They answered directly to the *SS-Oberleitung* or headquarters unit commanded by Schreck. Schreck in turn took his orders from the office of the Supreme SA Leader Franz Pfeffer von Salomon.

In 1926 Schreck stood down as *Reichsführer-SS*, being replaced by former junior army officer Joseph Berchtold. Schreck later became an *SS-Standartenführer* and continued to serve Hitler as his personal driver following Maurice's sacking for many years until his sudden death in 1936 from meningitis.

In 1927 *Reichsführer-SS* Erhard Heiden replaced Berchtold. Before 1929 the SS wore brown SA uniforms but with black ties and a black kepi adorned with the silver death's head skull and bones symbol borrowed from earlier Imperial cavalry uniforms. It was a miniscule organisation in comparison with the now 3,000,000-strong SA from which it recruited its members, but it was an organisation that owed its allegiance not to the Nazi Party but to the body and person of Hitler, and Hitler alone. The SS was the new Praetorian Guard and its men were the brightest and best that the SA had to offer, men whose loyalty to Hitler was sacred. Unlike the SA, a mostly working class organisation, many SS men came from the middle classes. Their motto, engraved on their silver belt buckles, was '*Meine Ehre heisst Treue*' ('My Honour is Loyalty'), and this was taken quite literally.

In 1929 the leadership of the SS changed when a 29-year-old, bespectacled Bavarian chicken farmer and former Imperial Army officer cadet took over – Heinrich Himmler. His loyalty to Hitler was pathological – he once said: 'If Hitler were to say I should shoot my mother I would do it and be proud of his confidence.' With men such as Himmler at his disposal, Hitler's protection underwent a revolution, evolving from a rough gang of street toughs and bruisers into a professional organisation that quickly gained both numbers and responsibilities.

Himmler changed the look of the SS to differentiate it from the SA. The SS uniform now incorporated black breeches, black boots and belts and black edges to the Nazi armband. In 1932 the organisation adopted a completely new all-black uniform. Although still a tiny organisation, the SS was nonetheless quickly gaining Hitler's trust and Himmler was building up and expanding his power base.

Before 1933 the threats to Hitler's life and person came from three general sources. Firstly there were the loners or mentally unbalanced people that all public figures have to contend with. Such persons were very difficult to identify until they actually made a move to carry out their plans, and Hitler was to survive several such attempts. This category of would-be assassin may have been mentally unbalanced, but some undoubtedly realised the truth, that the *Führer* was a great threat to Germany and the world at large. Members of this category could be called, to borrow a term from 1960s America, the 'lone gunman' or 'lone nut'. Loners made numerous attempts. For example, at the Hotel Kaiserhof in Berlin in 1932 an unknown assailant poisoned Hitler's food, though the attempt was foiled before the *Führer* took a bite. On 15 March of the same year someone fired several shots at the train Hitler was travelling on between Munich and Weimar, again without causing any injuries.[10] Such plots became more commonplace after Hitler's seizure of power in 1933.

The second group in opposition to Hitler could be broadly labelled 'The Left'. Socialists and Communists hated Hitler and the Nazis, and knew what would happen to them if Hitler ever gained power. But the Left was remarkably disorganised. The Socialists clung on to a belief in the democratic process and viewed political assassination as anathema, a position also later adopted during the war by the Western Allies until quite late in the conflict. The Communists took their orders from Moscow, which directed their best efforts against their ideological cousins the Socialists rather than against the Nazis. In spite of the political situation, some on the Left did manage to make attempts on Hitler's life.

The third, and potentially the most dangerous, group can be collectively termed 'The Right'. In 1931 this took the form of the SA. Leader of the SA, Ernst Röhm, frightened many Germans, particularly the *Reichswehr* general staff and prominent industrialists, when he constantly alluded to the SA replacing the regular army and creating a true socialist state. The SA numbered 3,000,000 while the Treaty of Versailles had limited the regular army to just 100,000 men. Generals and industrialists made representations to Hitler to curb Röhm's power, but Hitler initially was reluctant to move against the very people who had done so much to put him into power. Other Nazi leaders wanted the SA leadership smashed, chief among them Hermann Göring and Heinrich Himmler.

By 1931 the SA was starting to become a threat to Hitler's authority. A revolt against Hitler and the party organization by the SA under its deputy commander Walther Stennes was brought under control by Goebbels and Göring, and in 1933 an armed man dressed in SA uniform actually got inside Hitler's private Bavarian house, the Berghof on the Obersalzberg, but was speedily arrested by SS guards.

Hitler eventually moved against Röhm when Göring and Himmler fed a fabricated plot to him. This suggested that the SA was planning to depose Hitler as *Führer*. Hitler ordered the SA leadership to meet at the Hanselbauer Hotel at Bad Wiessee on 10 June 1934. Hitler, accompanied by his SS bodyguards, stormed into the hotel and placed the leaders under arrest. Elsewhere in Germany SA leaders were simply shot. Hitler initially reprieved Röhm because of his vital role in the early days of the movement but under pressure from Göring and Himmler, Hitler changed his mind. Röhm was offered suicide, but refused so two SS officers shot him to death in his cell. Altogether, upwards of 200 senior SA leaders were murdered in the purge and the Brownshirts brought severely to heel.[11] 'The Night of the Long Knives', when Hitler used his SS bodyguards to smash the power of the SA, was the event that would establish the SS as the new power in Germany.

After this, Himmler and his black knights were in the ascendant. The SA was severely reduced in numbers and although it survived until 1945, it was sidelined and most of its personnel drafted into the armed forces.

The focus of Nazi power in Germany in the early days was Munich not Berlin, which also became the spiritual home of the party until the end of the war. Munich was also the site of two important Nazi buildings. The first was the *Braunhaus* (Brown House), the headquarters of the NSDAP and named for the colour of SA uniforms. The building, a large, handsome three-storey house built in 1828 on Brienner Street was originally English-owned. Called Barlow Palace after the family of English wholesale merchants who built it, the Nazis acquired the property from the Barlows in 1930 after they had outgrown their original headquarters building. The palace was extensively remodelled, some of the work personally directed by Hitler, and paid for by the wealthy Fritz Thyssen. The Brown House was where the *Bludfahne* (Blood flag) was kept. During the Beer Hall Putsch the blood of Nazis shot by *Reichswehr* troops outside the Feldherrnhalle splashed onto this particular swastika flag and it had come to be revered as a holy relic. It was paraded each year on the anniversary of the Putsch. The Brown House contained Hitler's party office, as well as the offices of Hess, Himmler, Göring, Minister of Justice for Bavaria and Hitler's personal lawyer Dr. Hans Frank and Philipp Bouhler, Chief of the Chancellery of the *Führer*.

The second important Nazi building in Munich was Hitler's private apartment. Although Hitler had lived at several different addresses in the city since the First World War he eventually moved into a luxury apartment on Prinzregentenplatz, a large building that now houses the regional police headquarters. It was here that Hitler would live with his half-niece Geli Raubal and where he entertained British Prime Minister Neville Chamberlain during the 1938 Munich Crisis. For his protection, the SS had the building's basement transformed into a rein-forced air raid shelter equipped with metal bunker doors.[12] Himmler soon determined that the SS should assume full responsibility for protecting the new chancellor, and that would include not only at his office and apartment in Munich, but everywhere the *Führer* went. On assuming the political leadership of Germany Hitler's protection was no longer simply a Nazi Party matter, it was a national concern and the fledgling SS was still not powerful enough to circumvent or replace the established offices of state security.

Chapter 2

Ein Reich, Ein Volk, Ein Führer!

'I swear to you, Adolf Hitler, as Führer and Chancellor of the German
Reich, loyalty and bravery. I vow to you and to my superiors designated
by you obedience to the death. So help me God.'

(RSD Oath)

The Berghof, Hitler's private house in the Bavarian Alps, overlooking
his birthplace of Austria, was a rural idyll. One summer's day a man
passed through the entrance gate, which was carefully guarded by
hard-looking SS men in field grey uniforms and armed with automatic
pistols, and approached the large Alpine chalet-style building set on a
wooded incline above the approach road. The visitor, a man named
Kraus, had been granted the honour of personally delivering a petition
into the *Führer's* hands. He was dressed in the brown uniform and
kepi of the SA. Escorted into Hitler's presence, he stood to attention
and stared into the 46-year-old *Führer's* piercing grey eyes. Aides and
bodyguards stood close by. Kraus handed the petition to Hitler, the
Führer shaking his hand and muttering a few noncommittal words of
encouragement. Suddenly, Kraus reached into his pocket and pulled
out a pistol, pointed it in Hitler's direction and pulled the trigger. The
bullet cleaved the air close to Hitler but missed. Before the sound of
Kraus' shot had finished echoing off the wooden walls Hitler's bodyguards had cut the assassin down with a hail of lead from their own
weapons, killing the SA man instantly.[1]

The *Führer's* Irish sister-in-law, Bridget Hitler, first told this story.
She said it happened in 1935, just two years into Hitler's leadership of
Germany and a year after he had ordered the SA senior officers to be
liquidated during The Night of the Long Knives. Some believe that
Kraus came the closest of all Hitler's would-be assassins to actually
killing him. If the story is true, Kraus joins a very long list of men who
for a multitude of reasons decided that Hitler, now Chancellor of
Germany, must die. Many came almost as close as Kraus. It was up to
Hitler's constantly evolving security apparatus to prevent any of them

from succeeding. Guarding the world's most hated man was one of the busiest personal protection details in history.

On Hitler's assumption of the leadership of Germany in January 1933, his new home was the Old Reich Chancellery in Berlin, which was both the seat of government and his official residence for entertaining and impressing foreign heads of state and other dignitaries.

The Old Reich Chancellery was originally the Rococo-style city palace of the enormously wealthy Prince Antoni Radziwill, who died in 1833. The palace, which dominated the Wilhelmstrasse in Berlin's government quarter, was acquired by the newly unified German state in 1871 and its first inhabitant was the 'Iron Chancellor', Otto von Bismarck.[2] It was in this building, in Reich President Paul von Hindenburg's office, that Hitler was appointed chancellor.

The building was significantly enlarged in 1930 and once Hitler took up residence further extension was completed by 1935. Hitler's private apartments were redesigned and a large reception hall cum ballroom added, as well as a large conservatory known at the *Wintergarten*. The conservatory connected with a large cellar that was reinforced and became known as the Reich Chancellery Air Raid Shelter in 1936, later renamed the *Vorbunker* when Hitler's *Führerbunker* was constructed deep beneath it.

The Old Reich Chancellery's main entrance was on the Wilhelmstrasse. Gaining access to the Old Reich Chancellery before 1935 was not particularly difficult as in the beginning the complex was only lightly guarded, despite assassination attempts on previous chancellors and ministers during the Weimar period. A police sentry at the main street entrance who watched strangers carefully but did not actually check identification documents guarded Hitler's private apartments. This was done inside at the receptionist's desk. A second guarded gate gave access to the inner courtyard and Hitler's private apartments. The police officer at the second gate could not see the main entrance, so visitors and deliverymen were issued with metal tags to present to this guard before entering Hitler's private world. The gap in security was obvious, and a determined assassin could probably have overcome two policemen and a male receptionist to get at Hitler. The policemen were drawn from Berlin's 16th Police Precinct and were under the command of *Hauptmann* Koplien. There was a third security post located at the main vehicle entrance gate, where a policeman checked the identity documents of drivers and their passengers before permitting them entry. A single armed guard drawn from the *Leibstandarte SS 'Adolf Hitler'* (SS Lifeguard Regiment 'Adolf Hitler' or LSSAH) assisted him. This gate was kept locked between 9.00pm and 7.00am.

The wider Reich Chancellery complex was guarded by other Army, SS and police guards drawn from several different units and as time went on the security measures and the depth of protection for the head of state was steadily increased. The SS, in line with their increasing power in the Nazi state, also became more visible at the Reich Chancellery.

The LSSAH were the epitome of the Nazi ideal of the Aryan warrior. Tall, healthy and National Socialist, membership was exclusive and the selection process rigorous. All candidates had to prove Aryan ancestry back to 1750. The symbol of the *Totenkopf* (Death's Head) was chosen because of its association with older elite formations of the Kingdom of Prussia and later German Empire.

By March 1933 the SS had grown from 280 to 50,000 men. It was decided to form a new bodyguard unit to protect Hitler, the men mostly drawn from the *1st SS-Standarte* in Munich. Its new commander, a former army sergeant major named Sepp Dietrich, selected 117 men to form *SS-Stabswache Berlin*. Many of the 117 originals went on to spectacular careers during the war, three becoming divisional commanders and eight winning the Knight's Cross, Germany's highest gallantry award. Two training units were also formed, *SS-Sonderkommando Zossen* and *SS-Sonderkommando Jüterbog*. In September 1933 the three units were amalgamated into one and at a ceremony in November outside the Feldherrnhalle in Munich, a holy place in Nazi ideology because of the bloody events of the Beer Hall Putsch in 1923, the unit swore a personal oath of allegiance to Hitler and received the title – *Leibstandarte Adolf Hitler*. In April 1934 Himmler changed the unit name to *Leibstandarte-SS Adolf Hitler* to clearly differentiate the troops from the SA and the *Reichswehr*.

The LSSAH provided several sentries at the Old Reich Chancellery, who dressed in full black SS uniforms, red Nazi Party armbands and black steel helmets that were an intentionally intimidating sight. When the *Führer* was in residence the LSSAH mounted a 'long guard' consisting of one officer, three NCOs and thirty-nine men. When Hitler was elsewhere the guard was reduced to three NCOs and thirty-three men. They were on constant patrol armed with either automatic pistols or Mauser Karabiner 98K rifles. Four static guard posts were manned outside the Adjutant's Office, kitchen anteroom, garden front and garage entrance on Hermann-Göring-Strasse.

In 1932 Sepp Dietrich had also been ordered to create a permanent close protection group for Hitler during the crucial year the *Führer* spent campaigning for the Reichstag. Dietrich created the *SS-Begleit Kommando Des Führers* (SS Escort Command of the Leader), consisting of twelve ruthless and coldly efficient SS officers. Dressed in black uniforms and red party armbands, they accompanied Hitler everywhere. Later in the war they reverted to a standard field grey SS uniform with a special cuff band.

On 15 March 1933 Himmler, keen to place his men as close to Hitler as possible, founded a new unit that was also tasked with protecting the *Führer*. Called the *Führer Schutz Kommando* (*Führer* Protection Command or FSK), its commander was 35-year-old *SS-Standartenführer* Johann Rattenhuber. A Bavarian, Rattenhuber was a former policeman and First World War infantryman and would remain at Hitler's side until the very end. He only joined the Nazi Party *after* he was appointed to lead the FSK, his police skills being more important than his ideology. His deputy, *SS-Obersturmführer* Peter Högl had worked as a miller in Bavaria before the Great War, joined the army in 1916 and served on the Western Front rising to the rank of corporal. In 1919 he had joined the Bavarian Police, transferring to the criminal police in 1932 before joining the SS and being appointed to the FSK. Högl was one of several men in Hitler's inner circle who would remain with the *Führer* from just after the Nazi seizure of power until the bitter end in the Berlin Bunker in 1945.

From the moment Hitler moved into the Old Reich Chancellery he was a target. On 4 March 1933, shortly after Hitler had assumed the chancellorship, police in Königsberg uncovered a bomb plot against him. A local communist group led by Kurt Lutter, a ship's carpenter, held two meetings to plan planting a bomb in the speaker's dais when Hitler visited the city. As Hitler delivered his speech the bomb would be detonated. Unbeknown to Lutter and his co-conspirators one of their number was a police informer. The group was arrested and interrogated, but the police never found a bomb and none of the group confessed. Faced with no evidence, Lutter and his friends were released a few months later.[3]

Anti-Hitler organisations and groups developed throughout many levels of German society, even within the Nazi Party itself. Otto Strasser, a senior Nazi ideologue who had been ejected from the party by Hitler, led the Black Front, a Nazi organisation numbering 5,000 members by January 1933. Strasser hated Hitler, not least because his elder brother Gregor, a prominent SA leader, had been murdered during the Night of the Long Knives. He was the brains behind a plot to kill Hitler with a suitcase bomb at the party headquarters in Nuremberg in 1936. He recruited a young German Jewish student named Helmut Hirsch who was studying in Prague to carry out the task, but Hirsch was arrested at the German frontier and later executed. Strasser himself fled to Czechoslovakia and later to Canada.

In 1935, two years into Hitler's chancellorship, a Communist conspiracy, based in Vienna planned to assassinate Hitler. The group also planned to eliminate the Minister for War, non-Nazi *Generalfeldmarschall* Werner von Blomberg (ironically soon to be removed by Hitler himself following a manufactured sex scandal), Dr Joseph Goebbels, Nazi propaganda minister, Hermann Göring, creator of the concentration camps, and Deputy *Führer* Rudolf Hess, but the plot eventually came to nothing.

The FSK was mainly composed of former Bavarian police officers and was initially intended to protect Hitler whilst he was within the state of Bavaria, the 'birthplace' of Nazism. Bavaria was Himmler's realm. In 1934 the FSK replaced the *SS-Begleitkommando des Führers*, providing all of Hitler's personal security throughout Germany. In the beginning the FSK had been forced to guard Hitler at a distance, the *SS-Begleitkommando des Führers* being the only agency that Hitler permitted near him. One spring day in 1933 in Munich Hitler noticed a strange car following his own and his *SS-Begleitkommando* bodyguards' car. He ordered his driver, Erich Kempka, to speed up and lose the tail. Only later did he discover that the mystery car was full of FSK men.[4] This incident highlighted the sometimes farcical nature of Hitler's security in the early days.

The Nazi regime was notorious for its duplication of official positions and offices. Hitler believed in the theory of 'divide and rule', and he maintained his pre-eminent position of *Führer* by encouraging his subordinates to expend their energies fighting amongst themselves rather than contemplating replacing him. Nazi bureaucracy was highly inefficient precisely because of this duplication of roles and respon-sibilities, and when it came to Hitler's personal security the story is quite confusing. No single agency was solely responsible for guarding the *Führer* – instead, over time several different agencies developed, causing Hitler to have simultaneous layers of security often perform-ing overlapping or complementary functions.

An attempt was made in February 1935 to clearly understand who was guarding Hitler and whether some of these organisations should be merged or replaced. The FSK guard unit that looked after Hitler numbered eighteen men, headquartered in Berlin. Hitler was also guarded by four criminal police officers and four gendarmes from the Berlin Police, as well as thirty-one members of the LSSAH, the black uniformed, steel-helmeted sentries from Hitler's personal lifeguard regiment. The FSK also guarded Göring, Hess, Goebbels and Himmler, while other branches dealt with administration, combatting assassina-tion plots, protecting other Reich ministers when travelling, and also providing security for visiting foreign dignitaries. A total of seventy-six personnel performed these tasks.

On 1 August 1935 the FSK was renamed the *Reichssicherheitsdienst* (RSD – Reich Security Service). The early composition of the RSD reflected the multiplicity of interested organisations protecting the German head of state. A resolution in 1936 drawn up by the *Wehrmacht* High Command (OKW), the organisation that ran the armed forces, stipulated that all RSD members had to be *Wehrmacht* officers, but holding extra jurisdictional powers and privileges. This unit was formally the *Reichssicherheitsdienst Gruppe Geheime Feldpolizei z.b.V.* (the secret special purpose security field police service), effectively a collec-tion of army military police officers who wore SS uniform. The com-plex nature of the organisation meant that although they were part of the regular *Wehrmacht*, RSD personnel were technically also on *Reichsführer-SS* Himmler's personal staff. 'At first they wore black SS uniforms, but on the outbreak of war the whole SD changed to field grey. When serving in the Chancellery they carried 7.65mm Walther PPK automatic pistols and flashlights.'[5] They wore an 'SD' sleeve diamond on their left cuffs. Following SS doctrine, all members had to be of pure German descent.

In 1937, in a further consolidation of Himmler's power over the organisation, all RSD officers were fully inducted into the mainstream SS, breaking the link with the regular army and politicizing Hitler's personal protection provided by the state.

The RSD's orders came directly from Hitler via three of his closest subordinates: *SA-Obergruppenführer* Wilhelm Brückner, Martin Bormann or Julius Schaub. Of the three, Bormann was the major block preventing Himmler from assuming complete control. *Reichsführer-SS* Himmler was the official head of the RSD, with Rattenhuber and Högl running the day-to-day operations. Bormann was Chief of Staff to Deputy *Führer* Rudolf Hess until the latter's controversial flight to Scotland in May 1941. In August 1938 the scheming Bormann had been declared a member of Hitler's permanent entourage and he steadily expanded his influence until he controlled most of the Nazi Party organisation and was able to interfere in the operations of most government and military agencies. Two days after Hess fled Germany, Hitler created Bormann Head of the Party Chancellery, then a Reich Minister without Portfolio. He was also Hitler's secretary. Bormann's influence over Hitler's protection would be most particularly felt at the Obersalzberg, Hitler's private village in the Bavarian Alps. Bormann effectively ran the place, controlling access to Hitler, much to the frustration of other Nazi potentates.

In 1940 Bormann was probably behind an argument that led to Brückner being eased out by Julius Schaub from his post as Hitler's chief aide. Brückner joined the *Wehrmacht* and finished the war as a colonel while Schaub stayed with the *Führer* virtually to the end, rising to become an *SS-Obergruppenführer*.

Personal protection for Hitler at the Old Reich Chancellery in Berlin consisted of *SS-Begleitkommando*, RSD, and SD-Chancellery. This last unit was not part of the main *Sichersheitsdienst*, the intelligence agency of the SS and Nazi Party created in 1931 and led by Reinhard Heydrich, but was a special group of experienced police who were personally responsible for the prevention of all criminal acts and dangerous behaviour inside the complex. During the daytime the SD-Chancellery consisted of nine men working in shifts of three.

The *SS* guards were overseen by their own officers who visited several times a day from nearby Lichtefelde Barracks to inspect their men and check that everything was satisfactory. Unfortunately, many of the SS soldiers were very young, and standing on guard being one of the most boring jobs imaginable, some acted in a manner characterised by civil servants working at the Chancellery as 'juvenile'. For example, SS guards were reported for riding up and down in the lifts to pass the time. A complaint was also made that the SS were playing their wireless at full volume with the guardroom windows wide open.[6] Perhaps the most serious accusations concerned the misuse of firearms by SS guards. On several occasions guards accidentally discharged their pistols while playing with them.

The threat of intruders was real enough and often revealed serious security lapses or gaps. On 8 June 1936 guards apprehended two women who had climbed over a wall that separated a neighbouring garden from that of the Reich Chancellery. On 11 June 1937 a more serious security breach occurred when an unemployed salesman who was desperate to see Hitler scaled a construction site fence on Vossstrasse in broad daylight without being seen. He then managed to cross the Chancellery gardens and climbed into the building through an open toilet window. He was armed with a gas pistol but his demeanour alerted an SD guard and he was arrested. An additional LSSAH sentry was placed on the construction site fence.

Just over a month later on 14 February a thirty-three-year-old butcher named Franz Kroll was apprehended inside the Reich Chancellery when he suddenly appeared outside Hitler's private rooms and tried to push past the guards. He had a grievance with the police, and was attempting to appeal directly to his *Führer*.[7]

Even members of the SS could not be completely trusted. In 1937 Hitler addressed a rally at the Sportpalast in Berlin. A disgruntled SS soldier placed a bomb in the speaker's platform and waited for his opportunity. Knowing that Hitler would harangue his audience for several hours, the guard took the opportunity of slipping away to use the toilet. Unfortunately, someone locked the toilet block door while the SS man was still inside, and he was unable to activate the bomb's timer. Hitler was saved on this occasion by the call of nature.[8]

Hitler was dissatisfied with the Old Reich Chancellery, calling it 'fit for a soap company' but not for the headquarters of Nazi Germany and asked his architect, Albert Speer, to design for him a grand new Chancellery to be constructed close by. 'I shall have extremely important conferences in the near future, and I need huge rooms and halls with which I can impress especially the smaller potentates,' said Hitler. 'You can use the entire terrain along Vossstrasse, and I don't care how much it costs.'[9] In the end, Speer spent 90 million Reichsmarks on the project that was completed in 1939, employing 4,000 workers who laboured in shifts twenty-four hours a day. Speer's marshalling of labour and his success in creating the New Reich

Chancellery led Hitler to later appoint him Minister of Armaments, a position that gave him authority over slave labour.

The finished building was very impressive. A huge double gate led through reception halls into a 164-yard-long (150m) gallery. The main entrance was flanked by two huge bronze sculptures by Arno Breker, 'Wehrmacht' (Armed Forces) and 'Partei' (Party). At the end of the gallery, twice as long as the Hall of Mirrors at Versailles, was Hitler's gigantic 400 square metre office that was dominated by a huge over-size desk and a large marble top table. Hitler loved this room and used it often for military conferences in the latter part of the war. Hitler's apartments in the Old Reich Chancellery remained his official residence.

From a security point of view, the new building presented considerable challenges. Between forty and fifty people were free to enter the New Reich Chancellery to have lunch with Hitler if they first telephoned ahead. This group included Gauleiters (provincial governors), Reich leaders, ministers and Albert Speer. No military men were granted such access. The guards personally knew these party men by sight and by reputation.

Two LSSAH sentries armed with rifles guarded the main gate. A policeman checked all IDs. *SS-Begleitkommando* sentries guarded Hitler's office and private quarters. The New Reich Chancellery guard was beefed up by the addition of sentries from the *Wehrmacht*'s *Wachregiment Grossdeutschland* (Guard Regiment 'Greater Germany'), with one NCO and six men armed with carbines on the Vossstrasse entrance. Guests who were seeing Hitler mingled freely in an outer lounge and sitting rooms. The only check that these high-ranking Nazis were subjected to was a cursory search of their briefcases for handguns, bombs or other weapons. Military officers were forbidden from wearing their side arms in the *Führer*'s presence.

For outsiders, gaining access to Hitler was much more difficult, highlighting that any credible threat to Hitler's life would have to come from within the inner circle of Nazi officials and military officers who had regular access to him.

When Hitler left the Reich Chancellery on official business he was accompanied by the LSSAH who posted guards outside his hotels and residences. Regular soldiers replaced these SS guards on *Wehrmacht* Day and during a national mobilization.

Hitler's private quarters at the Old Reich Chancellery were well guarded. SS sentries patrolled the Winter Garden that was shared with the New Chancellery and Hitler's private entrance. Two were posted at the entrance to the Court of Honour, a vast hall just inside the New Chancellery's entrance, two in the Great Hall in front of Hitler's office, one at the entrance to the cupola hall and one at the side entrance on Vossstrasse that led to the Great Hall. Two sentries, either SS or *Wehrmacht*, stood to attention respectively in front of No. 4 and No. 6 entrances on Vossstrasse. If any special events or receptions were being held the number of guards was considerably increased. In addition to all of these sentries, RSD officers constantly patrolled the grounds and buildings.

One of the most famous attempts on Hitler's life occurred in 1939, shortly after the outbreak of the war. It was a plot that came very close to success and managed to completely circumvent all layers of the *Führer*'s personal protection. A 36-year-old German carpenter named Georg Elser came within minutes of killing Hitler. A quiet but sociable man, Elser was a bit of a paradox. He was a devout Protestant yet had flirted with communism. After the 1938 Munich Crisis Elser believed that Hitler was most likely leading Germany into another major war. Elser decided to stop him. Working entirely alone, Elser travelled to Munich to attend the annual ceremony to commemorate the 1923 Beer Hall Putsch. The focus of events was the Burgerbraukeller, a huge beer hall, where Hitler delivered his annual address to the party faithful. Elser noted that security in the building was lax. Returning home, Elser decided to kill Hitler at the following year's ceremony. He designed and built a time bomb and returned to Munich a month before Hitler's 1939 speech.

Each evening Elser would hide inside the Burgerbraukeller until the patrons had left and the hall was closed and then he set to work. He excavated a hole in a large pillar behind the speaker's podium, carefully removing all evidence of his nocturnal activities each morning before the hall opened for business. When the time came for Hitler's address, the bomb was ready and its timer began ticking down to detonation, an event that Elser had timed to occur midway through Hitler's speech. On the night of the attack Elser was nowhere near Munich. He was heading for the Swiss frontier.

Hitler was saved by fog. War had broken out on 1 September, and an extremely busy Hitler had decided to cancel his annual address in Munich. But characteristically, he had suddenly changed his mind. He would deliver the speech and then fly back to Berlin straight afterwards. But fog meant that he had to change his plans. Instead of flying, Hitler would have to take the train, so he delivered his speech early, leaving the hall thirteen minutes before Elser's bomb detonated. The explosion killed eight and wounded sixty-three. But for the weather, Hitler would have been blown to pieces in 1939.

German customs police arrested Elser for a separate reason thirty-five minutes before the bomb exploded as he tried to cross into Switzerland. After they searched his belongings they discovered articles that tied him to the bombing, news of which had been swiftly transmitted to all relevant security agencies of the state. Handed over to the Gestapo, Elser was horribly tortured until he confessed. Imprisoned in Sachsenhausen and Dachau Concentration Camps, Elser was shot on Hitler's express order on 9 April 1945, less than a month before the end of the war.[10]

The RSD protected not only Hitler but also the members of his government and inner circle, many of whom, such as Hermann Göring, had their own personal protection units drawn from other branches of the armed services or police. Johann Rattenhuber was responsible for security at all of Hitler's field headquarters once war had broken out in 1939. For example, an RSD battalion as well as other elite protection troops guarded Hitler's field headquarters in East Prussia, the gloomy Wolf's Lair. *SS-Obersturmführer* Peter Högl, Rattenhuber's 35-year-old deputy commander, was chief of RSD Bureau 1, making him the officer who was responsible for Hitler's personal protection on a day-to-day basis throughout the war. He later rose to the rank of *SS-Obersturmbannführer* but he remained Rattenhuber's subordinate.

Table 1. RSD Bureaus, 1939.	
Bureau No.	Assignment
1	*Führer* Protection – Obersalzberg, Munich, Berchtesgaden
2	Hermann Göring
3	Joachim von Ribbentrop
4	Heinrich Himmler
5	Josef Goebbels
6	Reich Minister of the Interior, Dr Wilhelm Frick
7	Reich Minister of Food, Dr Richard Darre
8	*Führer* Protection
9	*Führer* Protection

Table 2.   RSD Bureaus, 1944.

Bureau No.	Assignment
1	*Führer* Protection – Obersalzberg, Munich, Berchtesgaden
2	Hermann Göring
3	Joachim von Ribbentrop
4	Heinrich Himmler
5	Josef Goebbels
6	Reich Minister of the Interior, Dr Wilhelm Frick
7	Governor of Bohemia & Moravia, Dr Karl Hermann Frank
8	*Führer* Protection
9	*Führer* Protection
10	Reichskommissar in the Netherlands, Dr Arthur Seyss-Inquart
11	Reichskommissar in Norway, Josef Terboven
12	Grand Admiral, Karl Dönitz
13	Reichskommissar in Denmark, Dr Werner Best
14	Chief of the RSHA, Dr Ernst Kaltenbrunner
No number	Head of the German Labour Front, Dr Robert Ley
No number	Gauleiter Erich Koch of East Prussia
No number	Reich Chancellery, Berlin

Following the assassination of Himmler's deputy Reinhard Heydrich in Prague in May 1942 by a pair of British-trained Czech SOE operatives, RSD detachments were assigned to his successor as head of the Reich Main Security Office, Dr Ernst Kaltenbrunner, and to his successor as Governor of Bohemia and Moravia, Dr Karl Hermann Frank. Some other Nazi governors who were always top priority targets for assassination were also given RSD protection, as well as Hitler's naval chief, *Grossadmiral* Karl Dönitz. By 1944 there were seventeen separate RSD guard detachments protecting, and also keeping tabs on, the top Nazi leadership.

Chapter 3

Trains and Automobiles

'Hitler was a demonic personality obsessed by racial delusions. Physical disease is not the explanation for the weird tensions in his mind and the sudden freaks of his will. . .But he was in no sense mentally ill; rather he was mentally abnormal, a person who stood on the threshold between genius and madness.'[1]

Dr Otto Dietrich
Hitler's Press Chief

A Mosquito fighter-bomber roared down towards the long train that snaked through the dark forest of Eastern Germany. Behind the aircraft several more followed in tight formation, each driving home devastating attacks. The British aircraft, armed with bombs, rockets and cannon, screamed along the length of the train. Two steam engines hauled smart Pullman carriages at almost full speed. Cannon shells ripped through the surrounding treetops, or thudded like crazed hornets into the roofs of the carriages, gouging out great holes. Rockets and bombs smashed down, the train rocking as blasts impacted close by, uprooting trees and throwing huge showers of dirt high into the air. German anti-aircraft crews fed box after box of 20mm shells into the four-barrel guns mounted on special carriages at each end of the train, a constant barrage peppering the sky with black puffs of smoke. One-by-one the Mosquitos dived on the train, expending their munitions, many taking shrapnel hits from the intense flak screen, one peeling away with its port engine on fire before ploughing into the surrounding forest in a massive fireball. But suddenly the leading locomotive's boiler exploded as RAF cannon shells punched through it, and the train started to slow down. More Mosquitos piled in, one scoring a direct hit with a bomb on a carriage midway down the length of the train, its metal body absorbing the hit, the interior instantly reduced to a burning charnel house of wrecked furniture and smashed bodies. The train was strafed from end to end before a British air-to-ground rocket slammed into the second carriage, severely wounding Hitler and his closest staff who were crouched beneath the conference room's wooden table. RSD personnel fought their way into the burning carriage with fire extinguishers before rescuing their boss who had severe shrapnel wounds to the head and chest. As the last of the British aircraft made a pass, the train came to a shuddering halt while onboard the doctors desperately tried to stem the *Führer's* bleeding and the heavily armed RSD organised a hasty evacuation to the nearest town.

The attack related above never happened. But the scenario was one of three plans hatched by the British to kill Hitler whilst he was aboard his personal train. The others were to derail it with explosives or to poison its drinking water supply. Hitler continued to use his train until the last few weeks of the war even though the Allies had air superiority over the Reich, a move that was seen by many as an unnecessary security risk. Special Operations Executive, ingenious as ever, saw Hitler's train as the perfect target but in the end the British failed to launch an assault on the *Führer* Special.

Throughout the war Hitler travelled constantly. He used three methods to get around his empire: planes, trains and cars. As his security became more professional it was deemed important that Hitler no longer use public transport, where he would be vulnerable to assassination. Instead, the security agencies that protected the *Führer* began to acquire private means of transport that eventually resulted in Hitler being able to travel widely without having any contact with his people or those outside of his inner circle of advisors and generals. One of his favourite modes of transport was the train, and Hitler's train was a truly awesome sight.

Emperor Wilhelm II had had the use of several plush railway carriages that formed an Imperial Train before the end of the First World War. The German government during the Weimar period then re-used some of these carriages. Hitler ordered the construction of several special coaches between 1937 and 1939 for his own train. Each coach was constructed entirely from steel and weighed over sixty tons. The *Führersonderzug*, as Hitler's train was known, came in two configurations – peacetime and wartime. The peacetime train consisted of (in order) locomotive, baggage and power engine car, *Führer's* Pullman, conference car, escort car, dining car, two sleeping cars, Pullman coach, personnel car, press chief's car, baggage car and power-engine car.[2] Codenamed 'Amerika' until 31 January 1943, it was then renamed

'Brandenburg'. During wartime Hitler's train was officially a *Führer-hauptquartier* (*Führer* Headquarters – FHQ).

An FHQ, whether a mobile train or static headquarters complex, was a command facility for Hitler's use. The *Wehrmacht* always had its own headquarters nearby and liaison officers seconded to the FHQ. The FHQ was not a military headquarters in the strictest sense, but rather was so *de facto* because of Hitler's interference in the military command structure.

The Army, Navy and Air Force had received nominal oversight since 1938 by one unified organisation, the *Oberkommando der Wehrmacht* (Supreme Command of the Armed Forces – OKW). For most of the war *Generalfeldmarschall* Wilhelm Keitel acted as its commander, with *Generaloberst* Alfred Jodl as Chief of Operations Staff. In reality Hitler personally controlled OKW.

The German Army was under the command of *Oberkommando des Heeres* (Supreme Command of the Army – OKH), headed until December 1941 by *Generaloberst* Walther von Brauchitsch. Hitler sacked him after he failed to capture Moscow and appointed himself Supreme Commander of OKH. During wartime, OKH was responsible for strategic planning of Armies and Army Groups and the OKH General Staff managed operational matters. Both OKH and OKW were co-located in a huge bunker complex at Zossen outside Berlin, and both had large numbers of staff officers and adjutants attached to FHQ.

Little is known today about Hitler's wartime train, but an idea of its likely regular composition comes from information leaked in June 1941, when the *Führersonderzug* departed the Anhalter Station in Berlin for Hitler's gloomy pine forest HQ at Rastenburg in East Prussia. For the overnight journey the train consisted of fifteen carriages pulled by two large *Deutsches Bahn* K5E-series war locomotives. The *Führerson-derzug* was a self-contained rolling headquarters that enabled Hitler, much like the present British Royal Family and their Royal Train, to travel in safety and comfort to any part of his empire whilst remaining wired into the communications grid. If the train stopped, the *Führer*'s Pullman, dining car and sleeping cars could be quickly connected with the postal telephone network. When on the move, communications were conducted by encrypted radio.

Behind the two locomotives was a flatbed *Flakwagen* mounting two Flakvierling 38 four-gun anti-aircraft cannon manufactured by

Mauser. Sitting on a traversing platform, the Flakvierling 38 consisted of four individual 20mm cannons mounted together that were each fed by twenty-round magazines. In combat, the Flakvierling 38 could fire 800 rounds per minute (involving ten magazine swaps per minute on each of the four guns). The weapons' effective range was 2,200m. The flatbed was disguised to look like an ordinary wooden freight wagon, the guns being raised up when brought into action against low-flying aircraft. Each *Flakwagen* had five crew compartments for the seventeen gunners. The officers and men were drawn from *9 Regiment General Göring*, supplied to Hitler by the *Luftwaffe* chief.

Behind the *Flakwagen* was a baggage carriage, then the *Führerwagen*, Hitler's personal Pullman carriage that contained a bedroom, bathroom, sitting room, valet's quarters, and a conference room. Behind Hitler's carriage was the *Befehlswagen* or Command Car, where Hitler's staff officers worked. This carriage contained another conference room and a communications centre incorporating a 700-watt short wave radio transmitter. Next was the *Begleitkommandowagen*, a barracks on wheels for Hitler's twenty-two-man *SS-Begleitkommando* and RSD detachment. Behind this was the dining carriage, two guest carriages, the *Badewagen* or Bathing Car, another dining carriage, two sleeping cars for staff, then the *Pressewagen* or Press Car for Hitler's press chief, Dr Otto Dietrich, and his staff. Finally, another baggage carriage and another *Flakwagen* completed the train.

Using the *Führersonderzug* required several hours' notice. The train was usually kept at Tempelhof maintenance depot and was shunted to the chosen departure station, usually taking two hours. Security concerns meant that the number of railway employees who knew the departure and arrival times, the route and any stops planned along the way was kept to an absolute minimum. One time, Hitler's train pulled into a station and stopped beside a trainload of Jews who were being shipped off to a concentration camp. Whether he actually looked out of the window and saw this horrific sight is unknown. The blinds in his personal Pullman were usually kept lowered during the war.

The entire route that Hitler's train would travel was patrolled – railway policemen would each be allotted a short 'beat' beside the track, this precaution making it almost impossible for anyone to plant a bomb on or beside the tracks to attempt to derail the train. Only collusion by the police would have made such an attempt feasible, which was an unlikely scenario.

Table 3.   Nazi 'Special Trains'.

Type	User	Original Codename	Later Codename
Führersonderzug	Adolf Hitler	Amerika	Brandenburg
Ministerzug	Joachim von Ribbentop Heinrich Himmler	n/a	
Sonderzug	Wilhelm Keitel	Afrika	Braunschweig
Sonderzug	Hermann Göring	Asien	Pommern
Sonderzug	Karl Dönitz	Atlantik	Auerhahn
Sonderzug	Wehrmacht Operations Staff	Atlas	Frankern
Sonderzug	Chief of Luftwaffe Intelligence	Enzian	
Sonderzug	Army General Staff	Ostpreussian	
Sonderzug	Chief of Command Staff, Luftwaffe	Robinson I	
Sonderzug	Chief of the General Staff, Luftwaffe	Robinson II	
Sonderzug	Heinrich Himmler	Steiermark	Heinrich/ Transport 44
Sonderzug	Joachim von Ribbentrop	Westfalen	
Sonderzug	Army General Staff	Württemberg	

At every station enroute where Hitler's train was scheduled to stop the platform had to be kept completely clear of all luggage, packages or crates, anything that could conceal a bomb. Railway police guarded all entrances, exits, underpasses, bridges and stairways. Hitler's RSD commander, Johann Rattenhuber, assumed command of all railway police for the duration of the train's journey. Railway police also travelled aboard Hitler's train, and one of their jobs was to carefully search every carriage for bombs and concealed weapons before a journey commenced. Technicians also travelled on board to rectify any faults that occurred during the journey. At the end of the journey all the written orders, timetables and documents that had been distributed to interested parties were gathered up, counted and then destroyed, to make sure that no one could plan a future attack on the same route.

As well as Hitler, several other senior Nazis and military officers had special trains for their own exclusive use (see Table 3).[3]

One of the enduring images of Nazism is Hitler standing in the front of a large Mercedes-Benz limousine saluting as he is driven through dense throngs of adoring Germans. Hitler loved cars, took an interest in motor racing and enthusiastically supported the 1936 International Motor Show in Berlin. Hitler was the first world leader to use specially modified and armoured cars. The trend had begun in Prohibition America where gangsters like Al Capone paid huge sums to have their cars armoured and bullet-proofed. As with everything to do with Hitler, security considerations revolutionised VIP transport, resulting in some truly monstrous machines.

The giant limousines were often Hitler's first line of defence against lunatics and against more well-organised assassination plots. Throughout the 1920s and early 1930s Hitler was repeatedly shot at whilst he was on the move, and providing properly armoured vehicles became paramount once Hitler became chancellor in 1933.

The year before, while Hitler's small convoy of cars was negotiating a hairpin bend on the road near Stralsund in northern Germany, Hitler's car was ambushed by a group of unidentified armed men who opened a fusillade of shots at the vehicle narrowly missing the *Führer*. A year later another group of unknown assassins opened fire on Hitler's car on the road between Rosenheim and the Obersalzburg in Bavaria.

The *Führer* required serious cars, and German carmaker Mercedes-Benz was more than happy to accommodate his wishes, particularly his interest in personal security. Hitler had first owned a red Benz in 1923 – it was this car that he had used to drive to the Burgerbraukeller in Munich shortly before launching his abortive putsch. During these tumultuous years Hitler was even involved in a car accident. 'Rudolf Hess once told me that just before the seizure of power [in 1933], Hitler, Hess, Heinrich Hoffmann and Julius Schaub were all nearly killed in Hitler's Mercedes due to an error made by a lorry driver,' related Hitler's valet, Heinz Linge. 'Hitler was injured in the face and shoulder but with great composure calmed his co-passengers, still paralysed with shock, with the observation that Providence would not allow him to be killed since he still had a great mission to fulfill.'[4]

Hitler stated in 1934 that he 'did not tolerate a car manufactured by other companies in his escort and entourage,' a ringing endorsement of what was now called Mercedes-Benz (though not something they like to highlight today). Between 1929 and 1942 Mercedes-Benz delivered a total of forty-four cars to the Reich Chancellery, the majority during the Nazi period.

Before 1935 Hitler used ordinary tourers and unarmoured limousines but his vulnerability to assassination caused a change in vehicle type. One incident in particular forced a change. After attending the marriage of *Generalfeldmarschall* Werner von Blomberg, Hitler drove to Kaiser Wilhelm II's former mansion and hunting range on the Schorfheide to be with Göring. 'Himmler drove ahead of us,' recalled Hitler's valet Linge. 'Suddenly shots cracked out from the forest undergrowth. Himmler's car stopped after being hit. Himmler, deeply shocked and pale, told Hitler that he had been shot at. Driving on after the incident, Hitler said: 'That was certainly intended for me because Himmler does not usually drive ahead. It is also well known that I always sit at the side of the driver. The hits on Himmler's car are in that area.'[5] Following this incident, Hitler took delivery of three specially modified Mercedes-Benz 540KW24 limousines, known with good reason as the 'Swabian Colossus'.

Introduced at the 1936 Paris Motor Show, the 540K was one of the largest cars produced at the time. A total of twelve specially lengthened wheelbase cars were manufactured for use by the German government, huge six-seater convertible saloons. Hitler's three personal 540K *Paradewagens* were kept in service until 1943. The *Führer* had had the vehicles 'panzered' or armoured with 4mm steel body armour, a 25mm thick bulletproof windscreen and side windows and bulletproof tires. They weighed close to 4 tons each, reducing their top speed from 177 kph to 140 kph. They could withstand pistol and rifle fire and probably a bomb or grenade blast at close range. It was these cars that Hitler used to visit the Nuremberg rallies and one was even used to drive British Prime Minister Neville Chamberlain up to the Berghof in 1938 during crisis meetings over the future of Czechoslovakia. Hermann Göring and Heinrich Himmler also utilised 540Ks, and many were kept at the New Reich Chancellery motor pool for the use of visiting VIPs and government ministers.

Hitler also used the 520G4W31 and 131 models. These equally huge vehicles had three axles and were used for cross-country driving and for military parades. Protection included a 30mm thick windscreen, 20mm thick roll-up windows, rear side windows armoured to 30mm and the back of the rear seat was reinforced by 8mm of steel plate. But the security features on the cars were only as good as the security protocols that governed the cars' use. Hitler consistently toured around in armoured limousines with the top down. Although the side windows were rolled up, he was vulnerable to either a rifleman shooting from higher up (as in the case of John F. Kennedy in Dallas in 1963) or from a tossed grenade or bomb.

In 1942, following Reinhard Heydrich's assassination in Prague, when British-trained Czech agents ambushed the Reich Protector, one throwing a grenade which exploded against the open-topped vehicle, the German government ordered another twenty 540Ks for the exclusive use of Nazi ministers and other leaders. Hitler's protection, and that of his ministers and inner circle, became increasingly stringent as the war turned against Germany. Battlefield reverses left all of the Nazi leaders feeling increasingly vulnerable to assassination. In 1944 a final order for seventeen 540Ks was placed with Mercedes. The most famous 540K was probably 'Blue Goose', the car owned by Hermann Göring. Blue was the Reichsmarschall's favourite colour and his personal 540K had Göring's family crest emblazoned on both rear doors.

From 1938 Hitler upgraded his collection of 540Ks with the addition of the Mercedes-Benz 770K150. Seven of these enormous vehicles were often used during the war years as Hitler's personal transports. The chassis was twenty feet long and loaded down with 900kg of armour plating and bulletproof glass. With fuel, oil and radiator fluid each 770K weighed almost 4.5 tonnes. Side and floor armour consisted of 18mm of steel. The windows consisted of 40mm of armoured glass. Hitler allegedly tested the glass himself by firing a Luger pistol at it.

The 770K '*Grosser Mercedes*' was powered by a 230hp straight 8 with dual carburettors and dual ignition; superchargers would cut in automatically if the driver floored the accelerator. The armour reduced the vehicle's top speed to about 160 kph. Although fitted with 230-litre fuel tanks, Hitler's 770Ks made barely 1km per litre, giving a range of only 230km. There was a compartment in the front dashboard and two more in the rear seats to hold pistols and an armoured plate could be raised behind the rear passenger seat. Hitler's 770Ks were all painted midnight blue.

A typical example of Hitler's pre-war use of automobiles was his March 1938 visit to Austria in the few days following the *Anschluss*. On this occasion Hitler had decided to drive over the border into his homeland and visit his birthplace in Braunau am Inn as well as Linz and the Austrian capital Vienna.

Security for the trip was provided by two agencies: *SS-Standarten-führer* Johann Rattenhuber's RSD and *SS-Sturmbannführer* Bruno Gesche's *SS-Begleitkommando*. Rattenhuber was in overall command while Gesche acted as his deputy. In total, thirty-one bodyguards accompanied Hitler's cavalcade of vehicles as it progressed into Austria, with ten acting as drivers under Hitler's personal driver, Erich Kempka. Members of both units wore identical grey SS uniforms to confound assassins.[6]

Gesche, one of the original eight founding members of the *SS-Begleitkommando*, would suffer from several ignominious falls from grace during his career. A favourite of Hitler's, whom he had been protecting since 1932, Gesche had made a very powerful enemy during the early years of Nazism.

In October 1932 Gesche, then second-in-command of the *SS-Begleit-kommando*, had made some very disparaging remarks about a second SS unit sent by Heinrich Himmler to help guard the *Führer* during his election campaign. When Himmler heard what Gesche had said he took it as a personal affront and requested that Gesche should be demoted and removed from the *Führer* protection detail. Hitler would only agree to a mild reprimand. Hitler often joked that he was not comfortable with Gesche, who was slightly cross-eyed, sitting behind him in his armoured Mercedes, fearing that he would shoot him by accident rather than any potential assassin. But Hitler was loyal to those subordinates that he liked, and Gesche, though now the dread enemy of Heinrich Himmler, later the most powerful man in Germany after the *Führer*, was protected.

Himmler had to content himself with destroying Gesche's superior and commander of the *SS-Begleitkommando*, Kurt Gildisch, who was dismissed from his position and in 1936 actually thrown out of the SS for being a drunkard. Himmler's removal of Gildisch actually proved a boon to Gesche, who was promoted to be the unit's new commander in 1934.

In 1935, Himmler, a notoriously fastidious man, attempted to exercise control over the various security apparatuses of the early Nazi state, and he ordered that salaries due to the *SS-Begleitkommando* be withheld. Gesche responded by enlisting the help of another of the *Führer*'s favourites, Sepp Dietrich, the commander of the *Leibstandarte SS Adolf Hitler*, who managed to get the order reversed.

Many of Hitler's bodyguards were heavy drinkers and Gesche was no exception. Alcohol eventually led to his downfall. In 1937 Himmler enforced regulations forbidding SS men from drinking to excess. After gathering evidence against him, Himmler forced Gesche to sign a statement in September 1938 promising to abstain from all alcohol for a period of three years or face dismissal from the SS. Gesche signed but the ban was lifted when Hitler once more interceded on Gesche's behalf. It would be fair to say that Himmler was more determined than ever to destroy Gesche – it had taken on something of the character of a personal vendetta and Himmler was both petty and patient, a deadly combination. We will read more of Gesche and Himmler's feud during the war years.

Erich Kempka would remain as Hitler's personal driver until the end of the war. The son of a Ruhr Polish coal miner, Kempka had been one of the eight founding members of the *SS-Begleitkommando* in 1932. He was chauffeur to *SA-Obergruppenführer* Josef Terboven, Gauleiter of Essen, until 1932 when he was recommended to become Hitler's reserve driver. In 1936 Kempka replaced Julius Schreck on his death as Hitler's primary driver and chief of the car pool. He would rise to the rank of *SS-Obersturmbannführer* and was awarded the SS Honor Sword by Himmler, a straight sabre given for special merit and worn when in full dress uniform. When Hitler was being driven he always, unless he was travelling with some important guest, sat in the front passenger seat next to Kempka. His valet, Heinz Linge, would sit in the back. Hitler did not drive himself, but particularly enjoyed being driven at high speed, and Kempka was both skilled and reliable.

The bodyguards were divided into three details under Gesche, *SS-Obersturmführer* Högl (RSD Deputy Commander) and *SS-Hauptsturmführer* Schädle of *SS-Begleitkommando*. In all, there were twelve large Mercedes in the convoy. Five cars were required just to carry the bodyguards, weapons and luggage, plus more cars for Hitler and his entourage, a group that included his valet Heinz Linge, adjutants Schaub and Brückner, Press Chief Dr Otto Dietrich, the ever-present Martin Bormann, Hitler's personal physician Dr Karl Brandt, Heinrich Hoffmann, Hitler's 'court' photographer, and *Generaloberst* Wilhelm Keitel, Chief of the OKW.

The bodyguard detachment on the visit to Hitler's birthplace was well armed. Between them they carried fourteen MP38 machine pistols and every man also carried two automatic pistols. Hitler's personal adjutant, *SS-Sturmbannführer* Wernicke, was given two extra machine pistols with two full magazines each, just to be safe.[7]

The party drove from Munich after flying in from Berlin on 12 March 1938 aboard nine Junkers Ju-52s of the *Führer*'s personal squadron. After boarding their cars, the first stop was Mühldorf, headquarters of *Generaloberst* Fedor von Bock's VIII Army. Army and *Waffen-SS* troops sealed off the HQ from prying eyes. At Braunau am Inn, the small border town where Hitler was born in 1889, he was met, as he was everywhere in Austria, by huge and enthusiastic crowds of admirers who showered his car with flowers while he stood and gave them his trademark 'German greeting' from the passenger seat or reached down to shake upstretched hands. It was at moments like these that Hitler was most vulnerable to assassination, a fact that the RSD and *SS-Begleitkommando* were more than apprehensive about. But it proved extremely difficult to keep the adoring crowds back from Hitler's person, particularly when moving in a vehicle convoy where it was often impossible to cordon off roads. After passing through Lambach and Wels, the party arrived at the city of Linz, where Hitler's father had once been employed as a customs officer. There the *Führer* and his entourage spent the night.

On 13 March Hitler resumed his triumphal progress towards Vienna. As the caravan of vehicles passed a petrol station one man stood beside his car, his eyes narrowed with barely concealed loathing. Colonel Noel Mason-MacFarlane was the British Military Attaché in Vienna. He would later volunteer to assassinate Hitler once he was transferred to Berlin just before the German invasion of Poland, proposing to a horrified Foreign Office in London to shoot Hitler with a high velocity rifle from a window in the British Embassy when he was reviewing an annual military parade.[8] Mason-MacFarlane watched as two large Mercedes 'filled with SS bristling with tommy-guns and other lethal weapons, came by; they were closely followed by half-a-dozen super-cars containing Hitler and his entourage and bodyguard.'[9] The day ended with a large military parade in Vienna.

Regardless of how many bodyguards that he had with him, Hitler still remained vulnerable when travelling by car. The best way to protect him when he was on the move, whether by plane, train or automobile, was to maintain secrecy about the route he would take, denying his enemies the vital time needed to plan an effective ambush.

Hitler's vulnerability was startlingly clear when he drove into Austria. The *Wehrmacht* had only secured the towns that he visited a couple of days previously, and although enraptured crowds mostly greeted him in his homeland, there were those who would have liked to have seen him dead. The cordoning off of the streets through which Hitler's procession would pass was often inadequate and haphazard, the task falling mainly to rear echelon army signals detachments. This meant that people could get very close to Hitler and the party's vehicles, close enough that on several occasions they almost stopped the procession by sheer weight of numbers requiring RSD bodyguards to walk beside Hitler's car, three on each side, to try to create a little space between the *Führer* and his adoring throngs. People would hand Hitler bunches of flowers or baskets of fruit as he stood in the front passenger seat, one hand gripping the windscreen frame and any of these objects could have concealed a bomb. From a security point of view it was a disaster waiting to happen.

The situation got worse once Hitler started annexing countries that outright objected to German occupation. When he swallowed the remaining parts of Czechoslovakia in 1938 he boldly drove through Prague where he was greeted not by saluting, yelling and crying throngs, but by small crowds who stood staring at their new master in ominous, stony silence. Hitler sat for most of the time, only standing to salute German Army units, but his car was still open-topped, an inviting target for any Czech nationalists. In the event, no one attempted to kill him.

Once again, the entire party of Nazi bigwigs travelled in dark open-topped Mercedes, Hitler apparently as adamant as John F. Kennedy twenty-four years later that he should be clearly seen by both his admirers and his enemies. The *Führer's* party travelled in two groups. The first group consisted of Hitler's car followed by two *SS-Begleit-kommando* bodyguard cars, another car full of aides and adjutants, and *Generaloberst* Keitel and his adjutants. Hitler's immediate companions were his driver Kempka, adjutant Schaub, Hitler's chief military aide *Oberst* Rudolf Schmundt, *Hauptmann* Nicholaus von Below, his *Wehrmacht* adjutant, *Hauptmann* Engel and his valet Linge (who was armed with an MP38 machine pistol). The two trailing escort cars had MG34 machine guns mounted.

The second group consisted of the 'ministers' cars'. There was one car each for Foreign Minister Joachim von Ribbentrop, Head of the Reich Chancellery Hans Lammers, Heinrich Himmler and his aides and bodyguard, Dr Dietrich, plus one vehicle reserved for invited guests, an empty reserve car in case of breakdowns, a luggage car, mobile field kitchen and even a petrol tanker to ensure that so many massive gas-guzzling Mercedes didn't run dry.[10]

Further protection for the two groups of cars was provided by five motorcycle outriders mounted on BMWs who rode ahead of Hitler's group with an armed reconnaissance Horch truck followed by *Oberst* Irwin Rommel, commander of the *Führer*'s escort, in another car (Column 'K' (*Kommandant*)).

When Germany invaded Poland in early September 1939 Hitler soon drove into the conquered territory behind his advancing armies, keen to conduct a tour of inspection of his troops and the front lines. Expecting serious trouble, the RSD and *SS-Begleitkommando* took no chances and an enormous effort was made to protect Hitler's caravan of vehicles. Although it was early days in the evolution of Hitler's vehicular security, already the essential components were in place and would be instantly familiar to any American president today.

The combination of the *Führersonderzug* and the fleet of armoured Mercedes meant that for the Polish Campaign Hitler was able to keep moving his military headquarters. Hitler established his first *Führer* HQ in the East Prussian town of Bad Polzin after *Wehrmacht* HQ Front Units had been mobilised on 23 August 1939. His personal train was used, arriving at Bad Polzin station on 4 September. HQ troops and a force protection unit were drawn from the elite *Grossdeutschland Regiment* under the command of *Oberst* Rommel.

The *Grossdeutschland* traced its origins back to 1921, during the unsettled period following Germany's defeat in the First World War. The new *Reichswehr* was limited to only 100,000 men, and each of its divisions recruited from within a particular state. A guard regiment for the nation's capital was duly created, *Wachregiment Berlin*, recruiting men from across all nine *Reichswehr* divisions, and in the process becoming the only truly 'German' unit in the army. Its duties were primarily ceremonial – providing sentries at the Old Reich Chancellery and guards of honour for state occasions and visits. Shortly after formation the unit's name was changed to *Kommando der Wachtruppe* (Guard Troop Command) and it was based at Moabit Barracks in central Berlin. When Hitler came to power in 1933 he left the unit intact, though his ceremonial guards were largely from the *Leibstandarte SS Adolf Hitler*.

In 1934 the *Kommando der Wachtruppe* was renamed *Wachtruppe Berlin* and a small detachment supplemented the LSSAH guards at the Reich Chancellery as well as continuing to parade and perform ceremonials throughout the capital. It was particularly visible during the 1936 Berlin Olympics.

In 1937 the unit was renamed again, this time becoming *Wach Regiment Berlin*, with soldiers posted individually to the unit from all over Germany for six-month tours of duty. Hitler decided to change the name one last time in 1939 to reflect the national character of the regiment – thus it became *Infanterie Regiment Grossdeutschland*.

At Bad Polzin in Poland in 1939 the *Grossdeutschland Regiment* provided three security groups. Group 1 guarded Hitler's train and the Minister's Train that joined it on 4 September. This group also manned an outer security perimeter for 500m around the station. Although local people were still permitted to use the station, they were subjected to intense security scrutiny and forbidden to gather in groups.[11] Group 2 was held as a reserve while the Front Group comprised the troops who would travel with Hitler and his ministers by car. On the trip to the front in Poland in September 1939 Rommel's men provided five motorcycle outriders at the front and rear of Hitler's column, plus a signal corps platoon and an anti-aircraft platoon towing 20mm flak guns. The third and final part of Hitler's huge column trailed along five minutes behind the flak guns and was labelled Column 'M' (*Militarische* – 'Military') and consisted of a towed anti-tank gun, more cars, another anti-tank gun, and elements of the signal troop, all derived from the *Grossdeutschland*. Such a formidable array of firepower was not just a show of force but was probably sufficient to have beaten off a determined attack by almost any group of assassins.

Hitler's huge column of vehicles headed for the front at Topolno on the Vistula River. When he visited front line units his security was usually quite lax, to a degree that would seem almost incredible today. This was because neither Hitler nor his bodyguards believed that loyal *Wehrmacht* soldiers, riding high on victory, would try to kill their *Führer*. Only much later in the war, when the tide had turned against Germany, did Hitler become much more wary around his own men, and with good reason as it turned out.

In Poland in 1939 Hitler believed that he had nothing to fear from his generals and men. 'During briefings, Hitler's eight or nine bodyguards just stood about looking on, or talking among themselves, but not, as they should have been, facing out from where Hitler was, watching the scene.'[12] This apparent break with procedure was startling considering that Hitler was within a war zone.

Any real danger in 1939 came not from fellow Germans but from the enemy. At one point Hitler's convoy was stopped because Polish soldiers had ambushed a field hospital unit on the road only a few minutes before. After waiting for the all clear, the convoy drove on, meeting with another close call. The driver of an oncoming army truck was shot dead at the wheel by a Polish sniper, the vehicle smashing into one of the anti-aircraft vehicles guarding the *Führer*'s convoy.

As the convoy continued to the town of Pruszez, the Fieseler *Storch* plane that was flying reconnaissance for Hitler's convoy was shot at by German ground troops who mistook it for being Polish. On arrival at Topolno Hitler watched German troops make an assault crossing of the Vistula before retreating to Plietnitz where his special train was waiting to take him back to Germany after Polish planes began bombing ground targets only a mile from where Hitler was standing on the riverbank.

On 9 September the *Führersonderzug* and its attached HQ units moved south to Ilnan, near Oppeln in Silesia. Each time the train stopped, the *Grossdeutschland* set up a security perimeter around the station and the headquarters was connected to the local telephone exchange. The next day Hitler paid his first visit to the Polish front by air. Shortly after 9.00am six Junkers Ju 52/3m trimotors took off from Neudorf with his large entourage and landed at Bialaczow. Six Messerschmitt Bf 109 fighters escorted the *Führer*'s aerial armada. Travelling with Hitler aboard his plane was his usual retinue: *Oberst* Schmundt, adjutants Brückner, von Below and Engel, his doctor Brandt, driver Kempka and his valet Linge. Two Ju 52s each carried six bodyguards, one plane consisting of *SS-Begleitkommando* and the other RSD. The remaining three aircraft carried Keitel, *Grossdeutschland* Front Group commander *Oberst* Rommel, *Oberst* Bodenschatz (Hitler's Luftwaffe aide), von Ribbentrop, Bormann, Press Chief Dietrich, Schaub, and Personal Adjutant *SS-Untersturmführer* Max Wünsche, Himmler and their several adjutants and bodyguards.[13]

At Bialaczow Hitler met with *Generaloberst* Walther von Reichenau, commander of the Tenth Army. The cars and other vehicles that made up the *Führer*'s *Frontgruppe* were waiting to take Hitler and his large entourage to Maslow where enthusiastic soldiers and a few civilians mobbed him. In a major operation, Hitler's cars were driven from Germany to meet his aircraft, and this was also done throughout the war. Only the specially armoured Mercedes cars were used during Hitler's visits to the war fronts.

Permitting the *Führer's* car to be mobbed was a serious security breach, but one which Hitler tolerated and encouraged, feeling secure in the knowledge that his beloved soldiers would not harm him. As his convoy passed through recently occupied Polish towns and villages they were slowed to a crawl by huge numbers of soldiers, horse-drawn wagons and even trucks full of Polish prisoners-of-war that were being driven back from the front.

Hitler's headquarters moved constantly during the Polish Campaign. On 12 September the *Führer's* train *Amerika* arrived at Gogolin, 30km south of Oppeln. On 18 September it moved to Goddentow-Lanz near Lauenburg, 40km northwest of Danzig. Hitler returned to the Reich Chancellery aboard *Amerika* on 26 September.

Further steps were taken to create a dedicated *Wehrmacht* headquarters protection unit for the *Führer*. At the beginning of the Polish Campaign Rommel's troops wore a cuff band on their right sleeve that read 'Führerhauptquartier', indicating that they were special headquarters troops working directly for Hitler. The *Führer* decided on 28 September 1939, with Rommel's agreement, to change the name of the elements of the *Grossdeutschland* unit that guarded him to the *Führer Begleit Bataillon* (*Führer* Escort Battalion – FBB) and it was considerably expanded. The rest of the *Grossdeutschland* would continue as a separate army unit, eventually becoming a division. In January 1941 all FBB personnel were ordered to only wear their *Führerhauptquartier* cuff bands when not serving at Hitler's HQ – for example, when on leave. It was important to maintain a high level of secrecy around Hitler and advertising the location of his headquarters was deemed unwise. Instead, when on duty, FBB wore a '*Grossdeutschland*' cuff band on their right sleeve.[14]

Hitler now had four units providing him with protection. The RSD and *SS-Begleitkommando* provided bodyguards and valets, the LSSAH still had one company on guard duties at the Reich Chancellery and whenever Hitler visited the front he could expect a large FBB escort from the *Wehrmacht*. Four different units from two arms of service all dedicated to protecting one man and his inner circle of henchmen. Such multiplicity suited Hitler's belief in 'divide and rule' perfectly as each of the protection agencies vied with the other for more influence and power as the war progressed.

Although during his battlefront tours Hitler occasionally exposed himself to danger, particularly ambush by cut-off enemy troops or landmines, the most serious plot to kill Hitler in Poland occurred while he was driving through the capital Warsaw on 5 October 1939. It was planned that Hitler's car would cross today's Charles de Gaulle Square in the city centre as the *Führer* made his way to a victory parade. Polish resisters, the cut-off remnants of Polish Army units stranded in the occupied capital, planned to hide a massive Improvised Explosive Device (IED) along the route and detonate it as Hitler's Mercedes drew level. Fortunately for Hitler, human error meant that the IED failed to explode.

By the time Hitler started to visit the Western Front in 1940 security had been further tightened in the light of Georg Elser's failed bomb plot in Munich. *Oberstleutnant* Thomas had taken command of the FBB since Rommel's promotion to *Generalmajor* and transfer to frontline duty in France. The FBB became responsible for all luggages that were to travel with the *Führer*, conscious that this was an excellent method of infiltrating a bomb close to Hitler.

Three FBB men personally collected all bags and suitcases that were to travel with Hitler and his staff, whether by train, plane or car, from the hotel or apartment where the group was staying. Two fetched the luggage while the third man guarded the truck outside to prevent any interference. The luggage was always guarded and often kept under lock and key. The chance of someone managing to plant a device in any of the bags was extremely remote unless they used an inside man, and the FBB and RSD who guarded Hitler were totally loyal.

The car convoy also became more heavily protected than before. The *Frontgruppe* now consisted of fifteen Mercedes to carry Hitler and his entourage, protected by elements of an FBB infantry company, signals platoon, motorcycle platoon, armoured reconnaissance platoon (with radio car), two anti-aircraft platoons, two armoured cars each mounting 20mm cannons, two field kitchens, two fuel tankers and a supply section. Overhead was a Fieseler *Storch* spotter plane constantly moving ahead of the convoy looking for trouble and reporting on road conditions by radio.

Hitler made several visits to France during the invasion in 1940, but when Paris fell he cancelled a planned triumphal military parade on 20 July, a date that was to have great significance four years later, because he feared, rightly as it turned out, that the British planned a bombing raid. Sholto Douglas, Deputy-Chief of the Air Staff, proposed an attack in July 1940, only two weeks after the French capitulation.

Donald Stevenson, Director of Home Operations in the Air Ministry, picked up the idea and quickly proposed attempting to kill Hitler, who could be expected to be standing on a saluting base near the Arc de Triomphe. A salvo of bombs dropped by low-flying RAF light bombers was predicted to cause carnage. However, the British eventually dropped the idea, considering it unsporting to bomb an opponent's military parade.[15] Stevenson remarked: 'I am against the attack on Paris on this occasion. The triumphal march through Paris is in accordance with military custom – we did the same thing ourselves after the battle of Waterloo.'[16] Later in the war the British would be less prepared to play by 'Queensberry Rules' when it came to Hitler and his acolytes.

When Hitler did visit Paris he did so secretly and his whistle-stop tour of the French capital was extraordinary for the risks that he took. The tour happened before the planned victory parade, which was cancelled. At 3.30am on 23 June 1940 Hitler's party took off from an airfield in France and landed at Le Bourget Airport soon after. This time there would only be five cars – three for Hitler and his party and two for the SS and RSD bodyguards. The reason for the visit to Paris was primarily to indulge Hitler's love of architecture and for this reason the *Führer* was accompanied by his two court architects, Albert Speer and Hermann Giesler as well as the sculptor Arno Breker. Hans Baur, his personal pilot, was also with the party along with Bormann, Schaub and Keitel, and with the usual smattering of aides and valets.

The five-car convoy drove into central Paris in the early hours of the morning, just when the first Parisians were beginning to get up for work. *Oberst* Hans Speidel, a staff officer from Paris headquarters who would later be involved in plots against the *Führer* in 1943 and 1944, accompanied Hitler.

Security for Hitler's visit consisted of the bodyguards in the escort cars and nothing else. There were no cordons on the streets or troops presenting arms as he drove by. Nothing. Had the French known about this visit it is fair to say that Hitler would have presented an extremely juicy target for anyone with a rifle or a hand grenade. All of the Mercedes drove along with their roofs down, through streets lined with tall buildings. On several occasions Hitler got out of his car to stroll and sightsee.

The first building visited was the Opera, with Hitler actually leading the party around with the caretaker quickly unlocking doors. The *Führer* had previously studied the building's blueprints in detail. Then the convoy drove down the Champs Elysées, past the Madeleine to the Trocadero before stopping in front of the Eiffel Tower. Hitler strolled around near the tower's base, holding his cap peak and staring up at the great monument, deep in conversation with Speer and the other 'experts', and posing for photographs like any other tourist.

Back in the cars, the party next drove to the Tomb of the Unknown Soldier, before Hitler alighted again at the Dome des Invalides where he stood deep in thought before Emperor Napoleon I's tomb, the new conqueror of Europe paying homage to the old. Then it was on with the famous sights – the Pantheon, Place de Vosges, Louvre Museum, Palais de Justice and Sainte Chapelle. The convoy of large dark Mercedes cars powered down the Rue de Rivoli to the tour's final destination – the magnificent white Sacre Coeur that overlooks Montmartre. By 9.00am Hitler had left Paris for his field headquarters, *Wolfsschlucht I* at Margival. As for the inhabitants of Paris, they had either ignored the tyrant with a Gallic shrug or run away from him. Hitler's triumphal progress through the City of Lights had been unimpeded – it was probably the most insecure and dangerous visit Hitler ever paid outside of Germany and one of the greatest missed opportunities to have put an end to the man who was determined to expand the war on an almost unimaginable scale.

Chapter 4

Eagle's Eyrie

'I have striven, therefore, from the beginning to conduct the war wherever possible offensively. Wars are finally decided through the recognition by one side or the other that the war as such can no longer be won. To get the enemy to realise this is therefore the most important task.'

Adolf Hitler, The *Adlerhorst*
12 December 1944

The *Führersonderzug* pulled into Giessen Station in the German state of Hesse, a small, pretty town of large half-timbered houses. There were no adoring crowds awaiting the *Führer* – instead the platform was carefully guarded by SS. Outside, in the station courtyard stood a fleet of polished midnight-blue Mercedes-Benz limousines and more *SS-Begleitkommando* guards. Hitler stepped slowly down from his Pullman carriage, a black cape over his uniform tunic. It was blustery and cold and the *Führer*, walking with a slight stoop, headed straight for his car where Erich Kempka, his personal driver for so many years, sat waiting, the engine running. Hitler's entourage settled themselves into the fleet of cars, turning up their collars against the cold wind. Twenty minutes later the procession of gleaming vehicles swept uphill through the tiny village of Ziegenburg towards a large, gloomy Gothic castle that stood on a hill above the houses, perched atop a lofty promontory. It was 11 December 1944 and Hitler had arrived at the *Adlerhorst* (Eagle's Eyrie), his top secret Western Front headquarters. He was happy and excited, for he came with a new plan prepared that he hoped would win him a great victory against the Western Allies. As his car entered a narrow approach tunnel to Kransberg Castle, Hitler felt energized. As he stated to his generals that evening: 'If forced back on the defensive, it is all the more important to convince the enemy that victory was not in sight.'[1] At the *Adlerhorst* he would change the course of the war back into Germany's favour.

Hitler would have several military headquarters for his campaigns in Western Europe. They were built and used during three specific periods: the German invasion of France and the Low Countries during 1940; the Allied invasion of Normandy in 1944; and the Ardennes Offensive of 1944–45. Hitler spent most the war, over 800 days, at the Wolf's Lair in East Prussia demonstrating that his strategic focus was primarily upon the monumental fight with the Soviet Union. When not at the Wolf's Lair he was mostly to be found at his private house, the Berghof, in southern Bavaria. Because of this, his visits to the Western Front were often short affairs. But a considerable amount of money, effort and time was expended in finding and creating suitable headquarters for Hitler and his large entourage, the most significant but perhaps least known of the *Führer* Headquarters being the Eagle's Eyrie in western Germany, hidden as with most of Hitler's HQs, in a gloomy forested area with more than an element of the Brothers Grimm about the place.

On 10 October 1939 Hitler's first *Führer* Escort Battalion (FBB) commander, Irwin Rommel, was sent West to find a suitable location for a new *Führer* Headquarters for the forthcoming campaign against France and the Low Countries. Hitler also dispatched his architect Albert Speer along with the Reich Minister for Armaments and Ammunition, Dr Fritz Todt, to help with the search.

Speer and Todt recommended Kransberg Castle in Langenhain-Ziegenberg, 35km from Frankfurt-am-Main. The castle, looking like something out of a fairytale, sits in the densely wooded Taunus Mountains and was codenamed 'A' for '*Adlerhorst*' (Eagle's Eyrie) by the Nazis. Originally constructed in 1170, the castle had fallen into disrepair by the mid-nineteenth century. Extensively remodelled in the 1870s it was given a neo-gothic makeover in line with the then fashion for Germanic myth and legend. Acquired in 1926 by Austrian noblewoman Emma von Scheitheim, she used the castle for entertaining and society events until, in 1939, the government seized it for military purposes.

This was to be Hitler's showpiece headquarters for the campaign in the West and no expense was spared. Incredibly, the local villagers who lived below the Castle in Ziegenberg do not appear to have realized that it was now a *Führer* Headquarters. The Germans kept the secret well, using labour that was brought into the area to complete the building work.[2] As far as locals were concerned, Kransberg Castle was just another military installation during a time of war. The castle was extensively renovated and seven concrete bunkers disguised as half-timbered cottages were built in the grounds. These were connected with extensive underground bunkers which in turn were themselves connected with the main castle by tunnels. But when Hitler visited the site he rejected it as too luxurious and not in keeping with his image as a simple and frugal leader. He was particularly worried that after the war his loyal disciples would visit the castle as a kind of shrine and be dismayed to find out that their beloved *Führer* lived in such opulent surroundings while they suffered air raids and food shortages. Hitler demanded a different headquarters on a more modest scale.

The *Adlerhorst* would not be used until 1944, when Hitler finally moved in to direct the Ardennes Offensive, but although mothballed for the time being the site nonetheless still had to be carefully protected. Speer modified the complex for use by the Luftwaffe as their HQ for Operation 'Sealion', the planned invasion of Britain in 1940. After Hitler cancelled Sealion the castle was used as a recuperation centre for wounded German soldiers and as a private retreat for the corpulent Luftwaffe leader Hermann Göring.[3]

Hitler's RSD commander, Johann Rattenhuber, provided nineteen of his men to guard the *Adlershorst* complex, plus 106 military policemen – a considerable use of resources to guard an 'empty' headquarters. This activity served as a useful distraction from Hitler's real HQ, the considerably more basic 'F' or *'Felsennest'* (Mountain Nest) that was occupied at Rodert near the town of Munstereifel, 35km southwest of Bonn and only 45km from the Belgian frontier.

At the *Felsennest*, Hitler took over an already existing site that consisted of some anti-aircraft positions and a few wooden huts. Engineers built catwalks between the buildings so that Hitler and his officers did not have to wade through mud, renovated the existing structures, put up security fences and gates, and built some small bunkers and air raid shelters. Hitler's personal bunker was very small. It consisted of one room that he could use for meetings and military briefings plus a modest bedroom, bathroom, bedrooms for Keitel, adjutant Schaub and one manservant, and a kitchen.[4] 'Jodl, Dr Brandt, Schmundt, Below [*Luftwaffe* aide], Puttkamer [naval aide], and Keitel's adjutant were in a second [bunker]. The rest had to be accommodated in the nearby village.'[5] But the headquarters was in keeping with Hitler's simple nature, and importantly it reinforced his own image of the straightforward and frugal leader.

The complex was ready for Hitler to move in on 16 December 1939 but the *Führer* did not finally arrive at his new headquarters until the afternoon of 9 May 1940 when the *Führersonderzug* pulled in at

Euskirchen Station. The next day the German invasion of France and the Low Countries commenced.

One of the major concerns for the Germans was a British or French airborne assault on *Felsennest*. To counter this possibility strong anti-aircraft batteries were established throughout the area and the FBB formed a 234-man guard company that was split between Rodert, Munstereifel, Kreuzweingarten and the *Felsennest*. But such a small number of troops would not have proved very effective in a serious emergency. Local garrison troops were also to be used in the event of an attack by the British or French.[6] No such assault was ever contemplated or planned by London or Paris.

Once again, Hitler found himself in the front lines following his close calls during the Polish Campaign. The danger came not from paratroopers but from British and French aircraft. An air raid warning system had already been installed in the region before the war, and Allied aircraft often overflew the *Felsennest* on their way to attack other targets in Germany. On 25 May the HQ flak battery engaged an enemy aircraft overhead and the next night several batteries fired on aircraft in the vicinity. One plane was hit and bombs were dropped close to Hitler's HQ. Just after midnight on 27 May the batteries shot down a British bomber. On the night of 10/11 August British aircraft dropped leaflets over the *Felsennest* – RSD men at first light hastily cleaned these up before Hitler saw them. The next night incendiary bombs fell on a nearby airfield. Overflights, flak and occasional bombings continued right through August and September 1940. Hitler remained unconcerned and stated that he wished to move his headquarters further west behind his rapidly advancing armies.[7]

The FBB sent a detail forward to try and locate a suitable location while Fritz Todt was sent to the Maginot Line east of Avesnes to inspect recently captured bunker systems. These were judged to be unsuitable for Hitler's use. FBB commander *Oberstleutnant* Thomas and Dr Todt settled on a location at Bruly-de-Pesche, 25km northwest of Charleville, Belgium. Three large huts were swiftly built – one for Hitler, one dining hall and one for a section of the OKW high command staff. The site was codenamed '*Waldwiese*' (Forest Meadow). The local village's inhabitants were forcefully relocated and the FBB protection unit, most of Hitler's staff, adjutants and bodyguards moved into the vacated buildings. Hitler arrived on 6 June 1940 and the HQ was immediately renamed '*Wolfsschlucht I*' (Wolf's Gorge I). Hitler routinely used the name 'Wolf' for his military headquarters, and, indeed, during the so-called 'years of struggle' he had called himself by this name. His own Christian name Adolf was a variation of the Old German name 'Wolf'. He also saw himself as a lone wolf – a rather childish fantasy in the eyes of many of his enemies. Even one of his sisters took the surname 'Wolf' in an attempt to live incognito during and after the war.

Wolfsschlucht I was once again a painfully simple collection of wooden huts and damp bunkers. The name would be used again in 1943–44 when Organisation Todt workers built a *Führer* Headquarters complex near Margival, France. *Wolfsschlucht II* was on a grander scale than the first attempt and incorporated a huge tunnel for Hitler's train that could be sealed with bombproof blast doors. But Hitler only used his new HQ for one day, 17 June 1944, during the Battle for Normandy.[8]

In 1940 *Führer* HQ was moved from *Wolfsschlucht I* to Installation 'T' (*Tannenberg*) located in a dark spruce forest on Kniebis Mountain near Freudenstadt in Germany's Black Forest. Hitler arrived there by plane on 28 June. The site was difficult to protect as the thick forest impeded patrols by FBB, RSD and *SS-Begleitkommando*.[9] The HQ consisted of a few damp bunkers and air raid shelters and was in many regards a prototype for the later Wolf's Lair, also located deep in a thick dark fir forest. Hitler didn't spend much time at *Tannenberg*, visiting Strasbourg and some First World War battlefields.[10] On 5 July Hitler returned to the Reich Chancellery in Berlin, the campaign on the Western Front virtually completed. Headquarters moved to the *Adlerhorst* at Kransberg Castle to begin preparations for the invasion of Britain. They left Kransberg Castle on 25 November for Berlin after Operation Sealion was cancelled and Hitler's interest turned to the Soviet Union. On 12 December 1940 *Felsennest* was turned over to local army command.

Hitler visited the west again between 12 and 25 April 1941 when the *Führersonderzug* was parked outside a tunnel south of Wiener Neustadt near Monichkirchen – this mobile headquarters was code-named '*Frühlingssturm*' (Spring Storm). To protect Hitler from possible air attack the train's two locomotives were kept fully steamed up and ready, at a moment's notice, to shunt the train into the long tunnel.[11]

Hitler returned to the Western Front in June 1944, shortly after the D-Day landings in Normandy. His headquarters for his short visit was *Wolfsschlucht II* near Margival in France. He flew to Metz aboard his personal *Condor* aircraft on 16 June and then travelled by motorcade through the early hours of 17 June to his conference with *General-feldmarschalls* Gerd von Rundstedt and Rommel, his two Western Front commanders. The *Führer's* safety when airborne was assured by the grounding of all Luftwaffe aircraft along the route and an order that no German anti-aircraft batteries would be permitted to open fire. It should be noted that by this stage of the war Hitler was taking a considerable risk still travelling by air because the Allies had managed to achieve almost complete aerial superiority over Western Europe.

The meeting with von Rundstedt and Rommel was deeply acrimonious, Hitler blaming them for their failure to force the Allies back into the sea at Normandy. They first had lunch together. Hitler watched as his special vegetarian food was tasted for him before eating any himself. Two RSD officers stood behind Hitler's chair, their faces hard and their eyes constantly scanning the *Führer's* lunch companions. Rommel told Hitler that in his opinion the German Army would collapse in France, as well as in Italy, and Hitler should end the war as soon as possible. An air raid alert forced the group underground into Hitler's personal air raid shelter. Hitler was due to visit Army Group B front headquarters at the Chateau of La Roche-Guyon on 19 June but Hitler had suddenly departed for Germany on the night of the 17th. The reason for this was the impact of a brand new V1 flying bomb on the headquarters at Margival that night. V1 launches against London had begun on 12 June and by the 15th over 500 of these primitive cruise missiles were being launched daily. One malfunctioned and landed on *Führer* Headquarters, frightening Hitler enough that he decided to return to Germany and from there take his personal train back to his Eastern Front headquarters at the Wolf's Lair.

Hitler came West once again on 11 December 1944. His personal train arrived at Giessen Station in Hesse where a fleet of armoured Mercedes took him and his party to the *Adlerhorst*, the command complex that had been built several years before adjacent to Kransberg Castle. Although Hitler had previously refused to use the complex, complaining that it was too luxuriously appointed, by December 1944 he required a large headquarters base with excellent communications and a co-located army high command facility for the forthcoming Ardennes Offensive. His other Western Front headquarters were none of these things. The Eagle's Eyrie was the only *Führer* Headquarters in the West that met these criteria and so preparations had been made for Hitler's arrival.[12]

The *Adlerhorst* consisted of seven large 'cottages' set in a heavily wooded compound beyond Kransberg Castle's main entrance. In reality, each cottage was in fact a large two-storey concrete bunker that was disguised to look like a typical *'Fachwerk'* or half-timbered wooden cottage. Although constructed of concrete with walls 3 feet thick, the second storey included fake dormer windows with flower baskets under a sloped tiled roof. The interiors of the bunkers were kept simple, as befitting Hitler's personal taste. They were furnished in traditional German style, with oak floors, pine wall panelling, functional brown leather furniture, wall lamps, wall hangings depicting hunting scenes or Teutonic battles, and deer antlers.[13]

Haus I was the *Führer's* personal bunker. The decoration and furnishings were not embellished in any way. *Haus II* was also known as the "Casino", a German military term for an officers' mess. It consisted of a lounge and a café on the ground floor with bedrooms on the first floor. An entrance to the bunker below gave access to a secure situation room and communications centre outfitted with radio transmitters and Enigma coding machines. The Casino was connected to the *Führerbunker* by a short covered walkway so that Hitler could stay out of the elements.[14]

Haus III was occupied by a section of the *Oberkommando der Wehrmacht* (German High Command – OKW) and was the residence of the commanding general. At various times this building housed *Generalfeldmarschall*s Gerd von Rundstedt, Albert Kesselring and Wilhelm Keitel as well as *Reichsmarschall* Göring and *Generaloberst* Alfred Jodl.

Haus IV was known as the 'Generals' House' and was used by second echelon general staff, for example Hasso von Manteuffel, Ferdinand Schörner and Heinz Guderian.

Haus V was occupied by a section of Dr Goebbels' Propaganda Ministry while Reich Ministers and very senior Nazi officials including Martin Bormann, Alfred Rosenberg and Robert Ley used *Haus VI*. The final cottage, *Haus VII*, was known as the '*Wachhaus*' and was the largest of the seven. It housed Hitler's adjutants, bodyguards, personal secretaries and housekeeping staff. This building was connected to Kransberg Castle, as we have seen already previously converted into a secure army headquarters complex, by an 800-metre long tunnel.

The largest building in the *Adlerhorst* complex was called the *Kraftfahrzeughalle* (Motor vehicle hall) and this was located in the village below Kransberg Castle. It housed the armoured Mercedes limousines used by Hitler and his henchmen as well as fire engines, buses and ambulances. There was also *Fachwerk*-style accommodation for the families of personnel working at the *Adlerhorst*.

The entire site was carefully guarded, with disguised concrete guard bunkers covering all approaches and a network of anti-aircraft batteries sited around the surrounding hills. Above the Castle, located to the north in the hills, was a disguised *Wehrmacht* depot that housed additional army units for the defence of the *Adlerhorst*.

Hitler would use the Eagle's Eyrie between December 1944 and January 1945 during the Ardennes Offensive, his last gamble in the West. The *Adlerhorst* became Hitler's last field HQ after the abandonment of the Wolf's Lair to the advancing Soviets. The Commander-in-Chief West, Gerd von Rundstedt, moved into Kransberg Castle in October 1944 in preparation for the coming offensive, but when Hitler arrived by train at the *Adlerhorst* on 11 December, von Rundstedt and his headquarters moved forward to near Limburg in Belgium.

On the morning of 15 December Hitler hosted a planning conference to discuss the Ardennes operation attended by von Rundstedt, Keitel, Jodl and Gunther Blumentritt and the ground commanders including von Manteuffel and Sepp Dietrich. Many of these top commanders didn't even know of the existence of the *Adlerhorst* and before they had arrived they had been driven in an SS bus on a long and circuitous route through the mountains to deliberately confuse them about the headquarters location.[15]

After Christmas 1944 Hermann Göring arrived and took up residence inside the Castle. It was at a briefing inside *Haus II* that the Reichsmarschall destroyed his relationship with Hitler after he suggested, in light of the evident failure of the Ardennes offensive, that Hitler seek a truce with the Allies through neutral Swedish contacts. Hitler flew into a rage and threatened to have Göring placed before a court martial and shot.

On New Year's Eve, 31 December 1944, Hitler made a rare radio broadcast to the German people before going to *Haus* I to welcome in 1945 with his close intimates including Bormann, Dr Dietrich and two of his secretaries, Traudl Junge and Christina Wolf. Two inches of snow had fallen, giving the Castle and the surrounding pine forest a pretty and festive aspect. Hitler's Austrian dietician, Constanze Manziarly, had laid out a buffet and there were chilled bottles of *Mosel-Sekt*.

Whilst Hitler was preoccupied with the Ardennes Offensive, *Generaloberst* Heinz Guderian, Chief of the General Staff of the Army, had visited the *Adlerhorst* on several occasions trying in vain to warn Hitler of the growing Soviet threat on the Vistula River south of Warsaw. Intelligence summaries suggested that in the predicted main assault areas the Red Army would outnumber the Germans by 11-to-1 in men, 7-to-1 in tanks and 20-to-1 in guns. Hitler rubbished the intelligence and refused to transfer divisions east.

At 4.00am on 1 January 1945 Hitler attended a conference in *Haus* II to discuss his counter-offensive in the West, Operation North Wind. Launched at midnight, the counter-offensive ran out of steam by 25 January 1945 when it became clear that Germany had lost the battle and in the process used up its last remaining reserves of manpower and equipment. Also on 1 January Guderian attended another meeting with Hitler where he continued to plead for the transfer of forces east before it was too late. Hitler only permitted the transfer of four divisions, and promptly ordered them to Hungary instead of the threatened sectors of the front.[16]

On 9 January Guderian was back at the *Adlerhorst*, pestering Hitler again about the Eastern Front. At this time Hitler's great offensive in the west was faltering, and Hitler flew into a rage, refusing to transfer divisions or even to consider permitting exposed German formations to pull back to more defensible positions. It was at this point that Guderian made his famous remark: 'The Eastern Front is like a house of cards. If the front is broken through at one point, all the rest will collapse.'[17]

On 15 January, with the western campaign virtually ended and with increasing signs of an imminent Soviet assault across the Vistula, Hitler left the *Adlerhorst* for the last time. As he was leaving aboard his train, one wit among his staff pointed out that 'Berlin was preferential as a headquarters; it would soon be possible to travel from there both to the eastern and western front by suburban railway.'[18] Apparently Hitler actually laughed. He had probably been encouraged to move out of the *Adlerhorst* not only by the obvious failure of his offensive in the West and by the imminent Soviet onslaught from the East, but also by another close call with death. On 6 January an RAF Lancaster bomber, possibly in trouble, jettisoned a huge Blockbuster Bomb over Ziegenburg, the town that lay at the foot of Kransberg Castle. The late-war Blockbuster, known to the RAF as the 'Cookie', was the largest conventional bomb used by any of the Allied air forces. It was packed with 12,000-lbs of Amatol high explosive and designed to level entire city blocks with one strike. One bomber crew recorded that when they dropped one into the centre of Koblenz the tremendous explosion damaged their Lancaster flying at 1,800 metres. The explosion at Ziegenburg, which was not densely populated or built-up, killed four civilians, wrecked the local church and caused extensive damage to surrounding houses. If the bomb had landed on the *Führerbunker* Hitler could conceivably have been killed.

Chapter 5

The Führer's Squadron

'But for the war, I might have spent the rest of my life in an office.'
SS-Obergruppenführer Hans Baur

13 March 1943. An airfield set amongst dense forest just outside the Ukrainian city of Smolensk. Hitler and his entourage walked towards two huge Focke-Wulf Fw 200 *Condor* aircraft belonging to the Führer transport squadron. A young army officer, *Oberleutnant* Fabian von Schlabrendorff, walked slightly behind the large party of senior officers headed for Hitler's plane, carrying a medium-sized wooden box in his arms. As the Führer climbed a short ladder into the *Condor* followed by his senior staff members, *Generalmajor* Henning von Treskow reminded *Oberstleutnant* Heinz Brandt, who would be travelling with the Führer, to take the parcel. Unnoticed, Schlabrendorff had opened the top, crushed a short metal tube with a pair of pliers, resealed the package and then stepped forward smartly and handed it to Brandt. Inside were what appeared at first glance to be two bottles of French cognac. Treskow inveigled Brandt into taking the liquor to Germany for him as payment for a bet lost to *Generalmajor* Helmut Stieff, Chief of Organisation at Army High Command. Brandt was more than happy to oblige and such behaviour was not unusual among the senior military officers who worked around the Führer.

As the two *Condors* powered down the grass landing strip and headed off into the wide blue sky towards Germany Treskow and Schlabrendorff exchanged a knowing look. In thirty minutes Hitler would be dead and the plan to take back Germany from the Nazis would swing into action.

Due to the size of Hitler's empire, the most efficient way to get around it was by plane. As with so many aspects of Hitler's leadership style and security arrangements, he set a standard by using aeroplanes in an era when air travel was still a novelty. Hitler was the first modern politician to travel by aircraft, beginning during his election campaigning in the 1920s and 1930s. Once he became a war leader he utilised a fleet of aircraft to move speedily between his various headquarters, much like modern presidents and generals today. The speed of the modern battlefield dictated that if he wished to exercise effective command and control, and Hitler became increasingly 'hands on' as the war progressed much to his generals' indignation and frustration, then air travel was really the only way he could do this. But air travel is intrinsically dangerous, particularly during wartime, so extreme precautions were taken by the Germans to ensure that Hitler travelled not only in comfort, but also in safety, including some very novel emergency equipment designed to preserve the Führer's life if his aircraft was ever fatally damaged.

Hitler first flew to a war front during the Polish campaign in September 1939. Two modified Junkers Ju 52/3m transport planes, the tri-motor corrugated metal workhorses of the German armed forces, were used to fly Hitler and his military entourage to a recently captured Polish airfield, closely escorted by several Messerschmitt Bf 109 fighter planes. Following a short meeting at an army headquarters at the front Hitler was flown back to Berlin by his personal pilot and friend, Hans Baur.

Baur, who was born in Ampfing, Bavaria in 1897, had transferred to the flying service in 1915 as an artillery spotter. By 1918 he had claimed six aerial victories, plus three probables, and had been awarded the Iron Cross 1st Class for bravery. After the war Baur worked as a courier pilot and was one of the first six pilots employed by the fledgling German national carrier *Lufthansa*. In 1926 he pioneered *Lufthansa's* new 'Alpine Route' between Munich, Milan and Rome, one of his passengers being Tsar Boris III of Bulgaria. That same year Baur joined the Nazi Party and later came to Hitler's attention. He first flew Hitler during the 1932 elections. When Hitler became chancellor in 1933 he acquired a Junkers Ju 52/3m that he named '*Immelmann II*' in honour of a famous First World War German fighter ace. Baur was selected to be the Führer's principal pilot. At this time, because of the stipulations of the Treaty of Versailles, the *Luftwaffe* did not exist, so in order to give Baur some authority and power Hitler had him appointed an *SS-Standartenführer*. Because of this, Hitler's personal pilots were never *Luftwaffe* officers, always SS.

After the old Reich President Paul von Hindenburg died in 1934 Hitler was able to absorb the posts of president and chancellor into one new office, becoming '*Führer*'. He also reorganized the government and, with *Lufthansa's* help, acquired a further Ju 52/3m, which he christened '*Richthofen*' after the Red Baron. In 1935 '*Immelmann II*' was replaced by '*Buddecke*' and '*Richthofen*' was renamed '*Immelmann II*'.[1] Hitler used his new powers to create the *Regirungsstaffel* (Government Squadron) with Baur as its commander headquartered at Berlin's vast Tempelhof Airport.

The new Government Squadron was quickly expanded to include eight Ju 52/3ms, each capable of carrying seventeen passengers in relative comfort. These aircraft were to be used to ferry around Hitler, his senior inner circle of ministers and the all-important army generals. Some leaders were of such importance that they were assigned their own personal pilots, all of the flyers being former *Lufthansa* captains. Baur's second-in-command and co-pilot on Hitler's aircraft was Georg Betz. Deputy-Führer Rudolf Hess was assigned Kurt Schuhmann. Propaganda Minister Dr Goebbels' pilot was Max von Müller, while *Grossadmiral* Erich Raeder, professional head of the German Navy, was assigned Peter Strasser. An aristocrat, Count Schilly, flew the two chiefs of the army general staff, Werner Frengel and Walther von Brauchitsch.

Baur soon became one of Hitler's court favourites. Hitler knew how to extract personal loyalty from his immediate subordinates and Baur was no exception. To celebrate Baur's fortieth birthday in 1937 Hitler hosted a lavish dinner in his honour at the New Reich Chancellery in Berlin. He also presented him with a brand new Mercedes car as a present. It is small wonder that so many of Hitler's subordinates stayed close to the Führer until the regime's very bitter end.

In September 1939 Hitler ordered the government squadron renamed. It would now be called *Die Fliegerstaffel des Führers* (F.d.F), becoming in effect Hitler's private squadron.[2]

Hitler visited Poland for a second time by air shortly after the invasion began, this time the first part of the journey completed aboard the *Führersonderzug*, his personal train. Baur picked him up in a Ju 52 and flew the Führer along the front lines so that he could see his panzers racing into action.

On 5 October 1939 Hitler first flew in the aircraft that was to become his primary means of aerial transport during the war – the Focke-Wulf Fw 200 *Condor*. Baur had convinced Hitler that the *Condor* was a superior aircraft over the older Ju 52, as well as being much safer. Hitler, who often consulted Baur on matters aerial, including *Luftwaffe* strategy, was easily won over by his trusted subordinate. Originally proposed to *Lufthansa* as a transatlantic airliner by Kurt Tank of Focke-

Wulf, the aircraft entered service in 1937. In *Luftwaffe* service the *Condor*, named after the famous Andean bird because of its huge wing-span, was utilized as a transport, maritime reconnaissance aircraft and bomber. In the transport configuration a *Condor* could carry thirty fully-armed troops. With a length of 23.45m and a wingspan of 32.85m, the *Condor* had a maximum speed of 360km/h at 4,800m with a service ceiling of 6,000m. The aircraft's range was an impressive 3,560km.

As well as Hitler, some of the Reich's more important military com-manders were assigned personal aircraft, but not at this stage the new *Condor*. These aircraft were mostly converted Heinkel He 111, Junkers Ju 52/3m, Siebel Fh 104A or the small Fieseler Fi 156 *Storch* spotter plane.[3]

In 1939 Baur flew Hitler from Berlin to recently conquered Warsaw aboard Fw 200A-O *Condor* 'Grenzmark' for a special victory parade through the devastated Polish capital. Hitler was by now sold on the *Condor* and steps were taken to formally integrate more of the aircraft into the F.d.F. Baur also arranged for several Ju 52/3m transports to be transferred from their civilian operators to the *Luftwaffe* where two were to join Hitler's private squadron as back-up aircraft. As well as a few smaller liaison planes, Baur also had some *Luftwaffe* pilots and ground crew transferred into his squadron in addition to ground crew from the German national airline *Lufthansa*. Baur never joined Hermann Göring's *Luftwaffe*, remaining an SS officer throughout the war.

In Berlin on 10 November 1939 Hitler flew for the first time in his new personal transport aircraft – an Fw 200A-0 named '*Immelmann III*', taking off from Templehof Airport. The day before, Hitler had narrowly avoided being killed by a bomb planted by a carpenter called Georg Elser inside the Burgerbraukeller beer hall in Munich.

By 1942 Baur had requested three armed *Condor* aircraft for the F.d.F. At the Wolf's Lair at Rastenburg, Hitler's main Eastern Front HQ, the runway had been strengthened and also lengthened to accom-modate these larger aircraft. The first aircraft delivered was an Fw 200C-3/U9 marked KE + IX. This plane was not intended as the Führer's personal transport – instead it would act as a passenger plane for ferrying around Hitler's large retinue of staff when visiting the front. It was armed with a 13mm MG131 machine gun in an upper turret just behind the cockpit and a 7.9mm MG15 firing from a raised dorsal position aft of the main door. Another MG15 was mounted in the nose. Under its fuselage was a long gondola with a machine gun position. The other two aircraft were also delivered at this point. Of course, these weapons would be a last resort, for it was never expected that F.d.F. should have to fight it out with enemy fighters. When they were airborne these large transports were well protected by a strong *Luftwaffe* fighter escort.

Hitler's personal plane, the *"Führermachine"*, was an Fw 200C-4/U1 (CE + IB). It had the same comfortable layout as the older *'Immelmann III'*. Behind the cockpit was an equipment compartment containing the flight engineer's panel and positions for the radio operator and navigator. From here two of the gun positions could also be accessed. The next small compartment housed equipment, lubricants and fuel tanks, with a small toilet on the starboard side. Behind this, accessed through a door, was Hitler's specially insulated cabin containing an elaborate 'parachute seat' on the right facing forward, with a wooden table in front.

According to Baur the Führer's seat was fitted with a parachute harness. This harness was installed in the back of the seat cushions. The backrest was attached above by two buttons in the chair, and this had to be pulled forward to reach the stowed parachute. In an emergency Hitler would have donned the parachute harness in the back of the seat and pulled hard on a red lever on the wall. This would have opened a spring loaded escape hatch in the floor of the aircraft in front of him. The seat back cushion and seat bottom cushion remained attached to the jumper with the parachute harness. Hitler would then have climbed through the hatch and baled out. Once free of the aircraft he would have manually released his parachute and floated down to safety.[4] However, the likelihood of a middle aged and increasingly infirm man managing this in an emergency does seem a little far-fetched. Normal parachutes were stored in the cabin for Hitler's other passengers who would have presumably baled out through the main door or through one of the gun positions. Needless to say, none of this was ever put to the test in reality, though a *Luftwaffe* volunteer made a successful test of Hitler's parachute seat, proving the theory at least. All parachutes were checked at least once a month.

On the left side of the cabin were four seats, two side by side. The cabin was armoured against enemy machine gun bullets, cannon shells and anti-aircraft bursts. The walls, floor and ceiling were lined with 12mm thick armour plate and the windows were 50mm thick bulletproof glass.

The crew consisted of pilot Baur, co-pilot Betz, a flight engineer (who also doubled as a gunner), navigator/radio operator (also working as a gunner if required), and a steward. Moving aft beyond Hitler's cabin was another passenger cabin that was fitted with six seats, two on the right facing each other, and four on the left that also faced one another. Maximum passenger capacity on Hitler's personal aircraft was thirteen.

In both cabins the windows had curtains for privacy and to prevent sun glare and the interior was finished in highly polished wood so that it more closely resembled a railway carriage or a ship's cabin than an aircraft. 'The inside of Hitler's *Condor* looked like a gent's salon,' recalled *Hauptmann* Alexander Stahlberg, who flew in the aircraft in his capacity as an aide to *Generaloberst* Erich von Manstein in mid-April 1942 from his headquarters in the Crimea to a meeting at the Wolf's Lair. 'The walls were wood-panelled and the furniture leather covered. China and cutlery were solid silver and bore the NSDAP insignia. A steward was on board and served meals and drinks as desired.'[5]

At the rear of the plane was a small galley, located behind the rear gunner's position. No cooking was permitted on Hitler's plane; instead a specially insulated cabinet contained pre-heated meals that were similar to those found on today's commercial airliners. Hot coffee and hot water for tea were also available, though not alcohol. Luggage and clothing was stored separately in an unheated cargo hold and for safety each passenger had an oxygen tank under his seat.

The third *Condor* acquired by Baur for the F.d.F. was an Fw 200C-4/U2 (CE+IC). This plane was used primarily for transporting staff and guests but Hitler did travel on this and KE+IX occasionally. CE+IC was fitted with fourteen seats in a single large panelled cabin, but lacked a special parachute seat for the Führer.

Because of the added weight of bulletproof windows and armour plating, CE+IB and CE+IC had a maximum ceiling of 5,800m, a top speed of 330 kph (though they cruised at 280 kph) and normally loaded could travel just over 3,200km without refuelling.

Before every trip that carried the Führer was very carefully managed. In particular, measures were taken to prevent the use of bombs onboard the plane. The best type of bomb to be successfully smuggled aboard Hitler's plane would have been one fitted with a barometric fuse that detonated when the plane reached a certain altitude. This avoided the need for ticking parts in the bomb. To counter anyone trying something like this, before every trip Hitler's aircraft was taken for a ten or fifteen minute test flight, including up to cruising altitude. Of course, such measures were useless had anyone managed to smuggle a time bomb aboard Hitler's plane.[6]

The *Condor* also had a significant Achilles heel, a design fault that could have killed Hitler on several occasions. In June 1942 when his *Condor* landed at Michaeli near Wiborg in Finland so that Hitler could have a meeting with Finnish leader Field Marshal Mannerheim, Finnish ground crewmen were filmed running towards the plane's landing gear armed with fire extinguishers. The problem was in the design of the brake actuating cams. When the brakes were used 'forcefully', such as in landing, they overcentred and locked slightly in the 'on' position, with the brake shoes dragging on the drums. This friction could cause the linings to catch fire on landing. The problem could also manifest itself during take off as well. If the plane was parked overnight with the brakes on, or if the brakes had not released cleanly on parking, they did not free up fully when taxiing and this would lead to the linings catching fire on take off. This could be lethal, and several *Condors* were lost in *Luftwaffe* service because of this small technical fault. The wheels retracted into bays that were adjacent to the wing fuel tanks, the last place one would want to have a fire.

Air travel was dangerous, particularly during wartime, yet Hitler seemed to prefer the risks rather than using his train for most long-distance journeys. Hundreds or even thousands of railway workers, any one of whom could have been a potential assassin, would know about Hitler's train and its route, whereas air travel and Hitler's un-predictable changes in his plans better protected the Führer from plotters. But in flying he risked thunderstorms, burning wheels, foggy takeoffs and landings, soft ground[7], and, later in the war, enemy fighters and flak.

The plot that came very close to killing Hitler in the Ukraine in 1943 centered on the idea of destroying his *Condor* aircraft whilst it was in flight over the Soviet Union. It appeared that of all the methods of killing Hitler, a catastrophic high altitude explosion was the surest. But it was not the first method that was discussed. Henning von Treskow's plan was the result of several discussions that he had had with the hard core of anti-Hitler plotters who were centered around *General-feldmarschall* Gunther von Kluge and Army Group Centre head-quarters at Vinnitsa and Smolensk in the Ukraine.

Kluge's officers had carefully worked out three options to kill Hitler. The first idea was that an officer armed with a pistol would simply shoot Hitler dead during lunch when he next visited Army Group Centre headquarters. But the problem was that no officer could be found who was willing to do it. This was not only because it was clearly a suicide mission, but for a higher principle. It was not a question of courage, for all of the plotters were highly decorated combat soldiers, but a question of morality. These largely aristocratic Junkers could not countenance the idea of assassinating an unarmed man, particularly their commander-in-chief. They took the personal oath that they had sworn to Hitler very seriously, not because of the Führer as a man but because oath taking was part of their rigid code of honour. To break an oath was to impugn one's personal and family honour. It was unthinkable.

Von Treskow admitted, probably realistically, that any putative assassin would in all likelihood freeze at the vital moment when face-to-face with his supreme commander. This was not without precedent, for the year before a young *Luftwaffe* officer, less hidebound by military tradition, had concealed himself in woods at the Wolf's Lair in East Prussia planning to ambush Hitler during his morning walk accompanied by his pet Alsatian Blondi. When Hitler appeared the officer found that he could not move his arms. It may sound dramatic, but Hitler was more than just a man, he was a cult that loomed like a mental colossus over most of his subordinates. Few were immune from the invisible aura of power that surrounded the man. Junior officers, perhaps because they spent little time in close proximity to Hitler and never engaged him in 'normal' or relaxed conversation, unlike the field marshals and generals, could not view him simply as a man. To shoot Hitler face-to-face would require not only nerves of steel but also incredibly fast reactions and accurate shooting. Any hesitation during a heavily guarded lunch would result in the assassin being gunned down by Hitler's RSD escort within seconds of raising a weapon. Waves of arrests and interrogations would then follow, potentially destroying the entire anti-Hitler resistance. Of course, success would also mean death, as the RSD bodyguards would kill the assailant even after he had shot Hitler.

Rittmeister Georg Baron von Boeselager, the highly decorated 28-year-old deputy commander of cavalry regiments in Army Group Centre suggested that he kill Hitler using an entire unit of soldiers. Boeselager, a deeply religious man, had come to believe that Hitler was the anti-Christ and that it was his sacred duty to rid the world of this evil man and save Germany from further destruction. He was prepared to break his oath to Hitler for the higher ideal of the Fatherland.

Boeselager formed a cavalry "honour guard" consisting largely of fellow anti-Hitler officers. His plan was to intercept Hitler's fleet of cars as they drove from the airfield to the field HQ near Smolensk. The cavalry would then overwhelm and destroy Hitler's FBB and RSD escort and kill the Führer. *Generalfeldmarschall* von Kluge stymied this plan, objecting to the idea of German soldiers fighting each other, even if the other side were SS. Kluge also believed that Hitler's SS escort was too strong for Boeselager's men to overcome, leading to failure, great loss of life and the exposure of the remaining plotters.

The British inadvertently made the third option possible. The *Abwehr*, German military intelligence whose head, Wilhelm Canaris, was sympathetic to the Resistance, had captured several British Plastic-C time bombs from SOE agents who had been dropped by parachute into France. Sympathetic *Abwehr* officers passed some of this material on to the anti-Hitler movement.

The bomb was ingenious, but also so simple as to be virtually foolproof. An acid fuse contained within a slim copper tube was inserted into a slab of plastic explosive. Using a pair of pliers the assassin simply crushed the fuse, releasing the acid inside which slowly ate away at a wire. When the wire snapped it released a spring-driven hammer that struck a small percussion cap, setting off the explosive charge. The bomb was silent as there were no parts to make a telltale ticking sound, and the chemical fuse did not give off any smell as it burned. Therefore, it was virtually undetectable. The length of fuse determined the time delay before detonation, and for the attack on Hitler's aircraft Treskow selected a 30-minute fuse. All going well, Hitler's aircraft would be destroyed somewhere over Minsk. The loss of the *Condor* so close to the front could have been attributed to Soviet fighters, giving the conspirators more justification in taking immediate control of the Reich in the event of the Führer's sudden death.

Disguised as a parcel containing two bottles of cognac, *Oberstleutnant* Brandt unknowingly took Treskow's bomb aboard Hitler's *Condor*. He intended to hand the package to *Generalmajor* Stieff on arrival in Germany. Stieff, though sympathetic to the resistance, was not yet an active plotter. But he was Treskow's friend, so sending him the cognac as payment for a lost bet looked perfectly normal. Ironically, Hitler disliked the 42-year-old Stieff greatly. A small man,

Hitler called him a 'poisonous little dwarf'. Unsurprisingly, in light of his commander-in-chief's insults Stieff soon became more active in the plot to kill the Führer.

The 13 March 1943 should have been Hitler's last day alive. Brandt handed the parcel to the plane's steward, who placed it with the other luggage in the unheated cargo hold. This was in direct contravention of the accepted rules for loading Hitler's aircraft. All servicing, repairs and loading of luggage at any airport could only be done in the presence of the flight engineer or another member of the crew, as well as in the presence of RSD guards.[8] Brandt knew this full well, but as with many security procedures the people most likely to break them were those who lived within this restrictive arena day in, day out. Perhaps it was a case of familiarity breeding contempt.

As the two *Condors* taxied down the grass strip and lifted off into the clear blue sky Treskow and Schlabrendorff exchanged a look before settling into a radio truck to listen for news of the Führer's demise. In thirty minutes, with Hitler dead, they would institute a takeover plan. *General der Infanterie* Friedrich Olbricht in Berlin would order the Replacement Army to seize the capital as well as Vienna and Munich.

The Replacement Army was a sprawling organisation which provided reinforcements and replacements to the field army. Its garrison units would be used to overcome any SS resistance to the army high command seizing control, though whether individual generals and their subordinates would obey the orders of Olbricht and the other plotters is open to question. Many army officers were devoted Nazis, and the *Waffen-SS* and Gestapo very strong. The plan was for a new anti-Nazi government to be placed in charge and the senior Nazis either arrested or shot. A negotiated peace could then be made with the Allies and the war ended before Germany was militarily defeated and occupied.

At the airfield outside Smolensk the expected news that Hitler's plane had crashed did not arrive. Something had gone terribly awry. 'Treskow and I,' wrote Schlabrendorff, 'judging from our own experiments, were convinced that the amount of explosive in the bomb would be sufficient to tear the entire plane apart, or at least to make a fatal crash inevitable.'[9] No word came for two agonizing hours. The two men could not understand what had happened – the plan and the equipment appeared to be foolproof.

Treskow was suddenly informed by phone that the Führer's plane had landed safely at Rastenburg airfield. It was almost unbelievable. Schlabrendorff hurriedly took the next plane to Germany and retrieved the parcel before Brandt became aware of its true contents. When the bomb was examined it was found that it had actually worked perfectly. The acid had released the spring hammer and struck the percussion cap. But because of the intense cold inside the unheated cargo hold, the percussion cap had failed to detonate and the bomb had not exploded. Hitler had been saved from certain death once again by the tiniest of flaws, one conspirator commenting bitterly that he appeared to have a 'guardian devil.'[10] If the parcel had been carried inside the heated passenger cabin everyone onboard the plane would have perished. The explosives were returned to storage until they could be used for another attempt to kill Hitler.

The plot to destroy Hitler's aircraft was never discovered, and so the Führer continued to travel by air, oblivious of the potential dangers. But air travel was becoming risky for reasons other than the aristocratic plotters within the *Wehrmacht*. American B-17 Flying Fortresses had first bombed Berlin on 6 March 1944, followed by repeated American and British raids. When the promoted *SS-Brigadeführer* Baur, Hitler's personal pilot, flew the Führer from Rastenburg to Salzburg in early March, so Hitler could visit the Berghof, he had to fully coordinate the flight plan with the *Luftwaffe* air control centre to make sure that they did not encounter Allied aircraft or German fighters and flak en route.[11]

The same precautions were taken in June when Hitler received word of the Normandy landings whilst he was at the Berghof. Deciding to take battlefield command, Hitler was flown on 17 June from Salzburg to Metz and then driven in a heavily armed convoy of cars to his headquarters at Margival, near Soissons.

In early July 1944 Hitler, who had returned to Berchtesgaden, was flown to Rastenburg in order to coordinate efforts to stop the massive Soviet spring offensive that had filleted Army Group Centre. It was at the Wolf's Lair on 20 July that the German resistance struck again, coming closest to killing Hitler (See Chapter 9).

Following the July Plot, the German war situation entered terminal decline. Hitler's special transport squadron started to run short of spare parts for their planes. In the wake of the bomb at Rastenburg, security was so tight that even conducting routine maintenance on the flight's aircraft became difficult. Hitler's *Condors* were closely guarded twenty-four hours a day by the FBB and closely inspected for sabotage before every flight. The chances of smuggling a bomb aboard in a similar fashion to that at Smolensk in 1943 had decreased to virtually zero, as every item of luggage and cargo was minutely examined. The only possibility would have been someone wearing a suicide vest, and this was never considered, largely because the explosives and detonator could not be modified to be carried or let alone worn in such a way without attracting attention.

Due to the pressing war situation, most Nazi leaders had lost their personal aircraft, with the exception of Albert Speer and Heinrich Himmler. Speer, Minister for Armaments and War Production, needed to constantly visit factories, secret missile and aircraft projects and the regional Gauleiters, and could only do so efficiently by air. Himmler remained the second most powerful man in Germany, controlling the vast SS empire. *Generalfeldmarschall* Wilhelm Keitel, Head of the OKW, was permitted a Junkers Ju 52/3m BD+DH as the Reich's senior military officer.

In September 1944 Hitler was flown from Rastenburg to bomb-damaged Berlin for an important conference, the planning for Operation 'Watch on the Rhine', more commonly known to history as The Battle of the Bulge. But at the same time the Wolf's Lair was threatened, as the Soviet juggernaut continued its inexorable advance into East Prussia. Baur expected Soviet air attacks on the airfield at Rastenburg, and dispersed the F.d.F aircraft and supplies between the main airfield and a local airport. Knowing full well that an evacuation was inevitable, Baur obtained use of the large warehouse at an airfield in Pöcking, between Braunau and Passau in Bavaria, where he could relocate the F.d.F.[12]

In early December 1944 fifty personnel, spares, tools and engines were on their way to Pöcking by train when they were involved in a collision with another locomotive in western Poland. Seventeen members of the F.d.F were killed, its highest losses during the war.

Braun decided to disperse Hitler's squadron around Berlin. Small detachments were sent to carefully camouflaged airfields at Schoenwalde, Rangsdorf, Rechlin and Finsterwalde. Realising that Hitler must shortly move to Berlin, Baur flew *Condor* TK+CV to an airfield near Berlin. This aircraft would be kept ready for immediate use by the Führer should he need to flee the capital. In the event, Hitler chose to die in Berlin, but the F.d.F. remained a vital component in the hectic last few weeks of the war.

Chapter 6

Eagle's Nest

'Here my ideas mature.'
Adolf Hitler at the Berghof, 1938

The two men lay concealed beneath damp foliage at the edge of a wood. A light drizzle had been falling since before dawn, when the pair had silently hiked to their current position. For several hours the pair, dressed in German mountain troop uniforms that included camouflaged smocks, had carefully negotiated several tall wire fences and guard posts deep in the woods and skirted alpine meadows and farm houses, until they had settled into their hide. All around them great mountains soared up on the German-Austrian border. Pretty alpine chalets were dotted across the valleys above the town of Berchtesgaden.

The men waited patiently, laying still, their heads covered with green mosquito nets for added camouflage. One constantly scanned the terrain ahead with black binoculars, watching a path that snaked down through the valley, skirting another patch of woodland, towards a teahouse perched high on a rocky promontory. All was quiet. The other man had a Mauser 98K rifle propped against his right cheek, one eye peering through the weapon's telescopic sight. Their bodies ached from cramp and from the chilly mountain air, but they did not move or speak – they waited silently for their quarry to appear. The spotter glanced at his wristwatch for the thousandth time – 10.07am. If the great man were coming today he would be coming very soon.

Suddenly, they spotted movement – a small group of figures appeared from around a corner, strolling nonchalantly along the path. At the head of the group walked Hitler, dressed in a dark woolen suit and a grey fedora hat, holding a carved wooden walking stick in his right hand. Behind him walked his press chief, two female secretaries and an SS adjutant in field grey. There were no guards close to their leader, just as Hitler wanted it.

Taking careful aim, the sniper placed his scope's crosshairs over the *Führer*'s bobbing head, settling his rifle into his target's walking rhythm. His finger settled on the trigger while the spotter scanned the surrounding countryside for guards. 'We're clear,' whispered the spotter, 'go for the shot.' The sniper slowed his breathing, his eye never leaving the famous head that loomed large in his scope, his finger gently squeezing the trigger as he exhaled one long breath. The rifle butt slammed into his shoulder, and simultaneously Hitler's head was slammed violently back, a spray of blood and brains splattering his walking companions. As the high velocity rifle shot echoed off the surrounding mountains, the only sound to reach the two assassins was of screaming women. Hitler was dead.

Although the above never happened, it was thought about at the highest levels of the British government and green lighted by no less a figure than Winston Churchill. Special Operations Executive, set up in 1940 to assist the European resistance movements and sow mayhem behind the German lines, began seriously to consider assassinating Hitler after D-Day. Several German soldiers fell into British hands who had previously guarded Hitler, and one, surnamed Dieser, was able to elaborate on both Hitler's routine at the Berghof and his guarding arrangements. But killing Hitler at his private home was to prove a very difficult event to plan for, and Major H.B. Court, the SOE officer responsible for compiling a feasibility study, had his work cut out.[1]

Berchtesgaden is a pretty little Bavarian town located a stone's throw from the Austrian border. During the Nazi period the town was reserved for the most loyal party members and was, in effect, a private Nazi sanctuary high in the mountains. Around 30km south of Salzburg in Austria, Berchtesgaden is overlooked by Germany's third highest mountain, the 2,713m Watzmann and the nearby Kehlstein Mountain (1,835m) affording breathtaking and beautiful views across wooded and pastoral valleys set against a backdrop of high, craggy granite mountains. Hitler was drawn to this landscape and would spend a large part of his dictatorship looking down on Berchtesgaden and its adoring citizens from his own mountaintop perch on the Obersalzberg.

Hitler had first visited the area in the early 1920s. He would stay at inns in the tiny village of Salzberg near Berchtesgaden. Eventually he rented and then purchased a house of his own that came to be called the Berghof. This was Hitler's private home, and he was intensely proud of having purchased and extended the property courtesy of the royalties from his book *Mein Kampf*.

The Berghof, where before the war Hitler would spend six months of every year, held a special place in his heart. 'Throughout the early years during the many periods he spent on the Obersalzberg, Hitler enjoyed an almost carefree lifestyle. Here, in peace and comfort, he could escape the daily grind of political administration and public duties, which he disliked.'[2]

The Berghof represented Hitler's character in bricks, mortar and wood, its interior design indicative of his lower middle class and essentially conservative outlook. It was where Hitler felt most comfortable, and the surrounding area soon became a private gated community for his closest followers who were permitted to construct their own chalet-style houses, usually close copies of the Berghof. It was also Hitler's rest and relaxation area, where he could walk through alpine meadows, pine forests and along mountain tracks virtually unguarded, visit specially constructed tea houses perched atop precipitous mountains, entertain world leaders, artists, diplomats and musicians and, latterly, run the war. The Berghof fed into Hitler's own self-image. 'In these surroundings, Adolf Hitler projected an image of someone who loved nature and the great outdoors, a man of the people who enjoyed a simple and informal lifestyle.'[3]

From his lofty perch Hitler was often seen deep in thought on the Berghof's sun terrace, or in conversation with his henchmen, chief among them Heinrich Himmler, Hermann Göring, Albert Speer and Martin Bormann. The Berghof was also the only place where Hitler freely and publicly socialised with his long-term mistress, Eva Braun. At the Berghof he was shielded from the gaze of his people, and he could be himself.

Recently declassified documents have shed further light onto Hitler's private life at the Berghof, and his vast and complex security and travel arrangements. The Obersalzberg was the one place that Hitler regularly visited where the security, though tight, was not air-tight. The entire Hitler complex was simply too large and geographically challenging to guard to the same degree of thoroughness as at Hitler's other headquarters, notably the Reich Chancellery and the Wolf's Lair. And Hitler's own behaviour at the Obersalzberg actually increased the risk to his personal security. Hitler's aversion to being publicly guarded was particularly acute at this, his most private home, leading to more than one plan to kill him.

Hitler's mountaintop complex was approached from Berchtesgaden, 3km further down the mountain, by a single well-guarded road. The complex was largely the creation of Martin Bormann, whom the SS garrison soon dubbed 'The Lord of the Obersalzberg'. Over time, Bormann gradually removed local farmers and hotel owners from the area to create a carefully controlled security zone, in effect creating a private village for Hitler, built around the Berghof.

In the early days, security around the *Führer*'s house was considerably more relaxed than during the war years. Hitler and his entourage often used public paths through the nearby forests, normally accompanied by a few members of his inner circle and three or four RSD officers. He would take tea at the Mooslahnerkopf, a smaller mountain peak, and then be driven home in a low-key Volkswagen, a marked departure from the usual giant armoured Mercedes. Naturally, these excursions often brought him face-to-face with his adoring public. Until 1937 up to 2,000 people a day gathered at the security point near the Berghof to see Hitler as he left on a regular afternoon stroll between 3.00 and 4.00pm. As he passed by the adoring throng he might say a few words, perhaps tousle the hair of a suitably blond child, and photographers were on hand to capture everything for posterity. But the risks to his personal security were obvious should a member of the crowd have been bent on assassination.

In November 1937 Johann Rattenhuber, the RSD officer charged with Hitler's personal protection, was particularly worried after Hitler ordered the number of *Leibstandarte-SS* sentries around his property to be reduced as he particularly disliked being visibly guarded. A further problem was that the entrances through the outer security ring were not guarded by the SS but by civilian volunteers instead, called *Arbeitsposten* (Worker's sentries), who lacked the authority to stop and search people approaching Hitler's domain. At Post 1 at the privately owned Platterhof Hotel close to the Berghof visitors often witnessed unseemly verbal arguments between civilian guards, labourers and SS soldiers. Rattenhuber requested that all three checkpoints be taken over by the RSD.

The security arrangements at the Berghof still had some way to go before they could be described as completely satisfactory. This was evidenced by the case of Maurice Bavaud, a 22-year-old Swiss student who took it upon himself in October 1938 to kill Hitler.

Crossing the border into Germany, Bavaud, who was armed with a 6.35mm pistol and ammunition and a copy of *Mein Kampf*, initially attempted to stalk Hitler in Berlin but swiftly discovered that the *Führer* was hundreds of kilometres south on the Obersalzberg. When he arrived at Berchtesgaden in late October Bavaud quietly and unobtrusively questioned locals about Hitler's security and itinerary, but he discovered that Hitler had moved once again, this time north to Munich in preparation for the Beer Hall Putsch Memorial Parade, an annual Nazi pilgrimage. During this event Hitler would be at his most exposed, walking with other senior Nazis along roads crammed with spectators to lay a wreath at the Feldherrnhalle, where the *Reichswehr* had bloodily stopped Hitler's revolution in its tracks in 1923. At this location, a handful of aimed shots from the large crowd might just have been possible.

Incredibly, considering whose house it was, Bavaud was able to slip into the woods near the Berghof and spend *two days* practicing his shooting without being arrested. In 1938, only a small security zone surrounded the Berghof, with many of the valley's properties still in private hands. But it was nonetheless remarkable that repeated gunshots did not alert either the SS or civilian guards to Bavaud's presence. Even more incredibly, Bavaud struck up a conversation with *Hauptmann* Karl Deckert, one of the police officers in charge of security at the Old Reich Chancellery in Berlin and security officer to Dr Hans Lammers, State Secretary and Chief of the Chancellery.[4] The policeman had overheard Bavaud discussing his admiration for Hitler and his desire to meet him with two French language instructors. Deckert, who spoke French, was at the Berghof with his boss and told Bavaud, thinking that he was a 'fan', that if he wanted to see Hitler the best place would be during the upcoming parade in Munich. The only way he could meet the *Führer* was by a personal letter of introduction from a senior Nazi official.

On 31 October Bavaud arrived in Munich, rented a room, and plotted the route of the forthcoming march on a tourist map hoping to discover a suitable ambush point. He decided that one of the invitation-only grandstands near the Marienplatz afforded the closest vantage point of Hitler as he walked along the road. Bavaud obtained a ticket by pretending to be a Swiss reporter. Still concerned about his shooting ability he took himself off to a quiet forested area 40km from Munich to practice, again without raising suspicion.

The 9 November was a cold and clear day – perfect parade weather. Dressed in a heavy overcoat and with the pistol tucked into his pocket, Bavaud made his way through the huge crowd to his seat in the grandstand. The entire road was festooned with Nazi flags and bunting, the crowd was restless and excited and the route was lined with large brown-uniformed SA men. Suddenly a shout went up: 'The *Führer* is coming!' The crowd rose almost as one. Bavaud, in the front row, stood with one hand thrust deep into his coat pocket, gripping the pistol tightly. His heart was racing. Then the marchers came into view. Bavaud stared in scant disbelief – Hitler was not in the middle of the first rank of marchers as he had assumed, instead he was on the opposite side of the road from the Swiss assassin. The distance was around 15 metres, twice the range that Bavaud had trained himself to be comfortable with. Should he take the shot anyway? His mind raced, a dreadful uncertainty rooting him to the spot. No, he decided, he would probably miss and that would be the end of him. Wait for another opportunity. His hand released the concealed pistol and he watched as Hitler disappeared out of sight around a corner.

Bavaud decided to follow *Hauptmann* Deckert's advice about a letter of introduction and rather foolishly forged one from French Foreign Minister Pierre Flandin. Travelling back to Berchtesgaden by train, Bavaud rented a taxi to take him up to the Berghof. He was prevented from entering the security zone by SS guards who told him that Hitler was still in Munich. Bavaud rushed back to the station, boarded a train and arrived in Munich around the same time that Hitler was leaving on a train to Berchtesgaden.

Nearly out of money, Bavaud decided to give up on his plan to kill the *Führer*. Lacking the funds for a train journey to Switzerland, Bavaud hid on a train to Paris, where he hoped to obtain travel money from the Swiss Embassy. Caught by the conductor, he was handed over to the police in Augsburg. When searched, the police turned up the pistol and the forged letter that Bavaud had foolishly kept. Arrested by the Gestapo, after extensive interrogation Bavaud admitted the details of his plot to kill Hitler. On 14 May 1941 Bavaud was beheaded.

In 1938 Bavaud could have legally got quite close to the Berghof to have had a chance of shooting Hitler during one of his afternoon strolls. By the time Bavaud was executed no 'fan' would be permitted anywhere near Hitler's house.

Martin Bormann solved the *Führer's* security problems by steadily buying up all of the private properties in the valley, often intimidating farmers into selling. Through such methods the security zone around the Berghof was extended until eventually the entire area was under Bormann's personal authority.

The region's hotels provided the first layer of security. Any hotel close to the Obersalzberg was required to provide details of their guests to RSD Bureau 9, one of the three bureaus that protected the *Führer*. Bureau 9 would run a check on them. In this way, the RSD had a good idea of the strangers within the region at any given moment, and any who peeked their interest would be questioned by the Gestapo or politely told to leave. However, as demonstrated by the Bavaud case, this method of light screening was not foolproof.

Eventually, Bormann created a 'reserve' for the *Führer* at the Obersalzberg that measured 7km square. The entire area was wired off from the public with net mesh type fences, '200 to 220cm high, supported by steel tubes placed at intervals of three to five metres. The tubes are bent inwards at the top, the bent part supporting three or four strands of barbed wire.'[5] The fences, which were not electrified, were studded with numerous wire mesh gates, many watched by armed sentries.

The Obersalzberg complex was guarded by a system of SS and civilian patrols and piquets. The civilian guards 'are mostly Bavarian or Austrian,' recalled 19-year-old Austrian *SS-Schütze* Obernigg, a former LSSAH guard captured by the British near Caen during the Battle of Normandy on 19 July 1944. 'They look like ordinary workers and are very mixed types. They are reliable old Nazis who stand on duty in the sentry huts ... They wear civilian clothes without any distinguishing marks.'[6] (Obernigg's information was already out of date by the time he was taken prisoner.)These civilians, used until 1943, provided a screen through which anyone approaching the Obersalzberg would have to pass. Within the security zone were further civilians and also uniformed SS.

Obernigg's detailed report on the Obersalzberg complex was only recently declassified and adds a lot of detail to the existing literature. It is also interesting to see the complex and its inhabitants through the eyes of a young German soldier who, because of his job, was able to access most areas. Obernigg joined the SS in October 1942, serving initially with 3rd Company LSSAH at its depot at Lichterfelde Barracks, Berlin. The entire company was transferred to *Wachbataillon Berlin* on 15 December 1942 and tasked with providing ceremonial guards at the Reich Chancellery. Between early August 1943 and May 1944 Obernigg served in *SS-Wachkompanie-Obersalzberg*.[7]

RSD and sentries from *SS-Wachkompanie-Obersalzberg* guarded the three gates that gave access to this inner sanctum. This unit was the size of an infantry battalion and was permanently stationed in the area. When Hitler was in residence security was further augmented by the presence of the army's *Führer Begleit Bataillon* (*Führer* Escort Battalion – FBB).

The Obersalzberg area was divided into three districts or *Bezirke*. *Bezirk I* encompassed the area and buildings immediately adjacent to the Berghof and required a special red pass to enter. *Bezirk II* was all territory including the Berghof, but excluding the Kehlstein area, and a green-coloured pass was required to enter. RSD officers also manned the outer gates at the villages of Tengelbrunn, Klingeck and Au when Hitler was in residence, though the civilian guards were still used when the *Führer* was elsewhere until March 1943. *Bezirk III* covered the Kehlstein area. Only supply, maintenance and guard shift traffic was seen within this outer zone. Within all of these zones there were sub-zones, often fencing off construction sites or other utility or work areas.

There was near constant building work going on in the valley as Bormann ordered new buildings to be constructed. Military head-quarters were built, as well as more space for garrison troops. Sub-ordinate headquarters were established in the nearby alpine troops barracks at Strub near Berchtesgaden, and a new camp was built at Winkl on the Bad Reichenhall-Berchtesgaden road for the Army General Staff. This building mania meant that between summer 1943 and end of the war Bormann ordered the construction of seventy-nine bunkers, with a total area of 4,120 square metres, beneath the Ober-salzberg valley. They were well-appointed shelters, with proper drain-age, heating, gas and air-pressure chambers, marble, wood panelling, air-conditioning and carpets. Concrete machine gun posts protected their entrances. All this activity meant that large numbers of foreign workers from the *Organisation Todt* were always present, presenting security problems for Hitler's guards. Only thirty percent of workers at the Obersalzberg were Germans, the rest were French, Italians and Czechs. No Soviet prisoners-of-war or civilian forced labourers were permitted within the *Führerschutzgebiet* (*Führer* Protection Zone).

As cars drove into *Bezirk I* along the road from Berchtesgaden the first thing visitors would have seen was the Gutshof, an experimental farm created by Bormann. The specially selected farmers raised cattle, horses and pigs. There were bee hives, a milk cooling building, a blacksmith's shop and bucolic pastures. After the war the complex was taken over by the US Army and converted into a sports lodge, golf course and winter ski resort. Today one wing survives as a golf club house.[8]

Passing the Gutshof, visitors would find that the road to Hitler's residence was blocked by the main SS guardhouse that spanned the road with a solid wooden gate. Its stone foundations remain today. Once past the RSD and SS guards, the road ran past the Berghof, a handsome stone and wooden chalet set atop a small rise above the road with magnificent views across the valley to the Untesberg Mountains, a possible burial place of the Emperor Charlemagne, and of Austria beyond.

The Berghof was originally a much smaller chalet called Haus Wachenfeld constructed as a holiday home by wealthy German businessman Otto Winter in 1916. Winter rented the property to Hitler in 1928 and the *Führer* moved his half-sister Angela Hitler in as his housekeeper until the tragic suicide of her daughter Geli Raubal in Munich in 1931. This event proved to be something of a scandal for the *Führer*.

It is said that Hitler had become fixated on his half-niece, with rumours circulating of a less than healthy relationship between the two. Although enrolled at Ludwig Maximilian University to study medicine, Raubal was kept under very tight control by her uncle. When Hitler discovered that she was having a relationship with his driver, Emil Maurice, Hitler dismissed Maurice on the spot and became even more domineering and possessive towards Geli. Raubal wanted to go to Vienna to marry Maurice, but Hitler forbade her. Following a furious argument in Hitler's apartment Raubal shot herself in the chest with Hitler's own pistol and died. The event deeply disturbed Hitler and until his own death he kept Raubal's room at the Berghof exactly as she had left it, as well as having portraits of her in his bedrooms at the Berghof and Reich Chancellery. The true nature of their relationship remains a mystery to this day.

In 1933 Hitler was sufficiently rich to purchase Haus Wachenfeld from its owner and embarked on a complete rebuild and extension of the property, renaming it the Berghof. British *Homes & Gardens Magazine* ran a feature on the house in 1938, the same year Prime Minister Neville Chamberlain visited for a meeting with Hitler, and commented that it was 'bright and airy ... with a light jade green colour scheme.'

The entrance hall was lined with cacti in large majolica pots, the dining room was panelled in expensive cembra pine but the most famous room was the Great Hall. With white walls, low wooden panelling, a wooden latticework ceiling and red carpeting, the Great Hall was where Hitler held his meetings, guests often being seated on sofas arranged before a massive red marble fireplace at one end of the capacious room. A huge picture window dominated one wall, giving an expansive view across the valley towards the mountains beyond, and the entire window could be lowered into the floor on fine days. The furniture was largely eighteenth century German Teutonic, and on the walls were hung several masterpieces, including a great Gobelin tapestry and the sixteenth century Venetian old master *Venus and Amor* by Paris Bordone (this painting is now in the National Museum in Warsaw).

Outside there was a large sun terrace with colourful umbrellas where Hitler's intimates lounged, sun bathed or strolled. Hitler and his mistress Eva Braun, though she was officially lodged further down the mountain in Berchtesgaden, had interconnecting bedrooms at the Berghof with en-suite bathrooms. Hitler's secretaries and adjutants also lived inside the house along with several servants and other household staff necessary to keep the place running efficiently.

Hitler dominated the entire existence of his guests at the Berghof. 'Real informality was as good as impossible in his presence. And Hitler, for all the large numbers of people in attendance on him and paying court to him, remained impoverished when it came to real contact, cut off from any meaningful relationships through the shallowness of his emotions and his profoundly egocentric, exploitative attitude towards all other human beings.'[9]

The Berghof was one of only two buildings, the other being Hitler's luxury apartment in Munich, where Eva Braun was permitted to reside and be seen with the *Führer*. Hitler had first met Braun in 1929 in Munich when she was a 17-year-old assistant to the Nazi court photographer Heinrich Hoffmann. Hitler dominated his girlfriend, keeping her well away from the public eye. 'On the rare occasions she was in Berlin, she was closeted in her little room in the "*Führer* Apartment" while Hitler attended official functions or was otherwise engaged. Even in his close circle she was not permitted to be present for meals if any important guests were there. She did not accompany Hitler on his numerous journeys ...'[10] The Berghof was her home for most of the war, and if Bormann was 'Lord of the Obersalzberg' then Eva Braun soon became its 'Lady'.

Hitler was well protected from the possibility of air attack, something that became more likely with each passing month of the war. Directly beneath the Berghof, 15–20 metres underground, was a large air raid shelter. 'It zigzags at the entrance; turning left, left again, then right, one reaches the main passage,' recalled SS guard Obernigg. 'The shelter itself is 80 to 100m long, with rooms leading off on both sides. There are parquet floors, carpets, and the place is sumptuously furnished and centrally heated by a boiler which is underneath the shelter. The shelter is ventilated but there are no airshafts. It has three exits.'[11] To further protect against aerial attack, during the war all of the houses on the Obersalzberg were spray-painted, 'the disruptive pattern of which is changed every three months.' Finally, dummy trees were planted in most of the open spaces as further camouflage.

A short way along the road from the Berghof stands the Gästhaus zum Türken. Opened as a guesthouse in 1911, the hotel was a favourite haunt of celebrities including the composer Johannes Brahms, and Bavarian and Prussian royalty. The owner was forced to sell it to the Nazis in 1933 as Bormann began the process of removing civilians from the Obersalzberg area. Later the Gästhaus zum Türken was the headquarters and accommodation block for Hitler's RSD bodyguard detachment and the *SS-Wachkompanie-Obersalzberg*. It also served as the main Army High Command telephone exchange. When Hitler was at the Berghof nineteen RSD officers were stationed at the hotel. Armed with holstered automatic pistols, one officer always patrolled in front of the Berghof on a 3-hour shift. Another patrolled the buildings in the immediate vicinity, while two more patrolled the surrounding area between 8.00am and 8.00pm. One was always in his office close to the telephone in case of an emergency. The Gästhaus zum Türken was repaired after the war, and today is one of the most popular guesthouses in the area.

Beyond the hotel the road continued further down the valley. On the left stood Hitler's greenhouse. This was built by Bormann to supply fresh vegetables to Hitler's table and meet his boss's strict vegetarian dietary requirements. Its concrete foundations are still visible today near the new Intercontinental Hotel. A road branched off beside the greenhouse and led to Bormann's private residence. A large wooden chalet, the house was knocked down in 1951–52, though the underground bunker system has survived but is closed to the public.

Opposite the green house on the right of the main road stood the Kindergarten/Modellhaus. The twenty to thirty children of the Obersalzberg staff used the Kindergarten and they included those of Bormann. The daughter of a man who had died during the 1923 Beer Hall Putsch kept the Kindergarten. The Modellhaus was used as a store for Hitler's many architectural models, and there was also a building housing the *Führer's* private film collection, including many Hollywood productions banned in the Third Reich. These buildings were all razed in 1951–52 and their foundations removed in 2001–2002.[12]

The next complex on the right of the road beyond the Kindergarten was the *SS-Kaserne*, a large white barracks complex completed in 1937. This housed more members of the *SS-Wachkompanie-Obersalzberg* (actually in battalion strength) that patrolled the entire complex. It consisted of a large parade square enclosed by barrack blocks, kitchen, mess hall, vehicle maintenance facilities, gymnasium, and a staff headquarters building. The entire complex was pulled down in 1951. The basements, tunnels and air-raid shelters were torn out and filled in during 2001–2002.[13]

At the end of Hitler's greenhouse, opposite the *SS-Kaserne*, was a small road that branched left and wound upwards into the thick trees. The road divided into two, with one road leading to Hermann Göring's private house. Similar in design to the Berghof, Göring's chalet was decorated in 'fancy rustic'. This building has been pulled down. The second road led to the *Adjutanter Göring* (Göring's Adjutants' House) where Hitler's chief *Luftwaffe* aide *General der Flieger* Karl Bodenschatz and his staff lived and worked. There was a telephone exchange inside. This three-storey building remains intact and is currently a private home.

Turning right at the *SS-Kaserne*, a road led to a further complex of buildings. First on the right was the Platterhof Garage, a long building. Inside was stored a large assemblage of VIP vehicles, particularly the armoured Mercedes cars so beloved of the Nazi elite, while staff quarters were provided on the floor above. Only a retaining wall and the building's basement remains today.

Behind the garage stood the large Platterhof Hotel. Originally opened in 1877, the Platterhof was extensively remodelled by the Nazis and converted into a luxury guesthouse for visiting dignitaries.

In 1943 the building became a military hospital and convalescent home with beds for 80–120 soldiers. Within the Platterhof was the Bergschenke, a fairly inexpensive beerhouse-cum-restaurant with a kitchen underneath. The five or six waitresses were dressed in blue dirndl frocks, assisted by three or four foreign waiters. Refurbished by the US Army in the late 1940s, it was renamed the Hotel General Walker. The complex was torn down in 2000, though one side-building that was used as a restaurant by the US Army until 1995 survives intact. The hotel site is now a car park for the Obersalzberg Documentation Center and the Kehlsteinhaus bus ticket office.[14]

The nurses and staff from the Platterhof and the Bergschenke lived in the adjacent Gefolgschaftshaus. A barber operated a hairdressing shop under the Platterhof. *SS-Schütze* Obernigg called the barber 'an enigma'. He spoke fluent Italian and spoke German with a Bavarian accent and employed three Italian assistants. The garage beneath the Gefolgschaftshaus was used to store two buses for taking patients to the theatre in Salzburg and for other trips, and the SS also parked some of their trucks there.

On a short road that led away from the Platterhof Hotel was the Gästehaus. This building was used by Bormann's staff and also had VIP guesthouse facilities. Rebuilt after the war, the building is now the Obersalzberg Documentation Center with information about the Nazi period, the Holocaust and the Second World War. The bunker complex below the building is open to the public.

The last building of major significance was located on another small road beyond the Platterhof. This was the Kampfhausl, the cottage where Hitler wrote the second half of his book *Mein Kampf* after his release from Landsberg Prison in 1925. This building became a Nazi shrine and was pulled down in 1951. Its foundations are clearly visible in the woods across from the Documentation Center.[15]

There were several other buildings of less significance dotted around the area. These included Haus Speer, where Armaments Minister Albert Speer lived with his wife, children and nanny. There was a Post Office operated by an official wearing the Golden Party Badge with three girl assistants, a clerk and a postman who had lost an arm in the First World War.[16] Gästehaus Hoher Göll was used for guests and aides, and this is where Eva Braun 'officially' lived. It is interesting to note that among rank-and-file guards like Obernigg, they referred to Braun as 'Hitler's secretary',[17] though also noting that RSD men surrounded her. Frau Josepha, who was overseer of all women in the Obersalzberg district, kept the building, and Hitler's Press Secretary, Dr Otto Dietrich, would live here during his visits to the Berghof. It was equipped with a teleprinter.

There were also complexes of housing. The Vorderek consisted of two houses. The first house was the administration headquarters for the Obersalzberg area and was run by a Nazi Party man named Schenk. Second-in-command was *SS-Untersturmführer* Bredow. There were servants' quarters above and quarters for men from the *SS-Begleitkommando* who would live there when Hitler was in residence. The second house was where Schenk lived and was also the *LS Befehlsstelle* (Air Raid Control Room) under Bredow's command.[18]

There were two large housing complexes, the Klaushöhe and Buchenhöhe that were used for civilian housing or as married quarters for the men of the SS garrison. The Klaushöhe complex consisted of three rows of houses. The first row, Nos 1–6, consisted of a grocery shop at No. 1 and at No. 6 the women who worked in the SS barracks lived. The second row, Nos 7–14, were for German workers. The third row, Nos 15–22, included an SS doctor at No. 18, and Herr Grundner, who was responsible for rations at the SS barracks, at No. 22.[19] Most of these buildings, consisting of medium-sized white alpine chalets, remain intact and are rented out as holiday homes today. Some bombed ruins are scattered through the woods close by.[20]

Driving to Hitler's house on the road from Berchtesgaden, visitors would pass through a series of checkpoints, each requiring a special pass. The deeper one went into the protection zone, the more detailed the checks. At the outer checkpoint RSD officers would examine passes in detail. They checked that the pass matched the person who was carrying it, that it was genuine and that it contained the necessary weekly stamp. A record was kept of all comings and goings. It did not matter whether you were an SS private returning from leave or a field marshal attending one of Hitler's daily military conferences, all visitors received the same level of scrutiny. After the fall of Stalingrad at the end of January 1943 all hikers and tourists were banned from the area, so the only people the RSD encountered were persons with specific business or employment at the Obersalzberg.

Travel into the protected zone by car was only possible if the RSD had been given prior notification. Even the cars containing Nazi top brass like Himmler, Göring and Bormann were stopped and carefully inspected. Bormann was adamant that such scrutiny was necessary. 'If the gate guards open the gates upon the sounding of a horn, then this is the most outrageous carelessness, because sounding a horn is not identification.'[21] Neither was a uniform considered identification, no matter how exalted the rank of the wearer. Only the pass was important. This level of security meant that the chances of infiltrating a doppelgänger into the complex, perhaps disguised as a senior Nazi official or military officer, was unlikely to be successful.

The most senior security personnel had 'access all areas' passes. These special passes were coloured dark blue, 'and all require a stamp (which is numbered) to be affixed every week,' recalled *SS-Schütze* Obernigg, the former guard at the Obersalzberg complex. 'Passes bear the imprint of Bormann's or Rattenhuber's signature.'[22] SS personnel carried a special pass stating that they were members of the guard company and were allowed into the *'Führerschutzgebiet'* when on duty. Interestingly, although Bormann was most emphatic about everyone being carefully checked, former guards have admitted that fellow SS were mostly recognised by the RSD and civilian guards and not properly checked, particularly if senior Nazis like Bormann were not around. 'Children under 5 require no pass. The milkman, an employee of the Gutshof, and the woman who delivers the secret letters are never checked,' stated Obernigg to his British interrogators, indicating that familiarity caused security lapses despite Bormann's best efforts.

Those permitted to enter *Bezirk I*, the Obersalzberg's inner sanctum containing the Berghof, had their passes inscribed: *'ist berechtigt, das Führergelände und den Berghof zu betreten'* – 'is entitled to enter the prohibited *Führer* zone and the Berghof'. This observation was required for an individual to pass through SS sentry posts 1 to 6 as well as any RSD personnel in the area. The inhabitants of the Gutshof, Bechsteinhaus, Atelier Speer, and the Haus Speer possessed passes. They were marked: *'ist berechtigt, die Posten Tengelbrunn und Altenberg zu passieren'* – 'is entitled to pass the sentries at Tengelbrunn and Altenberg'.[23]

Passes were also required to enter the SS barracks area, theatre and Göring's house. 'Whilst Göring is there, Picquet Göring 1 is instructed to be particularly conscientious,' recalled Obernigg. 'All officers who visit Göring must produce evidence of having been invited.'[24] Göring was as paranoid as Hitler regarding assassination, and as Hitler's chosen successor since Rudolf Hess's flight to Britain in 1941, he had good reason to be cautious.

Some armed sentries walked particular patrol routes. For example, 'Patrol 1' consisted of a single SS soldier who would move between the

Berghof and the Mooslahnerkopf Teehaus. 'The stretch takes 15 to 20 minutes. Patrol usually chats for a long time with the civilian picquet at the Mooslahnerkopf,'[25] recalled a guard.

Hitler would visit the Mooslahnerkopf Teehaus almost every afternoon during his stays at the Berghof. The walk was less than a kilometre across the Obersalzberg Valley to the wooded Mooslahnerkopf Hill where the circular teahouse had been built in 1937. The path was mostly wooded and at one point passed a scenic overlook of the entire valley, enclosed by a wooden railing and with a bench where the *Führer* often sat and discussed matters of state with his intimates. Hitler often fell asleep at the Mooslahnerkopf and was always driven back to the Berghof while the rest of his intimates strolled back on foot in the late afternoon. Because of its close association with Hitler the teahouse was knocked down after the war by the West German authorities.[26]

Confusingly, there is another teahouse in the valley that is also closely associated with the Nazi regime. Known today in English as the 'Eagle's Nest', the Kehlsteinhaus is a chalet structure commissioned by Bormann in 1938 and presented to Hitler on his fiftieth birthday in April 1939. It perches atop Kehlstein Mountain near Berchtesgaden and the final 124 metres to the summit are made inside the mountain via an ornate lift that was bored directly through the granite. The lift, of polished brass and green leather, contains expensive Venetian mirrors. A huge red Italian marble fireplace that was a gift from fellow dictator Benito Mussolini dominates the main tearoom. The fireplace was heavily defaced by American troops in 1945, when they chipped off sections of the marble as souvenirs.

During the Nazi period the teahouse was known as the '*D-Haus*' or Diplomatic Reception House. Unfortunately for Bormann, Hitler preferred the Mooslahnerkopf and only visited the Eagle's Nest around ten times. 'He complained that the air was too thin at that height, and bad for his blood pressure. He worried about an accident on the roads Bormann had had constructed up the sheer mountainside, and about a failure of the lift that had to carry its passengers from the large, marble-faced hall cut inside the rock to the summit of the mountain.'[27]

But although Hitler didn't much care for Bormann's gift, the property was nonetheless carefully guarded by the RSD. A wire fence surrounded the entire Kehlstein Mountain, within *Bezirk* III, with single-patrol guards who were armed with rifles being relieved every two hours. 'Some lumber-jacks and a game keeper wander around the Kehlstein,' according to a contemporary witness. 'The place is com-

Hitler being driven by Julius Schreck in the early 1930s. Hitler almost always sat in the front passenger seat during car journeys.

The approach road to Hitler's mountain retreat, the Berghof, on the Bavarian-Austrian border. He purchased this house from royalties earned on his book *Mein Kampf*.

Hitler and his girlfriend Eva Braun pictured with their dogs on the sun terrace at the Berghof, 1936. Hitler kept his mistress out of the public spotlight on the Obersalzberg.

The Great Hall at the Berghof.

Reich Chancellery guards from the elite *Leibstandarte SS Adolf Hitler*, Berlin, 1938.

Hitler greeting his adoring public whilst standing in the passenger seat of one of his Mercedes-Benz armoured limousines.

The results of Georg Elser's failed assassination attempt on Hitler at the Burgerbraukeller in Munich, 1939.

Hitler being greeted by *Generalfeldmarschall* Keitel at the Wolf's Lair. On the left stands *Oberst* Count von Stauffenberg, the man who would come closest to killing the Hitler.

Hitler at the Wolf's Lair
pictured with some of his
SS-Begleit Kommando and RSD
bodyguards. Second from right
is the controversial Bruno
Gesche.

Henning von Treskow, one of
the central plotters against
Hitler in the *Wehrmacht*.

Hitler's Focke-Wulf Fw. 200 *Condor*.

Hitler addressing Reich Gauleiters in a conference hut at the Wolf's Lair, 4 August 1944.

(*Left to right*) *Generalfeldmarschall* Wilhelm Keitel, *Reichsmarschall* Hermann Göring, Hitler and *Reichsleiter* Martin Bormann pictured at the Wolf's Lair the day after Stauffenberg's bomb attempt. Hitler is holding his injured arm.

Hitler's black uniform trousers shredded by the bomb blast on 20 July 1944.

Hitler presents medals to Hitler Youths in the Reich Chancellery Garden, 20 March 1945.

The *Führerbunker* emergency exit (block house on the left). Hitler's body was cremated in a shell hole near the doorway on 30 April 1945.

pletely wired off, and there are always one or two RSD personnel in the tea house at the top, which is very difficult to reach except by the lift.' Visitors required a special pass that was clearly stamped '*und Kehlsteingebiet.*'[28]

The most significant event that occurred at the Kehlsteinhaus was the June 1944 wedding of Eva Braun's sister Gretl to *SS-Gruppenführer* Hermann Fegelein, Heinrich Himmler's dashing representative at *Führer* Headquarters. Today the Eagle's Nest is a restaurant with an outdoor beer garden and remarkably little changed from Hitler's day.

The wider Obersalzberg region was formidably guarded. Apart from the SS guard battalion and RSD troops near the Berghof there were several *Wehrmacht* mountain troop units and depots close by. The SS troops were on five minutes standby to react to any threat within the three Obersalzberg security zones. The Allies never seriously considered a *coup de main* against Hitler's mountain eerie, primarily because the geography was extremely hostile to parachute or glider landings. Hitler's greatest fear, and one that he shared at all of his military headquarters, was an Allied air raid. Bormann had assuaged this fear to some degree by constructing so many shelters and bunkers, but he also made sure that the SS provided plenty of anti-aircraft coverage.

By July 1944 the Obersalzberg was defended by twelve 105mm, eighteen 88mm and twenty-seven 37mm anti-aircraft guns manned entirely by SS Artillery and not by the *Luftwaffe* who was normally responsible for anything to do with aircraft. There were also six 20mm cannon and six 20mm quadruple flak guns.[29] In addition, an ingenious smoke-generating unit could fill the valley with virtually impenetrable fog using large machines, disrupting any Allied raid and concealing the Berghof and other targets. This was coupled with attempts to camouflage the buildings from aerial reconnaissance with disruptive pattern paint schemes, netting and dummy trees. The one drawback of the SS smoke generators was that the artificial fog completely obscured the flak batteries aim, but Bormann solved this by moving most of the batteries to new positions higher up in the mountains. Unfortunately, this meant that the gunners suffered more from the elements during the winter.

For all its tight security features, the Obersalzberg complex had one very significant problem – Hitler. The *Führer's* dislike of being guarded actually made him seriously vulnerable in the very place where he should have been safest, at home. When the British interrogated *SS-Schütze* Dieser and Obernigg, former members of Hitler's guard unit captured in Normandy in 1944, they soon realised that there existed a very good chance of killing Hitler. He was much more vulnerable there than at his military field headquarters.

On 27 and 28 June 1944 meetings were held of the SOE Council to debate the idea of assassinating Hitler. Major General Colin Gubbins, Director of SOE, decided to order a feasibility study.[30] The file would grow to include a huge amount of material on the Obersalzberg region, Hitler's appearance, his habits and routine, his guarding arrangements, and details about his special train, the *Führersonderzug*.[31]

Three possible attacks were considered. The first was an attempt to derail Hitler's train, but the limitations here were firstly gaining access to the track, which was guarded for the entire length of the train's journey, and secondly whether a derailment would actually kill the intended target. It seemed a rather imprecise form of assassination. The second method also involved Hitler's train. An idea was mooted to somehow introduce poison into the train's drinking water tanks, but as the plan relied on an inside man that the British did not have, this idea was rejected. The third and final idea was to shoot Hitler at the Obersalzberg during his daily afternoon walk.

It was soon known that Hitler enjoyed walking to the Mooslahner-kopf Teahouse from the Berghof every day that he was in residence. Dieser and *SS-Schütze* Obernigg told SOE that Hitler's RSD bodyguards were under orders to stay back when Hitler was walking with his small group of intimates. At one point during his stroll he passed close to a patch of woodland that placed him out of line of sight of the static SS sentry posts around the Obersalzberg. This meant that there was a window of opportunity to kill Hitler.

When Hitler arrived at the teahouse he would chat with his intimates, sip camomile tea and nibble on apple cake before invariably dozing off in his comfy armchair while the rest of his party chatted quietly around him.[32] After an hour or so Hitler would be driven back to the Berghof while his companions walked the 1,500 metres back.

The idea was so attractive that SOE considered extending the operation to killing Himmler, Göring, Goebbels or Bormann, and similarly detailed investigations into their movements, habits, routines and guarding arrangements were made.

Working with the information on Hitler, Major Court of the SOE, and his colleagues in London, began to work out how to assassinate Hitler at the Obersalzberg. It soon became clear that the most reliable method was a sniper attack when Hitler was walking along the path to the teahouse, and was very lightly guarded. The outline of the plan was for a German-speaking Pole and a British sniper to parachute into Austria. Dieser said that his uncle Heidenthaler, who was strongly anti-Nazi, would hide the two assassins in his house in Salzburg. From there, the two-man rifle team would infiltrate the Obersalzberg dressed in German Army mountain troop uniforms. There were mountain troops based quite close to the Obersalzberg, and of course the uniforms were only designed to divert the attention of locals and patrolling guards – the men would not try to enter the Obersalzberg security zone through any of the guarded gates, as they would not have the necessary documentation.

Once inside the enclosure, the sniper team would lie up in the woods close to the path that Hitler regularly walked. The Pole would act as spotter, using powerful binoculars, while the sniper would be armed with a Mauser Karabiner 98K rifle fitted with a Zeis Zielvier 4 × (ZF39) telescopic sight. The rifle had an effective range of 1,000m, but the shot would be taken much closer, at a range of around 300m. A British officer, Captain Edmund Bennett, was mooted for the role of sniper and may have begun training in England against moving targets.[33]

An alternative scenario was to have the second assassin concealed along the road used by Hitler's car to bring him back to the Berghof from the Mooslahrnerkopf Teahouse. This assassin would be armed with a PIAT anti-tank weapon to destroy the car should the rifleman have failed to get off a shot at Hitler walking.

In November 1944 Major Court presented his plan, codenamed Operation 'Foxley', but it was turned down after some heated argument. At this stage of the war, many senior officers felt that Hitler alive was doing more damage to the German military than Hitler dead. There were also some reservations about making Hitler a martyr through assassinating him. Foxley was by this stage anyway a theoretical exercise because Hitler had left the Berghof for the last time on 14 July 1944. However, postwar analysis of the plan suggests that although German security forces would most probably have captured the two-man sniper team before they were able to get into position, if they had managed to conceal themselves along the path between the

Berghof and the Mooslahnerkopf Teahouse, they could have killed Hitler with relative ease.

The main problem was that the plan came too late. SOE lacked intelligence about Hitler's routine until after D-Day when they captured a few low-ranking former guards who had been returned to active service. By the time SOE had managed to thrash out an assassination plan, Hitler had managed to frustrate them by moving away from the target area.

After the war had began, and following Bormann's stringent efforts to beef up security around the Berghof and prevent day trippers and hikers from getting anywhere near the place, any real threat of assassination had to come from insiders. Hitler was to face some serious attempts by members of his own armed forces to kill him whilst he was at home on his mountain. The resolve of his opponents to carry out their plans was severely tested by Hitler's formidable security apparatus. Killing Hitler soon became virtually a suicide mission for the few people who were prepared to act.

Chapter 7

Wolf's Lair

'Our enemies are not human beings any more, they are beasts.'
Adolf Hitler
The Wolf's Lair, 14 July 1941

The 'Wolf's Lair' conjures up images of danger, of hidden menace, of evil power. It was named by Hitler, playing on his own preoccupations with the wolf as metaphor for himself. Hidden beneath a canopy of fir trees, in the summer the complex of huge above ground concrete bunkers and net covered walkways was alive with the buzzing of mosquitos that thrived in the humid and unhealthy local conditions. During the winter the forest was silent and heavily laden with snow, the surrounding lakes frozen solid in the bitter cold.

The Wolf's Lair was well named, hidden as it was deep in the gloomy East Prussian forest, 8km east of Rastenburg (now Ketrzyn, Poland). It was here that Hitler would spend most of the war, over 800 days in total, directing the monumental fight against the Soviet Union. But the Wolf's Lair was not Hitler's only Eastern Front headquarters. As with his command facilities in the West, Hitler used several different headquarters at different times, and they all differed markedly in design and comfort.

One of his first was a truly enormous civil engineering project in occupied Poland built to protect his mobile headquarters train, the *Führersonderzug*. In November 1940 Hitler had sent Dr Fritz Todt east with a collection of military aides to find three possible locations for a permanent military HQ for the coming Soviet operation. Two sites in today's Poland were quickly selected: *Anlage Mitte* (Installation Centre) near Tomaszow and *Anlage Sud* (Installation South). Both were basically enormous shelters for the *Führersonderzug*. Only the latter was actually used by Hitler.

Anlage Sud consisted of a pair of gigantic reinforced concrete tunnels built by Polish slave labourers sent from nearby concentration camps that worked under the direction of *Organisation Todt* engineers and guards. The tunnel bunkers were located close to the main railway line between Rzeszow and Jaslo. One tunnel was built near the village of Stepina, 45km south of Rzeszow, the other at the town of Strzyzow, 30km southwest of Rzeszow. Each tunnel was 480m long, 8.3m wide and 12m high. The concrete walls were 2m thick, making for a formidable structure.[1] Around each tunnel bunker were wooden huts, more bunkers and wooden watchtowers, as well as fences, protected by the usual FBB, *SS-Begleitkommando* and RSD detachments. Each tunnel contained a railway line and a platform, so important trains could be completely hidden from observation and aerial attack. The portals that gave access to the tunnels could be sealed with gigantic steel doors with firing positions. In the event of parachute assault or partisan attack the tunnels could be sealed and defended while reinforcements were sent from military bases nearby to relieve *Führer* Headquarters.

Completed in the summer of 1941, *Anlage Sud* was first used on 27 August when Hitler met with Italian dictator Benito Mussolini to discuss the war in the Soviet Union. The *Führersonderzug* was parked in the tunnel at Strzyzow while Mussolini's private train was hidden in the second tunnel bunker at Stepina. Mussolini's party was then driven to meet Hitler aboard his train inside the armoured tunnel, the *Führer* never stepping foot on the platform during his entire visit. Hitler visited once more in October 1941, this time attending meetings in the surrounding complex of bunkers and huts. [2]

The third site chosen by Dr Todt was codenamed *Anlage Nord* (Installation North), which eventually became known as the *Wolfsschanze* (Wolf's Lair). A one-track railway and a road ran through the Wolf's Lair connecting the town of Rastenburg with Angerburg and Lotzen where other headquarters staffs were located.

The Wolf's Lair complex, initially a collection of concrete bunkers and wooden huts, was in the middle of a dense fir forest. The complex covered an area of 6.5 square kilometres and was divided into three security zones, or *Sperrkreis*. Where trees were felled to create space for buildings, artificial trees and camouflage netting were installed to maintain a continuous tree canopy. A company from Stuttgart was brought in to disguise the buildings, planting bushes, grass and artificial trees on the flat roofs. Roads were also partly disguised by camouflage netting and fake trees. The Germans carefully photographed the completed site from the air to test the camouflage, but the Soviets were soon aware of the existence of the headquarters and of its purpose.

Hitler's train was kept under more nets and trees at *Bahnhof* Görlitz, the Wolf's Lair's private station.[3] Hitler first arrived at the Wolf's Lair by train on 24 June 1941 and would stay, with some large breaks when he was in Berlin, Munich, and Berchtesgaden or at *Werwolf*, another Eastern Front headquarters, until 20 November 1944.

Visitors could arrive at the Wolf's Lair using four methods. The first method was by train, arriving at Görlitz Station. Every night two identical courier trains left from Silesian Station in Berlin and the town of Angerburg in East Prussia, passing Görlitz en route, and arriving at the opposite destination the next morning. The second method was by plane, arriving at Rastenburg Airfield southwest of the Wolf's Lair. Thirdly, the headquarters complex could be approached by road from the west, south or east. Fourthly, a rail trolley, a kind of tram, commuted between the Wolf's Lair and the OKH (Supreme Army Command) *'Mauerwald'* command complex near Angerburg with stops at Görlitz Station and at the eastern entrance gate near the *Luftwaffe* liaison offices.[4]

In order to enter *Sperrkreis I*, the complex's inner sanctum where Hitler lived and worked, one would have to pass through at least four security checkpoints.

Sperrkreis III was the outer security area consisting of fences, gates, slit trenches and guardhouses. The perimeter was extensively mined. After the war the Soviets removed 54,000 landmines from the complex. Close by, to the northeast of *Sperrkreis III*, was a *Wehrmacht* operations staff facility and army headquarters. Additional troops were stationed 72km away in case of an emergency. This unit, a *kampfgruppe* (battle-group), was under the command of highly decorated combat officer *Generalmajor* Walter Denkert. It was later envisaged that *Kampfgruppe Denkert* would be used to garrison proposed *Festung* (Fortress) Lotzen. Denkert's troops had responsibility for guarding the area outside of *Sperrkreis III*.[5]

The FBB was responsible for guarding and defending *Sperrkreis III*. The unit was expanded in April 1943 by the creation of a second unit, the *Führergrenadierbataillon* (FGB) from selected *Grossdeutschland* personnel. The FBB and FGB had tanks, anti-tank and anti-aircraft units, and mechanised infantry with which to defend the Wolf's Lair.

Within *Sperrkreis III*, like a Russian doll, sat *Sperrkreis II*. It was a self-contained fenced area lying north and south of the Angerburg road. It contained concrete and brick one-storey houses of the *Wehrmacht-führungsstab* (Armed Force Leadership Staff) and the headquarters of the Wolf's Lair Commandant and his staff. There were two messes, heating plants and a communications centre. East of the buildings, and south of the road, were more concrete and brick houses containing the *Kriegsmarine* (Navy) and *Luftwaffe* liaison offices, a two-storey building for drivers with a large garage on the ground floor to store and maintain Mercedes limousines, two tall air raid bunkers, FBB barracks, and the barracks for the *Führer-Flak-Abteilung* (*Führer* Anti-Aircraft Detachment). *Sperrkreis II* also contained housing for some of the senior Nazi leaders including Hitler's Armaments Minister Albert Speer and Reich Labour Front leader Fritz Todt (until his death in a plane crash in February 1942).

Sitting like the yolk at the heart of the Wolf's Lair egg was *Sperrkreis I* – the holiest of holies. Within *Sperrkreis I* was the *Führerbunker* as well as a collection of ten concrete bunkers or concrete and brick houses for the inner circle and their staffs. These consisted of bunkers for *Generalfeldmarschall* Wilhelm Keitel, Head of the Armed Forces (OKW), Press Chief Dr Otto Dietrich, Martin Bormann, a second communications centre, *Generaloberst* Alfred Jodl, Chief of the OKW Operations Staff, *Reichsmarschall* Hermann Göring, the Army Personnel Office, and the Adjutants Office. There was a house for the shorthand writers who transcribed all of Hitler's conversations and orders. Each bunker was above ground, the marshy soil precluding very many subterranean constructions, and each was built of steel reinforced concrete with 2m thick roofs to protect from aerial bombs. Hitler became increasingly and somewhat morbidly fascinated by the idea of an Allied bombing raid on the Wolf's Lair and once remarked to his secretary Traudl Junge: 'They know *exactly* where we are, and sometime they're going to destroy everything here with carefully aimed bombs. I expect them to attack any day.'[6]

To ensure his survival Hitler had *Sperrkreis I* extensively rebuilt in 1944, Albert Speer spending 36 million *Reichsmarks* reinforcing the bunkers. The *Führerbunker* was turned into a veritable fortress containing a large maze of passages, rooms and halls. The roof was increased to a thickness of 7 metres, with a layer of gravel within designed to provide a cushioning effect and prevent the cracking of the inner bunker shell if struck by large aerial bombs.[7]

Within *Sperrkreis I* were also several RSD command posts, Hitler's personal air raid shelter, the Secretariat under Philipp Bouhler, Johann Rattenhuber's RSD security headquarters, a post office, radio and telex buildings, vehicle garages, a siding for Hitler's private train, a cinema, and generator buildings. There were quarters for Hitler's personal physician, the fat and unpopular Dr Theodor Morell, Hitler's chief *Luftwaffe* adjutant *General der Flieger* Karl Bodenschatz, Walter Hewel of the Foreign Ministry, *Vizeadmiral* Hans Voss of the *Kriegsmarine*, and, after 1943, *SS-Brigadeführer* Hermann Fegelein, representing Himmler's SS. Martin Bormann, always close by his *Führer*, had a nearby staff accommodation house and an air raid shelter in addition to his personal bunker. Hitler's bunker was located at the northern end with all of its windows facing north to avoid direct sunlight. Hitler, Keitel and Jodl's bunkers had built-in conference rooms.

For relaxation *Sperrkreis I* also had an officers' mess, a mess room, teahouse, sauna, heating plant and a communal air raid shelter. The interiors were Spartan, as Hitler intended all of his field headquarters to reflect his own personal tastes and his concern to distance himself from his 'official' home in the grand and ostentatious Reich Chancellery in Berlin. Hitler always wanted to appear as a humble and frugal man in front of his people, though ironically his security needs ended up absorbing huge amounts of money and manpower that could have been more profitably used helping the war effort. For example, in 1944 alone, Bormann had 28,000 forced labourers working on improving Hitler's various headquarters.

To guard further against the possibility of air attack there was a radar system that was able to locate incoming enemy aircraft up to 100km away, giving several minutes warning of an air raid, though the Wolf's Lair was never seriously targeted by either the Red Air Force or the British and Americans. The *Führer-Luft-Nachrichten-Abteilung* (*Führer Air Intelligence Detachment*) had many observation posts to back up the radar system. If a plane was detected inside the security zone an alert list of key persons were immediately evacuated to shelters by the RSD or *SS-Begleitkommando*. Soviet planes did drop a few bombs on *Sperrkreis III* on one occasion, but other than this one nuisance raid the enemy left the Wolf's Lair in peace.

Certain senior Nazis were prevented from having offices inside the Wolf's Lair by Bormann, most notably Heinrich Himmler and Joachim von Ribbentrop. The OKH was also located elsewhere, only having adjutants at the Wolf's Lair and regular visits by army commanders.

Göring, the Deputy *Führer*, established his own Eastern Front headquarters elsewhere. Göring's HQ was a rather modest affair and quite out of keeping with the man himself. He had a place for his special train, *'Robinson'*, created in Rominten Forest northeast of the town of Goldap. The Luftwaffe High Command had a separate headquarters in Goldap itself.

In June and July 1941 *Reichsführer-SS* Himmler lived aboard his special Pullman carriage from his personal train, *'Heinrich'*, parked on a modest siding near Grossgarten (now Pozezdrze). Ribbentrop also had his carriage parked there. The platform was equipped with five small bunkers *cum* air raid shelters that were not habitable. Because of space considerations, both Himmler and Ribbentrop were forced to work inside their stuffy and uncomfortably hot railway carriages throughout the summer.[8]

Ribbentrop, who had a fondness for the finer things in life, decided to find a permanent and considerably more comfortable Eastern Front base and relocated to Steinort Manor, a large house 8km northeast of the Wolf's Lair and 10km from the main OKH headquarters.

On 16 September 1941 Himmler moved into a farmhouse and in the autumn had *'Hochenwald'* built, his own mini-*Wolfsschanze* in a dry pine forest 11km north of Grossgarten. The area was much healthier than the location chosen for Hitler's HQ, and it was also more comfortable during the summer and much more attractive than the 'breezeless, fetid swamp'[9] at the Wolf's Lair. *Hochwald* was a *Feldkommandostelle* (Field Command Post) and consisted of a railway siding for *Heinrich*, bunkers, barracks, garages, a central kitchen etc.

The OKH Eastern Front HQ was codenamed *'Mauerwald'* and consisted of two sections that were separated by the Rosengarten–Angerburg road. *'Fritz'* contained the General Staff offices and bunkers while *'Quelle'* housed the supply section and general administration offices. The HQ was decentralised for security reasons, some personnel living in barracks in Angerburg, Lotzen and other local towns. In total, around 1,500 officers and men worked at *Mauerwald*. The generals and other senior officers were guarded by sixty secret military police and the entire site patrolled by two companies of older *Wehrmacht* soldiers who were unfit for frontline duty.[10]

Hitler was always concerned about enemy parachute attack on his headquarters or those of the army high command and other important complexes close to the Wolf's Lair. Hitler had sited his Eastern Front headquarters in dense forest in an attempt to discourage the Soviets from attempting this form of assault, because paratroop units that jump into forests generally suffered huge casualties from injuries sustained when striking the canopy, or proved easy targets for defending forces when strung up in the trees. The area around the Wolf's Lair contained few open spaces big enough for the kind of enemy force that would be required to overwhelm the FBB units defending the *Führer*. But in winter this was not the case. The large lakes, including the nearby Moy-see and Zeiser-see, that dotted the marshy East Prussian landscape froze solid, providing perfect drop zones for paratroopers or glider-borne commandos.

There was also a small landing strip for Fieseler Fi-156 *Storch* spotter planes south of the facility. Also located nearby, and separate from Hans Baur's *Führer* Squadron (F.d.F) was the *Führer Kurier Staffel* (*Führer* Courier Squadron) under the command of *Luftwaffe Hauptmann* Talk.[11] This unit consisted of between six and twelve fighters that could be used to quickly move around documents or dispatches and to ferry messages.

The threat from paratroopers was limited to some extent when the FBB dug in 20mm anti-aircraft cannons around the lakes to be used in the ground role, and to punch holes in the ice in the event of a sudden enemy landing. In the town of Goldap, 70km northeast of the Wolf's Lair, was a German paratroop battalion that was kept in a high state of readiness. If enemy forces or partisans penetrated the Wolf's Lair's security zone, these German paratroopers had orders to fly directly to Hitler's aide and jump into action over *Sperrkreis I, II* and *III*, Hitler apparently having no qualms about the casualties that these elite troops would suffer jumping into a forest canopy or landing on minefields. Hitler and his staff would seal themselves inside their gas and bomb proof bunkers and await relief. Other nearby troops included *SS Anti-Tank Training and Replacement Battalion 1* in Rastenburg.

As at the Berghof in Bavaria, so life for Hitler at the Wolf's Lair was fairly relaxed and very routine. Hitler was remarkably indolent for a man attempting to hold his crumbling empire together, and usually rose late in the morning. After rising, washing and being shaved by his valet and taking breakfast Hitler would walk his Alsatian dog Blondi within *Sperrkreis I* between 9.00 and 10.00am. He did this alone with only his own thoughts for company. At his military headquarters Hitler always wore a form of uniform unique to him. Before the war Hitler was often seen dressed in a brown tunic with red and gold Nazi Party armband and black trousers, but he never wore this uniform once the war began. Instead, he would wear a high double-breasted military-style field-grey tunic with a golden German eagle on the left upper arm, white shirt, black tie, black trousers, leather shoes and a grey and brown peaked cap with gold embroidered eagle and national cockade. When he was walking outside he usually also wore kid leather gloves. On the left side of his tunic were three badges – his Iron Cross 1st Class, his Wound Badge in Black from the First World War, and his Nazi Gold Party Badge. He was entitled to wear four other First World War decorations (the Iron Cross 2nd Class, the Bavarian Cross of Military Merit 3rd Class with Swords, the Bavarian Medal of Military Service 3rd Class, and the Honour Cross of the World War 1914–18 with Swords) but never did. He was very proud of his Iron Cross and wore it, along with his Wound Badge, to demonstrate his wartime courage and service to the 'Fatherland'.

At 10.30am the mail was brought in to him. At noon he would walk across to Keitel and Jodl's shared conference room for the first of the two daily situation briefings delivered by the military high command. This event, known as the 'situation discussion' was the most important event of the day. Depending on the news, this meeting might last for up to two hours. Lunch was served in the dining room promptly at 2.00pm. Hitler usually sat in the same place, between press secretary Dr Otto Dietrich and *Generaloberst* Jodl. Opposite usually sat Keitel, Bormann and *General der Flieger* Bodenschatz. This arrangement was changed after a heated argument between Hitler and Jodl one lunch-time in early September 1942. Afterwards, Hitler ate alone or with two of his secretaries until he became bored and a fresh list of lunch companions was drawn up.

Following his vegetarian meal Hitler would deal with non-military matters, particularly any meetings or receptions. He frequently had important international guests to talks at the Wolf's Lair. Some of the notable visitors included Tsar Boris III of Bulgaria, Admiral Miklos Horthy of Hungary, Admiral Pierre Laval, Prime Minister of Vichy France, Finnish statesman Field Marshal Carl Mannerheim, Mussolini, and the Japanese Ambassador, General Hiroshi Oshima.

At 5.00pm Hitler would call the two female secretaries that he took with him to the Wolf's Lair in to take coffee with him, as well as some of his military aides. 'A special word of praise was bestowed on the one who could eat the most cakes.'[12]

At 6.00pm sharp there occurred the day's second military briefing delivered by Jodl. Dinner was served at 7.30pm, often dragging on for two hours as Hitler subjected his guests to one of his infamous monologues. Afterwards, Hitler and his inner circle, and any high-ranking guests that were visiting him, usually repaired to the cinema to watch films and newsreels. Then Hitler would retire to his personal quarters, usually with Bormann and his two female secretaries, and talk or listen to music until the early hours. 'Sometimes, it was daylight by the time the nocturnal discussions came to an end.'[13] As the war started to go badly for Hitler the atmosphere changed. Towards the end Jodl was to describe the Wolf's Lair as halfway 'between a monastery and a concentration camp.'[14]

Hitler's two secretaries at the Wolf's Lair, Christa Schroeder and Gerda Daranowski (later Christian) were given very simple living quarters. 'The sleeping section of their bunker was no larger than a compartment in a railway carriage. It had a toilet, a mirror, and a radio, but not much else. There were shower rooms.'[15] They were also under-employed in the almost exclusively male-dominated world of the Wolf's Lair, drawing criticism from many of the adjutants. But it appeared that Hitler liked to have females around for company. 'They had as good as nothing to do. Sleeping, eating, drinking, and chatting filled up most of their day.'[16] The job of being Hitler's secretary was not, apparently, a particularly happy one. 'We are permanently cut off from the world wherever we are,' complained Schroeder in a letter to a friend in August 1941, 'in Berlin, on the Mountain [Obersalzberg], or on travels. It's always the same limited group of people, always the same routine inside the fence.'[17]

Security and guard duties along the fences of *Sperrkreis I* and *II* were primarily the responsibility of the FBB. *Hauptmann* Gaum, an FBB officer, made this point emphatically to his British interrogators in late 1944.[18] Three guard companies were on active duty at any given time, day or night. Inside *Sperrkreis I* the primary bodyguards were RSD and *SS-Begleitkommando*. RSD Bureau I worked in cooperation with the SS. An *SS-Begleitkommando* officer was responsible for guard changes and patrols by both services as well as guards at the cinema, the issue of passwords, and supervising guards details in their quarters before they came on duty. Permanent guards were mounted as follows:

1. *SS-Begleitkommando* guard in front of the *Führerbunker* day and night.
2. RSD officer on constant patrol around the *Führerbunker* day and night.

3. RSD officer in front of the shorthand writers' building day and night.
4. RSD officer patrolling throughout *Sperrkreis I* between 10.00am and 6.00pm.[19]

Hitler's permanent adjutants were empowered to use the RSD guards for small errands as required. Anyone leaving one bunker to visit another bunker had to have permission. Officers were not permitted to wander freely around *Sperrkreis I*. Identity papers could be demanded at any time. The RSD would check them thoroughly and the person would then be escorted to his destination or to an exit gate into *Sperrkreis II*. The RSD guards were not supposed to stand around chatting or to walk in pairs. When Hitler was walking his dog or strolling the grounds in conversation with a member of the inner circle or a guest, the RSD officer on roving patrol was supposed to keep other people out of earshot of Hitler, and also make sure that he stayed well back. RSD guards were also not permitted to enter the *Führerbunker* unless they were escorting in a workman or a maintenance engineer. Any messages or packages for the *Führerbunker* were handed to one of Hitler's adjutants at the main door.

Although it appeared that the guards always followed strict protocol regarding passes, *Hauptmann* Gaum noted that this was not always rigorously applied for the top Nazis. 'If a person such as Himmler or Göring were seen approaching slowly in a car, he might possibly be let by without being checked by the sentry, but in that case the sentry would ring the IC of the Camp Commandant, who was the official responsible for issuing passes to persons before entering the FHQ.'[20]

Heavy drinking appears to have been a feature of life for Hitler's elite bodyguards and would lead to the dismissal of the head of the *SS-Begleitkommando*. In early 1942 Bruno Gesche, while blind drunk, pulled out his service pistol and took a few potshots at a fellow SS officer. For years Himmler had borne a grudge against Gesche. This time he had grounds for dismissal, and leaping at the opportunity had him dismissed from the *SS-Begleitkommando*. At the age of thirty-seven, with no previous combat experience, Gesche was sent to the *5th SS Panzer Division Wiking* on the Eastern Front. But contrary to what Himmler expected, Gesche proved to be neither a disgrace nor easy to kill. During the German retreat from the Caucasus in October 1942 Gesche was wounded in action and evacuated back to Germany. Awarded the Iron Cross Second Class and the Wound Badge in Black,

Hitler was delighted with his former bodyguard's performance and, overruling Himmler, reinstated Gesche as commander of the *SS-Begleitkommando* with the rank of *SS-Obersturmbannführer*. Hitler also ordered, in light of Gesche's experience, that no members of his guard detail would be permitted to serve on the Eastern Front for fear of capture by the Soviets. The Soviet security police would have thoroughly interrogated any such prisoner for every scrap of information about Hitler, his various headquarters and their security arrangements. It was too much of a risk.

In December 1941 work had commenced on Hitler's most forward headquarters, codenamed *Werwolf* (Werewolf). It was constructed 12km north of the town of Vinnitsa, Ukraine, on the Kiev highway between the villages of Stryzhavka and Kolo-Mikhailovka. Completed in June 1942, *Werwolf* was another mini-Wolf's Lair. The *Wehrmacht* had established its regional HQ in Vinnitsa while the *Luftwaffe* had a huge airbase at Kalinovka, 20km from Hitler's new lair. Once again, the collection of buildings and bunkers were located inside a deep, dark pine forest of the sort much favoured by Hitler, his headquarters often appearing oppressive places lurking in the woods like some fairytale grotto.

Werwolf consisted of a modest log cabin village that was built around a private courtyard with its own concrete bunker for Hitler and his intimates. Hitler's cabin or 'Führerhaus' was very carefully guarded. The RSD even searched the building's walls for microphones and explosives before he moved in.

Surrounding *Sperrkreis I* were another twenty wooden cottages and barracks and three smaller concrete bunkers. *Werwolf* was equipped with a teahouse, sauna, bathhouse, cinema, barbershop, and even an open-air swimming pool that Hitler never used.

The German company Zeidenspiner established a large vegetable garden within the complex to supply Hitler's dietary needs, and fresh water came from two deep artesian wells. Hitler's obsession about his diet and his fear of poisoning led the RSD to enact some intense security protocols. At *Werwolf*, his personal chef, *SS-Hauptsturmführer* Fater, had to go out to select the vegetables for Hitler's meals himself. 'Any other vegetables destined for the *Führer*'s plate had to be dug up under the eyes of an appointed courier who then brought the produce directly to the kitchen. All the food was chemically analysed before cooking, and sampled by a taster before it reached his plate.'[21]

The water supply was sampled several times a day by the RSD. Mineral water had to be bottled in the presence of couriers, and brought in. 'Even the laundry was X-rayed to ensure that no explosive had been concealed.'[22]

Hitler's obsession with poisoning was also much in evidence at the Wolf's Lair. He never really trusted his own inner circle and allies, and realised that because his security was so tight and thorough any attempt to kill him would probably have to come from those in closest proximity to him, and in positions of trust. When Romanian dictator Marshal Ion Antonescu sent Hitler caviar and sweets Hitler ordered the RSD to destroy them. Hitler remarked to *Generalmajor* Rudolf Schmundt, his chief *Wehrmacht* adjutant, *Generaloberst* Jodl and his aide Engel in November 1942 that there were 'groups busy trying to destroy him and his work, and he also knew that there were designs against his life; so far, he had managed to make life miserable for those who were out to get him.'[23]

Hitler was also frightened of the noxious vapours that were given off from his ferro-concrete bunker walls at both the Wolf's Lair and *Werwolf*, so the RSD maintained oxygen tanks outside the bunkers ready to pump in fresh air. These tanks were regularly tested. The bunkers were also fitted with anti-gas chambers to prevent the enemy or any would-be assassins from pumping poison gas into the bunkers through the air ventilation system.

The usual concentric barbed wire fences and access gates at *Werwolf* were strengthened with minefields, anti-aircraft batteries, an anti-tank ditch and a very well armed FBB detachment that included tanks.

Werwolf was built using mostly Soviet POWs working under *Organisation Todt* supervision. According to one account, Hitler ordered *Oberstleutnant* Thomas, commander of the FBB, to liquidate the workers on completion of the project, Hitler remarking: 'They must all be shot. There is not a moment to lose. They know too much about my HQ.'[24] Thomas apparently carried out this order faithfully, for there are large grave pits at the nearby village of Stryzhavka.[25]

The new headquarters was connected to Germany by air and rail. A daily 3-hour flight connected Berlin Tempelhof with the airbase at Kalinovka, while a train connection ran from Berlin-Charlottenburg to 'Eichenbein' Station at *Werwolf*, with a journey time of 34 hours.

Hitler, who spent most of his time directing the campaign on the Eastern Front from the Wolf's Lair, only stayed at *Werwolf* for three short periods as compared to the over 800 days that he spent at

Rastenburg during the war. He first arrived on 16 July 1942 and stayed until 30 October. The summer temperatures were punishingly hot, with daytime recordings of 45°C.

During this first visit Hitler contracted a very bad dose of the flu, his own temperature touching 40°C. Hitler was not only feverish from his illness, but also perhaps because he believed that the Red Army was about to collapse. He was pressuring his generals to take the city of Rostov as the panzer spearheads reached the Don River deep in the Soviet Union. It was while ill that Hitler had made the disastrous decision to split Army Group South into two parts, attempting to capture Stalingrad and the oilfields in the Caucasus simultaneously, leading eventually to the German defeat at the great city on the Volga and the demise of *Generalfeldmarschall* Friedrich Paulus's 6th Army. It proved to be a major turning point of the war.

Hitler's second visit to *Werwolf* between 19 February and 13 March 1943 almost cost him his life. It was while he was at *Werwolf* that *Generalmajor* Henning von Treskow managed to smuggle a bomb on to Hitler's *Condor* at Kalinovka Airfield. But, as we have seen, though Treskow and his aide Schlabrendorff had managed to penetrate Hitler's tight security screen, mechanical failure saved Hitler from what looked to be certain death. Hitler's last stay at the site was between 27 August and 15 September 1943.

After Hitler left *Werwolf* only minimal security was maintained, unlike at the Wolf's Lair which was fully guarded and maintained even when Hitler was not in residence. At Werwolf a small RSD security detachment remained under *SS-Untersturmführer* Karl Danner, while a second line of defence was provided by *Landesschützen Bataillon 318*, a *Wehrmacht* unit consisting of over-age or invalid soldiers who were unfit for the rigours of frontline service.

On 20 September 1943 Hitler, now back at the Wolf's Lair, decided to further tighten up his security arrangements. Rudolf Schmundt and *NSKK-Gruppenführer* Albert Bormann, Martin Bormann's brother and one of Hitler's closest aides, issued a new directive to further intensify security and secrecy within *Sperrkreis I*. A new inner sanctum was created called *Sperrkreis A*. It included Keitel's bunkers and annexes, Hitler's personal adjutants building, Mess No. 1, the teahouse, the *Führerbunker*, Martin Bormann's bunker, the *Wehrmacht* Adjutants' Office, and the Army Personnel Office. Only those serving with Hitler directly or those who had offices within *Sperrkreis A*, or those who lived there, were allowed in regularly. New passes were issued by the RSD.

Additional passes could be issued by HQ Commandant only on the authority of Schmundt or his deputy in consultation with Hitler's aide *SS-Obergruppenführer* Schaub or his deputy. The guard could issue day passes only after a personal or military adjutant of the *Führer* had given his permission.[26] No one was allowed inside *Sperrkreis A* without a valid pass. Anyone found without the proper documentation, regardless of rank, would be immediately arrested by the RSD.

Three gates gave access to *Sperrkreis A* – one by Keitel's bunker, one next to the Adjutants' House and one by Bormann's building. One RSD officer and one FBB NCO manned each gate. The FBB was responsible for checking passes, and the RSD man assisted. In addition, one RSD officer was on constant patrol within *Sperrkreis A*.

A special list of thirty-eight persons was created by the RSD. These men and women were permitted to dine with the *Führer* at lunchtime in Dining Room No. 1, and Hitler would select several each day from the list who were then issued with passes for *Sperrkreis A*. In addition, a further forty-three aides, valets, typists and shorthand writers were on another list permitting them to dine in Dining Room No. 2 inside *Sperrkreis I*.[27]

These new security precautions made any attempt to kill the *Führer* considerably more difficult. An assassin would firstly have to have a valid reason to enter the Wolf's Lair complex, and would have to pass through four identity checks before gaining direct access to Hitler. Very few people were given passes for *Sperrkreis I*, let alone the new inner sanctum of *Sperrkreis A*. But those determined to kill Hitler were resourceful and often well-connected individuals who were prepared to use Hitler's security precautions to their own advantage. During 1943–44 trusted men who were close to Hitler tried to kill him on several occasions. It would only take the right circumstances for one of these brave men to succeed and change Germany and the world's destiny in an instant.

Chapter 8

Enemies Within

'Hitler is the arch enemy not only of Germany but of the world. . .A man's moral worth is established only at the point where he is ready to give his life in defence of his convictions.'

Generalmajor Henning von Treskow, 1944

His back ramrod straight, Rudolf von Gersdorff raised his right hand in the Nazi salute as Hitler entered the large covered courtyard. Outside, the thunder of applause still hung in the air from Hitler's rousing and defiant speech to the assembled party faithful. Gersdorff looked at Hitler, careful to keep his face blank, as the *Führer* approached him. Hitler, who was slightly stooped by this stage of the war, was dressed in his customary field grey jacket and black trousers, his valet Heinz Linge just a step behind him carrying Hitler's grey and brown cap. Flanking the *Führer* were several tough-looking RSD bodyguards in grey SS officers uniforms, their gloved hands never straying far from their pistol holsters. Gersdorff's right hand remained in its rigid 'German greeting' while his left hand quickly and surreptitiously reached into his tunic pocket.[1] He set the fuse to the bomb that he was carrying and spoke: *'Heil, mein Führer!'* Hitler barely acknowledged him, just slightly raising his own right hand in a perfunctory salute. Gersdorff smiled inwardly – in just a few minutes this monster would be dead and Germany would be saved.[2]

Resistance to Hitler was, by 1943, centred on two interlinked groups. The first was a group of civilians and former military officers led by Dr Carl Goerdeler, former Reich Price Commissar who had fallen out with Hitler, and *Generaloberst* Ludwig Beck, the former Army Chief of Staff who had been removed from his post by Hitler in 1938. Others in this influential group included Ulrich von Hassell, the former German Ambassador to Italy, Johannes Popitz, Prussian Finance Minister under Göring, and Jens Jessen, a former Nazi and professor of politics and economics in Berlin. But to get rid of Hitler these older men came to rely upon a group of younger, mostly aristocratic patriots.

The second group was labelled the 'Kreisau Circle' by the Gestapo and included Helmuth James Count von Moltke, an admirer of Britain and a descendant of Bismarck's famous chief of staff; Peter, Count Yorck von Wartenburg, a lawyer; Adam von Trott zu Solz, a former Oxford Rhodes Scholar, as well as an increasing number of serving army officers centred on Army Group Centre on the Eastern Front. The liaison between the military and civilian opposition to Hitler was Fritz-Dietlof, Count von der Schulenburg, a lawyer and former high-ranking Nazi official.

Like Caesar, enemies surrounded Hitler. Many of the men who regularly visited the Berghof or the Wolf's Lair were either active members of the German Resistance or at the very least sympathetic to their cause and were all part of a vast and somewhat disorganised plan to induce Hitler's demise and to end the war before Germany was completely destroyed and occupied by the Allies.

Some of the senior plotters among Hitler's army staff included 57-year-old *General der Nachrichtentruppe* Fritz Fellgiebel. Although Hitler did not fully trust the bespectacled Fellgiebel, he needed him nonetheless for his expertise. Appointed head of Hitler's signals unit, Fellgiebel had introduced the revolutionary Enigma encryption machine to the *Wehrmacht* and he was privy to every military secret of the Reich including the top secret V weapons programme at Peenemünde. What Hitler did not know was that Fellgiebel had been an active plotter against him since 1938, when he watched his friend and superior *Generaloberst* Beck, Chief of the German General Staff, resign following his increasingly rancorous and vocal stand against Hitler's belligerent foreign policy. Fellgiebel then became friends with Beck's successor, *Generaloberst* Franz Halder. Fellgiebel would play a major role in the attack at Rastenburg on 20 July 1944 as he was in charge of Hitler's communications with the outside world.

General der Artillerie Eduard Wagner, 50-year-old Quartermaster General and Deputy Chief of the General Staff of the Army was another senior *Wehrmacht* officer who was in regular proximity to Hitler. On the face of it Wagner was the last person one would suspect of harbouring a death wish against his *Führer*. In July 1939 he had drawn up orders giving permission for the *Wehrmacht* to take and execute civilian hostages during wartime. He had vocally supported the invasion of Poland and most disturbingly had involved the army officially in the murder of the Jews when in May 1941, shortly before the invasion of the Soviet Union, Wagner had encouraged army units to cooperate with the *SS Einsatzgruppen* murder squads. But at some point Wagner had changed his mind about Hitler and had become an active plotter in the resistance movement.

It is easy to assume that those army officers who stood against Hitler were white knights, but many had blood on their hands from Germany's brutal campaigns in the East. They were motivated by different reasons. There were some, particularly younger officers who had served in the field, who were appalled by the massacres perpetrated against defenceless civilians by the SS and others. They viewed such criminal behaviour as impugning the good name of the German people and the armed forces. But others were motivated by fear that Hitler would lose the war, ushering in Soviet occupation and the destruction of the German Army and their own privileged status at the top of German society. Others still were men of deep religious faith who saw Hitler as the anti-Christ. So while some were genuine white knights, some inhabited shades of grey, and in the case of Wagner would have faced trial for war crimes had he survived the war. Collectively, these men represented Germany's last hope of avoiding utter destruction and occupation.

Other plotters with regular access to Hitler were *Generalmajor* Helmuth Stieff, Chief of Organisation at OKH, 56-year-old *Admiral* Wilhelm Canaris of the *Abwehr*, and even *Generalfeldmarschall* Erwin Rommel, Germany's most celebrated general and ironically the man who had been responsible for Hitler's security during the Polish Campaign. Canaris had been in contact with Britain's MI6 since 1938 and had already been involved in two failed plots to topple Hitler. He had been outraged on learning of SS atrocities in Poland and the Soviet Union and secretly kept detailed records on Nazi crimes.

With the debacle of Stalingrad in early 1943 finally revealing Hitler's military incompetence, as well as his evident willingness to sacrifice hundreds of thousands of German soldiers in a needless battle, the mood in Germany was both depressed and shocked. It was probably the best time to launch a coup against the Nazi government. 'A successful undertaking at that time might, despite the recently announced "Unconditional Surrender" strategy of the Allies, have stood a chance of splitting them,' notes Sir Ian Kershaw. 'The removal of the Nazi leadership and offer of capitulation in the west ... would at any rate have placed the western Allies in a quandary about whether to respond to peace-feelers.'[3]

But the plotters had much to lose, and although they schemed and encouraged, they were unlikely to raise a hand personally against Hitler. Any attempt on the *Führer*'s life would have been suicidal, and such self-sacrificial behaviour was left to more hotheaded junior officers. This posed a serious problem for the resistance, for, as the war continued, Hitler's security began to limit the numbers and the ranks of the officers who could be in his presence, perhaps sensing a latent threat from particular groups.

No officer was permitted to wear his service firearm in the *Führer*'s presence. Officers visiting the Berghof and Wolf's Lair left their pistol belts on racks along with their uniform caps before entering the conference area. This ensured that no officer, from field marshal to second lieutenant, had the tool necessary to dispose of his commander-in-chief. Hitler's SS valets, who always wore holstered automatic pistols, carried the only weapons permitted close to the *Führer*'s person. These men were absolutely loyal to Hitler, owing their position and advancement to him alone.

None of the plots against Hitler ever originated from the RSD, *SS-Begleitkommando* or the *Wehrmacht*'s FBB. Hitler's valets received regular target practice sessions with the RSD. Although the valets, cooks and bodyguards that served Hitler were the best placed to kill him, none ever attempted it. The motivation was simply not there. Hitler made sure that his servants were well looked after. When they married he sent substantial personal wedding gifts. At Christmas he was generous to both the men and to their families. On his birthday Hitler would invite all of his servants along with their spouses and children to take coffee and cake with him. Hitler talked to everyone, making even the lowliest servant feel appreciated. 'He cultivated their loyalty and love.'[4] He was, in many respects, an ideal boss.

The real threat to Hitler came instead from the Kreisau Circle, who felt, particularly after the debacle at Stalingrad, that the *Führer* was a liability who was leading Germany towards complete destruction. Amongst these '*vons*', as Hitler derisively termed his largely Prussian military officer class, was a hard core of younger officers who were determined to rid Germany of the beloved *Führer* by the most direct method available – assassination. As several of these plotters had regular access to Hitler and his military headquarters and residences, one of the first attempts was made at the Berghof.

The man who volunteered to kill Hitler inside his own private house was a 33-year-old cavalry officer, *Rittmeister* Eberhard von Breiten-buch. He had originally served as an aide from August 1942 on the staff of *Generalfeldmarschall* Gunther von Kluge, commander of Army Group Centre on the Eastern Front. The famous attempt to blow up Hitler's plane (recounted in Chapter 5) while it was airborne over the Soviet Union on 13 March 1943 had been preceded by some other assassination plans hatched from within Army Group Centre. Von Kluge was fully aware of what many of his subordinate officers were up to, led by his own Operations Officer, *Generalmajor* Henning von Treskow. Hitler visited Smolensk to discuss the forthcoming offensive at Kursk with Kluge and other army commanders. Hitler was, in effect, unknowingly entering the belly of the beast when he entered Army Group Centre. It was probably the most dangerous location that the *Führer* visited, where he would find himself surrounded by dozens of officers who would not have thought twice about putting a bullet between his eyes. As we have seen, one officer did object to such a move – von Kluge. The original plan had been to shoot Hitler dead while he was taking luncheon with the headquarters officers. When Kluge was informed of this plan he was outraged: 'One could not just shoot the man at his meal.'[5] Also Kluge and other senior officers were afraid of getting caught in the crossfire during the inevitable shoot out with Hitler's SS bodyguards; and the conspirators were averse to risking their commanding general's life, as he would be needed in the post-Nazi government.

An alternative plan was to ambush and kill Hitler as he walked the half-kilometre from his car to the dining hut. As related, *Oberstleutnant* von Boeselager, commanding Cavalry Regiment Centre, had found enough officers and NCOs who were willing to do this. But this plan also came to naught after Hitler refused to follow the assigned paths. Eventually, Treskow had decided upon a bomb aboard Hitler's *Condor*, a brilliant idea that ultimately also failed.

After von Kluge was injured in a car crash in October, *Rittmeister* von Breitenbuch became aide to *Generalfeldmarschall* Ernst Busch of Army Group B. His job meant that Breitenbuch accompanied Busch to all military conferences at *Führer* Headquarters, giving him unfettered access to both the Berghof and the Wolf's Lair. Breitenbuch had now become Treskow's new and best hope for disposing of Hitler.

Breitenbuch had been in contact with the shadowy conspiracy against Hitler for some years. He had decided to throw in his lot with them and move to direct action in 1942 after he had witnessed 'anti-partisan actions' conducted by German forces in the forests of eastern Poland, where thousands of civilians had been brutally rounded up and shot. 'What I had previously suspected [of the Nazi regime] I now knew for sure,'[6] he said later. Breitenbuch had contacted the then *Oberst* von Treskow, one of the central anti-Hitler plotters, and told him that he would have access to the Berghof when he accompanied Busch to meetings there. Treskow immediately supplied him with British-made plastic explosive in the hope that Breitenbuch would be able to plant a bomb near Hitler, but the younger officer demurred in favour of a pistol. Breitenbuch distrusted the explosive's reliability and preferred to try and smuggle an automatic pistol into Hitler's presence and at some point during a meeting shoot the dictator through the head. Naturally, Breitenbuch was outlining a suicide mission, for he would have been shot down by Hitler's bodyguards seconds after drawing his weapon. The pistol Breitenbuch selected for the task was a 7.65mm Browning, and this was hidden in his trouser pocket. Fortunately for all concerned, RSD personnel were not frisking visitors to *Führer* Headquarters at this time.

On 11 March 1943 Busch's party arrived by *Condor* plane at Salzburg Airport, the main airfield for visitors to the Obersalzberg. The party was then driven to the Berghof by car. On entering the *Führer*'s residence all of the officers removed their caps, belts and sidearms in the presence of the ever-vigilant RSD. Breitenbuch had earlier removed his watch and wedding ring to be sent to his wife. The Browning, loaded and already cocked, and with the safety catch off, felt heavy in his trouser pocket. He was almost sick with nerves, struggling to maintain his composure in front of the SS and senior Nazis. 'My heart was beating in my throat as it was clear to me that, within half an hour, I would be dead,'[7] he said.

A joking *Reichsmarschall* Hermann Göring went through to the conference room followed by *Generalfeldmarschall* Wilhelm Keitel, *Generaloberst* Alfred Jodl and the limping *Reichsminister* Dr Goebbels. Busch's party followed on behind but was suddenly stopped by RSD officers. Busch was informed that no aides would be admitted to the room. Breitenbuch was forced to 'endure Busch's vain and unwitting attempts to negotiate his entry, and was finally turned away, still with the pistol ... in his pocket.'[8] Standing on the sun terrace with another dismissed aide, nervously smoking, Breitenbuch felt ill from the stress and the anti-climax. He never again volunteered for a mission against Hitler and survived the mass arrests and executions that followed the 20 July 1944 bomb plot.

To kill Hitler was a virtual suicide mission, but Breitenbuch was not the only young patriot to step forward and volunteer to do the unthinkable. One such officer summed up the feeling among the German Resistance: 'Since the generals have up to now managed nothing, the colonels have now to step in.'[9]

One such colonel was *Oberst* Rudolf Christoph Baron von Gersdorff who said to von Treskow a few days after Breitenbuch's failed attempt on Hitler's life: 'It must be done. This is our only chance ... Hitler must be cut down like a rabid dog.'[10] Gersdorff, Head of the Staff Section at Army Group Centre had just volunteered to become a suicide bomber.

Gersdorff volunteered to kill Hitler when he discovered that he had been selected to act as a tour guide while the *Führer* perused captured Soviet weaponry at the Zeughaus, the old Berlin Arsenal, on the Unter den Linden. It was part of the celebrations for Heroes Memorial Day. Gersdorff believed that he had a real chance at killing Hitler because he would be close to him for about thirty minutes. He ruled out using a pistol, as he believed the security would be too tight at the event and that Hitler's RSD bodyguards would shoot him down before he had a chance to take proper aim. It was also suspected by the plotters that Hitler routinely wore a bulletproof vest underneath his tunic.[11] Gersdorff first decided to blow Hitler up by planting a bomb in the speaker's rostrum shortly before he arrived to deliver his annual speech.

Gersdorff flew to Berlin on 20 March with *Generalfeldmarschall* Walther Model, Commander-in-Chief of the Ninth Army, who would also be attending the ceremony. He carried two Clam Mines, small but powerful British explosive devices about the same size and thickness as a paperback book. Treskow had given these to him after he had retrieved them following the failed attempt on Hitler's plane.

Gersdorff carried out a quiet and unobtrusive reconnaissance of the Zeughaus on the afternoon of 20 March and soon realised that planting a bomb was out of the question. Wherever Hitler would walk, stand or sit was carefully guarded or watched, so Gersdorff rejected any notion of a Georg Elser-style attack on the *Führer*. Instead, Gersdorff decided upon a radical course of action. He would conceal one of the clam mines in his pocket. As soon as Hitler entered the glass-covered Zeughaus courtyard where the exhibition of weaponry had been set up, Gersdorff would start the timer. He would then stand as close to Hitler as possible and die in the resulting explosion, hopefully taking Hitler with him.

Gersdorff faced several significant problems. Firstly, he had no idea of Hitler's security and guarding arrangements and whether he would be permitted to stand close enough to Hitler for the bomb to be lethally effective. He had noticed that the covered inner courtyard where the display was to be held was huge and airy – any detonation by a small bomb would be quickly dispersed. Secondly, and most importantly, he could not find a sufficiently short fuse; the best he could manage was one of ten minutes. This meant that Gersdorff would have to closely shadow the *Führer* to keep him in range of the bomb blast. Would the RSD permit an officer to trail along behind Hitler after the *Führer* had moved on from Gersdorff's section of the exhibit? It appeared un-likely, so Gersdorff resolved to try and engage Hitler in conversation whilst demonstrating the Soviet weapons, and try to keep him close while the fuse counted down to destruction.

Gersdorff stood next to Model as Hitler entered the covered court-yard at the head of practically the entire senior Nazi leadership circle. Behind Hitler was Hermann Göring dressed incongruously in a white uniform of his own design, and wearing red leather jackboots and makeup. Heinrich Himmler's cold eyes stared out from behind his wire-framed glasses, lips pursed and disapproving while Hitler's two senior military commanders, the tall, pompous and slightly rotund *Generalfeldmarschall* Keitel, and *Grossadmiral* Karl Dönitz, both grasp-ing their ornate rank batons in their right hands, followed behind.

Hitler had already delivered his short speech outside, and Gersdorff had listened as the German national anthem was played followed by the *Horst Wessel*, the Nazi's unofficial anthem. Hitler now had thirty minutes to use up at the exhibition before the wreath laying ceremony commenced once more outside the Zeughaus.[12]

Hitler moved towards Gersdorff's section of the exhibition, the gallant Baron arming his bomb as the *Führer* approached. Gersdorff had ten minutes left to live and, determined to kill Hitler, he smiled and attempted to interest the *Führer* in the display of Soviet weaponry laid out on table before him. Hitler, a disinterested scowl on his face, moved along the tables with Gersdorff staying as close to Hitler as pos-sible, all the time trying to talk to him.[13] It is a measure of Gersdorff's incredible bravery that he showed absolutely no outward sign of the impending violent end of his life, carrying on as if everything were absolutely normal. The RSD guards never suspected a thing. But suddenly Hitler, instead of asking questions about the weapons, 'went – or rather ran – out of the side door,' recalled Gersdorff. 'During his short tour around the exhibition, he had barely looked at anything and had not said a word.'[14] A tour that was supposed to have taken thirty minutes had lasted for barely two. Gersdorff considered attempting to follow Hitler from the courtyard but quickly realised that this for-bidden behaviour would only alert the RSD and *SS-Begleitkommando* guards in the *Führer*'s vicinity and have led to his apprehension. Instead, Gersdorff made his excuses and locked himself inside a toilet cubicle. Frantically, he disarmed the bombs, succeeding with only seconds to spare.[15]

Later that same day a fellow army officer approached Gersdorff and jokingly explained how he could have 'killed Adolf today.' Hitler, he said, 'drove very slowly in an open top car down Unter den Linden, right in front of my ground-floor room in the Hotel Bristol. It would have been child's play to heave a hand-grenade over the sidewalk and into his car.'[16] Gersdorff, white faced, just stared at him blankly. The following day Baron von Gersdorff was transferred back to Army Group Centre on the Eastern Front and his plot to kill the *Führer* was never discovered. Gersdorff survived the war, dying in Germany in 1980.

The next man to step forward with a plan to kill Hitler was *Hauptmann* Axel Baron von dem Bussche-Streithorst, a 25-year-old half-Danish aristocrat who had been serving in the German Army since 1937. Standing 2 metres tall, the blonde haired, blue-eyed Bussche-Streithorst was selected to model some new winter uniforms before Hitler at the Wolf's Lair, the event scheduled for 18 November 1943. The young officer seemed to epitomise the Nordic ideal that the Nazis aspired to, but in reality Bussche-Streithorst had been a bitter opponent of the regime since witnessing a mass shooting of 3,000 Jews at Dubno by the SS in 1942. Deeply traumatized by this horrific event Bussche-Streithorst reasoned that he had three ways to preserve his honour. He could die in battle, desert or rebel against the government that perpetrated such inhuman acts. He chose the latter option.

Bussche-Streithorst's plan was simple – he would emulate Baron von Gersdorff. He would conceal a landmine in one of the pockets of the uniform that he would model for Hitler, fitting the bomb with a fast-reacting hand grenade detonator, thereby overcoming the fusing problem that Gersdorff had faced during his attempt at the Zeughaus in Berlin. As Hitler approached him, Bussche-Streithorst would set off the detonator, embrace the *Führer* in a death grip and kill both of them. Courage ran in his family, for his first cousin was the Danish soldier Anders Lassen, who would win a Victoria Cross serving with the British Army in Italy in 1945.

Arriving at the *Wolfsschanze*, Bussche-Streithorst waited for two days for the display to commence. But then crushing news arrived. The uniforms had all been destroyed during a huge British air raid on Berlin the night before the exhibition was to be held. It was a bitter blow. Bussche-Streithorst's plan would most probably have succeeded. He volunteered to try again in February 1944 but before this could be arranged Bussche-Streithorst was severely wounded on the Eastern Front, losing one of his legs. He was permanently out of the assassination business, but he too survived the war, dying in 1993.

At this point a brave new volunteer stepped forward – *Hauptmann* Ewald-Heinrich von Kleist-Schmenzin, a 22-year-old officer from a family with a long history of active opposition against the Nazis. Another exhibition of uniforms was scheduled for 11 February 1944. Kleist-Schmenzin decided to modify the Bussche-Streithorst plan slightly by using a mine concealed inside a briefcase, hoping somewhat optimistically that he could survive the blast that would kill Hitler by tossing the briefcase, with the mine's detonator already triggered, at the *Führer*'s feet creating a little distance between himself and his target before the explosion. Again, such a plan, pre-July Bomb Plot, had a good chance of success, for the RSD was not yet completely vigilant regarding officers' bags – they were more concerned about sidearms being carried in the presence of the *Führer*. But this ingenious plan failed because Hitler kept postponing the event before he finally cancelled it altogether. Von Kleist-Schmenzin was transferred back to regular duties. Unlike Gersdorff and Bussche-Streithorst he did not survive the war. He was arrested in the wake of the July Bomb Plot, and guillotined.

With the failure of the Breitenbuch, Bussche-Streithorst and Kleist-Schmenzin plots, concern was growing amongst the resistance that very few officers still had regular access to Hitler, and therefore the opportunity to attempt an assassination was diminishing. And with senior officers' aides now banned from conferences the chances of successfully introducing a bomb into Hitler's headquarters or private home were growing ever more remote. What was needed was an officer of sufficient rank who would attend military conferences and still be in close proximity to the *Führer*. By mid-1944 only two men fitted this description. One was 43-year-old *Generalmajor* Helmuth Stieff, a man who was described by one senior plotter as 'as nervy as a racing jockey.'[17] The other was a man of immense personal courage, the new leader of the resistance movement who had played such an important part in recruiting the men who had already attempted to kill Hitler, *Oberst* Claus Schenk Count von Stauffenberg. Germany's latest saviour was also its last great hope – the only plotter senior enough and brave enough to stand next to Hitler and kill him.

The Stauffenbergs are one of southern Germany's oldest and most distinguished aristocratic families. Claus von Stauffenberg was born at the family castle at Jettingen near Augsburg in 1907. He was commissioned into the *Reichswehr* in 1930 and took part in the invasion of the Sudetenland in 1938. He wrestled with his conscience regarding Nazi ideology, on the one hand supporting many of Hitler's foreign policy goals, and on the other despising the brutality and racism of the Nazis. His strong Catholic faith was deeply offended by the ill treatment of the Jews, a reaction shared by many of his brother officers and fellow plotters.

In 1939 Stauffenberg served with distinction in the Polish Campaign, and it was during this campaign that the anti-Hitler resistance first approached him. His uncle, Nikolaus Count von Uxkull-Gyllenbrand, spoke to him at length about the aims of the Resistance, but at this stage Stauffenberg was averse to breaking his oath of allegiance to Hitler and declined to join. As with many of his class, the breaking of an oath was practically inconceivable under any circumstances because it impugned an officer's family honour.

Stauffenberg won the Iron Cross First Class during the invasion of France, but what he saw and heard in 1941 during Operation Barbarossa, the invasion of the Soviet Union, both appalled and disturbed him. The mass execution of civilians, the roundups and the deliberate alienation of conquered populations, disgusted Stauffenberg leading him to finally join the Resistance in 1942. His conscience overrode his strong sense of patriotism and loyalty when the true amoral nature of Nazism was revealed to him. But like all of the other plotters, overcoming a reluctance to commit treason was a terrible internal struggle, as Kershaw notes: 'In a war, distinct from treachery against one's own country, from betrayal to the enemy, was chiefly a matter of individual persuasion and the relative weighting of moral values.'[18]

Posted to the Organisational Department of OKH, Stauffenberg tried to soften German occupation policies, also attempting to recruit local volunteers for the German armed forces. He wrote a proposal concerning the correct treatment of Soviet prisoners of war. Unfortunately, none of his proposals were adopted, adding to his frustration and determination to affect a change of leadership.

Posted to the *Afrika Korps* in Tunisia in 1942, he was promoted to *Oberstleutnant* and made Operations Officer of the 10th Panzer Division. During Rommel's advance through the Kasserine Pass in early 1943 Stauffenberg's job meant that he was constantly driving between units in his Horch staff car. On 7 April Royal Australian Air Force P-40 Kittyhawk fighter-bombers pounced on the convoy that he was travelling in. Stauffenberg suffered appalling injuries including losing his left eye, right hand and several of the fingers on his left hand.

After three months of hospitalisation in Munich, Stauffenberg recovered and was awarded the Wound Badge in Gold and the German Cross in Gold, one of Nazi Germany's most prestigious awards for bravery. After a suitable period of convalescence, he was promoted to *Oberst* and appointed Chief of Staff to *Generaloberst* Friedrich Fromm, Commander-in-Chief of the Replacement Army. Fifty-five-year-old Fromm could be best described as a 'fence sitter'. He never fully committed himself to Stauffenberg's plotting but he did agree to keep quiet in return for a high position in any post-coup government. In the end, when push came to shove, Fromm sided with Hitler with devastating consequences for Stauffenberg and the other plotters.

The Replacement Army had a dual role in Nazi Germany. Its primary job was to train soldiers as replacements for first line divisions. Secondly, in the event of a coup against Hitler, or internal disorder, the Replacement Army was to activate Operation 'Valkyrie'. The original Valkyrie plan, as created by *General der Infanterie* Friedrich Olbricht's staff, would see Replacement Army formations activated to guard vital points across the Reich. Awarded the Knights Cross for personal bravery during the invasion of Poland, Olbricht had been appointed Chief of the Armed Forces Replacement Office at OKW in 1942.

Olbricht had been wary of the Nazis since the early 1920s, and joined the plotters.

Unfortunately, only Fromm could activate Valkyrie, so from the beginning the plotters, led by *Generalmajor* von Treskow and Stauffenberg, sought to enlist a reluctant Fromm to their cause. After the failure to assassinate Hitler on his plane ride back from Smolensk on 13 March 1943, Olbricht felt that the original Valkyrie plan was inadequate and that the Replacement Army should be used to overthrow Hitler and his government even without Fromm's cooperation. Treskow created 'Valkyrie II', providing for the swift gathering of army units into battle groups ready for action.

During August and September 1943 Treskow revised and further expanded the plan, issuing new secret orders. The operational orders now began with the words: 'The *Führer* Adolf Hitler is dead! A treacherous group of party leaders has attempted to exploit the situation by attacking our embattled soldiers from the rear to seize power for themselves.'[19] There followed detailed instructions for Replacement Army battlegroups to occupy the main government ministries in Berlin, Himmler's headquarters at the Hochenwald in East Prussia, radio stations and telephone exchanges, other Nazi offices and the concentration camps. The plan relied upon tricking the Replacement Army into working for the plotters in eradicating the Nazi government by creating a false coup attempt by the SS. The ordinary troops would believe that the Nazi leadership was traitorous and had to be removed. Treskow was confident that the troops would obey as their orders came from Replacement Army Headquarters and looked genuine.

The Allied invasion of Normandy on 6 June 1944 convinced 36-year-old Stauffenberg that the writing was on the wall for Hitler's Germany. In his opinion, it was the sacred duty of loyal German officers to get rid of the *Führer* and to conclude an immediate armistice with the Western Allies to prevent further pointless bloodshed and the ultimate destruction of Germany.

From September 1943 Stauffenberg had been the driving force behind the resistance, and behind every plot to kill Hitler. As the failures mounted, Stauffenberg was becoming increasingly doubtful that the resistance would succeed. 'The assassination must be attempted,' urged Stauffenberg's friend and fellow conspirator von Treskow. 'Even if it fails, we must take action in Berlin.' Treskow believed that they had to show the Allies that not every German was like Hitler.

Stauffenberg had first met Hitler in person on 7 June 1944, the day after D-Day. He accompanied his boss, Fromm, to a military meeting at the Berghof. Hitler greeted the war-scarred hero warmly, carefully taking the Count's one remaining mangled hand into both of his and staring intently into Stauffenberg's one eye, as was his wont with new faces at headquarters. Stauffenberg was unfazed by Hitler's intense greeting and could not see the so-called 'hypnotic magnetism' that so many other officers claimed that Hitler exuded. The meeting was limited, aside from Fromm and Stauffenberg, to Hitler, Göring, Himmler, the crawling sycophant Keitel, and Albert Speer. Stauffenberg presented a revised draft of Operation Valkyrie to the *Führer* for his approval and signature, though this plan was not the one that Treskow, Olbricht and Stauffenberg would actually transmit to the Replacement Army. Hitler listened attentively and then signed the plan into official policy, undoubtedly pleased that he was so well protected by his *Wehrmacht* forces.

During the meeting Stauffenberg was afforded the opportunity to study Nazi Germany's most powerful leaders up close. He was disgusted and repulsed by what he saw. 'He ... described the atmosphere as degenerate and foetid and claimed that he had found it hard to breathe. Of his fellow participants, he noted, only Albert Speer gave the impression of normality. The others ... were "patent psychopaths."'[20]

On 6 July Stauffenberg was summoned from Berlin to the Berghof for a second time. On this occasion he brought British plastic explosives and time pencil fuses with him inside his briefcase. He hoped to persuade Stieff to attempt an attack on Hitler during a scheduled demonstration of uniforms at Castle Klessheim near Salzburg, but Stieff lost his nerve and demurred. The only plotter determined enough to attempt assassination and with direct access to Hitler was now Count von Stauffenberg. His war injuries had thus far kept him from becoming an assassin, but now he was left with no choice.

Stauffenberg made his first personal attempt to kill Hitler at the Berghof on 11 July 1944. He had returned to the Obersalzberg for another conference but this time had taken the precaution of stationing a plane at Salzburg Airport ready to fly him straight back to Berlin once Hitler was dead. In Berlin, Olbricht was ready to illegally activate Operation Valkyrie once he had received news from Stauffenberg of the *Führer*'s demise. The bomb, again inside Stauffenberg's briefcase, was carried into Hitler's presence without his RSD bodyguards being any the wiser. But Stauffenberg noticed that Himmler was absent from the meeting. In a quiet conversation with Stieff, his fellow plotter persuaded him to postpone the attack until such time as the entire Nazi leadership was present. Stauffenberg reluctantly agreed, completed his briefing and left for Berlin. On reflection, he felt that he should have killed Hitler when he had had the opportunity and allowed the Replacement Army to deal with Himmler and the SS. A bomb inside the large living room at the Berghof would probably have succeeded. Hitler had once again escaped death.

Stauffenberg was not prepared to wait much longer. In the meantime, Hitler had changed headquarters once again, moving back to the Wolf's Lair in East Prussia, and it was here that Stauffenberg was given another opportunity to kill the *Führer* and enact Operation Valkyrie.

Chapter 9

Valkyrie

*'It is now time that something was done. But the man who has the
courage to do something must do it in the knowledge that he will go
down in German history as a traitor. If he does not do it, however,
he will be a traitor to his own conscience.'*[1]

Count von Stauffenberg, 1944

Oberst Claus Schenk Count von Stauffenberg carefully placed his
brown leather briefcase against one of the thick wooden table supports, making sure that it was as close to Adolf Hitler as he dared. The
hot and stuffy conference room was crowded with senior officers,
aides and stenographers, the huge wooden table festooned with maps
and charts. Hitler, pale and drawn and wearing spectacles, stood halfway along the table listening to the latest bad news from the Russian
Front. His marked stoop and greying hair made him look older than
fifty-five. It was evident to all those gathered in the room that the
Führer was becoming increasingly agitated, as *Generalleutnant* Adolf
Heusinger, Chief of the General Staff of the Army, presented his pessi-
mistic strategic assessment and recommendations for the Eastern
Front.[2]

The conference hut windows were open, for it was another hot and
sticky day deep in the marshy East Prussian forest. The date was
20 July 1944 and Hitler had only minutes to live. Stauffenberg stood
erect a few paces from his *Führer*, standing next to 37-year-old *Oberst*
Heinz Brandt, Heusinger's aide and brilliant equestrian who had
won a gold medal at the 1936 Olympics. Stauffenberg's calm exterior
masked his rising panic. Stauffenberg was the epitome of the kind of
Wagnerian hero so adored by the Nazis. The Count was handsome,
with a military bearing, but horribly disfigured by his war injuries.
He wore a black eye patch and his right hand was missing from the
wrist. Most of the fingers of his left hand were also gone. This crippled
but proud warrior represented the last chance for Germany. Both
Stauffenberg and his fellow plotters had come so close to killing Hitler
on numerous occasions. They felt sure that Hitler's uncanny ability to

sidestep death could not last forever – one of their attempts would be bound to get him.

Inside Stauffenberg's briefcase was a bomb, a British bomb. It was the same slab of explosives that had already been unsuccessfully used to try and destroy Hitler's plane over the Soviet Union in 1943. Stuck into the Plastic-C was a British time pencil chemical fuse and it had already been crushed – acid was slowly eating through a spring holding back a firing pin. A detonation was imminent but the weapon was not precise, it could go off early due to the warm temperatures at the Wolf's Lair. Stauffenberg knew he had only a few minutes to leave the conference hut before the bomb detonated. Stauffenberg had no intention of dying alongside his *Führer* – he intended to survive so that he could play a central role in the military coup to be launched against the Nazi state in the wake of Hitler's successful assassination – Operation Valkyrie.

He glanced to his left at his target, the maniac who was dragging sacred Germany into the abyss. Stauffenberg's face betrayed no emotion. He looked around at *Generalfeldmarschall* Keitel's adjutant, *Major* John von Freyend and muttered something about a telephone call. Freyend and Stauffenberg stepped out of the conference. They went into the telephone operator's room where a call was placed to *Generalmajor* Erich Fellgiebel's nearby communications centre. 'This is Stauffenberg,' he announced curtly into the phone, appeared to listen for a few seconds, then calmly replaced the receiver in its cradle. Not pausing to retrieve his cap and belt with its holstered automatic pistol, Stauffenberg quickly left the conference building and started to walk towards his staff car parked close by outside. He expected the deafening explosion at any second. This time Hitler would not escape his fate.

Stauffenberg had been presented with an opportunity to attack Hitler at the Wolf's Lair because he was a member of the *Führer*'s inner staff. However, even someone as trusted as the Count faced virtually overwhelming obstacles to kill Hitler. Security at the *Führer*'s Eastern Front headquarters was formidable in comparison to the discreet arrangements at Berchtesgaden. It was designed to be overt and intimidating so that visitors were in no doubt that they were entering Hitler's nerve centre for his most important front. It was also relatively close to the Front, so security had to be tight to prevent a surprise Soviet attack. *SS-Begleitkommando* and RSD personnel guarded all the conference rooms.

On the morning of 20 July Stauffenberg was to have a meeting with *General der Infanterie* Walter Bühle, Chief of Staff of OKW in Jodl's House within *Sperrkreis I*. Afterwards, the participants attended another meeting in Keitel's Bunker. Stauffenberg was then due to report on new Replacement Army units at the *Führer*'s midday situation conference.

At 12.30pm Keitel's adjutant, *Major* von Freyend, reported that *Generalleutnant* Heusinger, who was due to deliver a report on the Eastern Front at the conference, had just arrived on the trolley from the nearby *Mauerwald* Headquarters complex. Keitel announced that it was time to go to Hitler's situation room near the Guest Bunker. At this point Stauffenberg managed to excuse himself from the group, as *Major* von Freyend led him to somewhere private where he could wash his face and change his shirt. Freyend led him to a private room but Stauffenberg appeared again shortly afterwards looking for his aide, *Oberleutnant* Werner von Haeften, who was carrying the bomb materials in his briefcase.[3] While Stauffenberg and von Haeften worked feverishly to put their bomb together Keitel and the others waited outside the building. Stauffenberg, who only had three fingers on his one remaining hand, struggled to crush the time pencil fuse that Haeften had pushed into the 1kg slab of plastic explosive. Using specially prepared pincers, Stauffenberg managed to set the fuse off. At this point an orderly, FBB Sergeant-Major Werner Vogel, tried to enter the room to find out why Stauffenberg was taking so long. The Count was nervous and curtly ordered him out, but *Major* von Freyend called out from the front of the building: '*Herr Oberst* Stauffenberg, *do* come along now!' Stauffenberg quickly left the room with only one bomb prepared, armed and fused, stuffed into his briefcase while von Haeften still had the other slab of explosives and time pencil.[4]

Keitel, having grown impatient waiting for Stauffenberg, had gone on to the conference hut, but the Count quickly joined Freyend and the others and started walking towards the security gate. Freyend offered to carry Stauffenberg's briefcase for him, but the Count, looking tense, curtly refused. But as they approached the security gate that led into *Sperrkreis A*, Stauffenberg handed the briefcase and its live bomb to Freyend and asked him to place him as close to the *Führer* as possible because his injuries had left him hard of hearing.

Outside the conference hut was an *SS-Begleitkommando* sentry and nearby lurked an RSD officer on patrol. Inside, a sergeant from the FBB manned the building's telephone switchboard. As the officers entered the hut they removed their caps and belts with their holstered service pistols and placed them on racks outside the conference room. No-one's briefcase was searched and Hitler's bodyguards did not frisk the visitors for weapons. A few days after the bombing the RSD concluded its report on the incident, writing: 'Any failure of security measures *provided* against an assassination attempt cannot be discovered, since the possibility had never been taken into consideration that a General Staff officer who was summoned to the situation conference would lend his hand to such a crime.'[5]

There were two SS officers present in the room: *SS-Sturmbannführer* Otto Günsche, Hitler's personal aide, and *SS-Gruppenführer* Hermann Fegelein, Himmler's SS liaison at *Führer* Headquarters. The other twenty men in the room were all army or navy officers, apart from two shorthand writers who would record everything that was said, and Minister Franz von Sonnleithner, Foreign Minister Ribbentrop's liaison man. Keitel introduced Stauffenberg to Hitler, who shook his mangled hand briefly before turning back to the conference table.[6]

Stauffenberg excused himself from the meeting barely two minutes after stepping into the room, on the pretext of making a telephone call. Stauffenberg asked Freyend to arrange the connection for the call that he said he still had to make to Fellgiebel. Freyend did as he was asked and Stauffenberg was left alone in the telephone operator's room to speak to Fellgiebel. As soon as Freyend had gone back into the briefing, Stauffenberg hung up and left the building.

When Stauffenberg left the conference room Hitler was leaning on the table, his chin cupped with one hand, his elbow on the desk as *Generalleutnant* Heusinger described the worsening situation on the Eastern Front.[7] Stauffenberg walked out of the building and across to where Fellgiebel waited in the doorway of the communications centre with von Haeften. At 12.50pm, just as Stauffenberg reached the building, a loud detonation went off behind him in the direction of the conference hut.

Oberleutnant Ludolf Sander, a communications officer in Fellgiebel's department, was standing near to Stauffenberg and von Haeften when the bomb went off. The Count and his adjutant were anxiously making arrangements for a car. The explosion was deafening. Fellgiebel gave Stauffenberg a startled look, but the Count just shrugged his shoulders. Sander was unsurprised by the detonation – tens of thousands of mines had been sown around the Wolf's Lair complex and wild animals often set them off by accident.

The explosion inside the conference hut was tremendous – the British Plastic-C explosive packing a mighty punch. Flames, debris and bodies were flung through the open windows while the detonation reverberated off the surrounding buildings. All hell broke loose as security personnel, shouting at the tops of their voices, raced towards the hut and an alarm siren started its mournful wail. FBB medics rushed to tend the injured while Stauffenberg and von Haeften hurried towards a nearby staff car.[8] The two plotters witnessed the scene of confusion as a huge cloud of black smoke and dust completely obscured the conference hut. Several guards looked skyward, expecting to hear the drone of aircraft engines, for it seemed as though the bomb had to have come from above. Stauffenberg climbed into the back of the black Mercedes believing that no one in the conference room could have survived such a catastrophic detonation.

Inside Hitler's conference hut the pleasant room had been reduced to a complete shambles. The huge map table had collapsed and was partly on fire. Bits of paper and dust twirled in the disturbed air. The walls and ceiling had also partially collapsed and the window frames had disintegrated, with wood and glass spread over the grass outside. But the bomb had not done its work. Stenographer Dr Heinrich Berger had taken the full blast of Stauffenberg's bomb, losing both of his legs. He died later that day. *Oberst* Brandt lost one of his legs and died the following day. *Generaloberst* Gunther Korten, Chief of the General Staff of the *Luftwaffe*, was speared by a piece of wood and also died the next day. Chief of the Army Staff Office, *Generalmajor* Rudolf Schmundt, was severely wounded, losing an eye and a leg, and also suffered burns to his face. He died in hospital several weeks after the attack. But most of the participants survived with injuries that ranged from serious to superficial – unfortunately for Stauffenberg and the plotters Hitler fell into the latter category.

The problem for Stauffenberg was the venue – if the situation conference had been held in the windowless concrete *Führerbunker* the explosive power of the 1kg charge would have been magnified and probably killed everyone in the room. But because of the stifling July heat, the venue had been changed to the cool and shady conference hut. The use of the term 'hut' is a little disingenuous as it was built of concrete and brick, but it had large windows and was wood and plaster lined, so some of the power of the blast dissipated through the windows and doors or was absorbed by the plaster and wood interior.

Hitler was blown off his feet by the blast. After the initial shock of the blast, Hitler, a veteran of the trenches, established that he was all in one piece and that he could move. He made it through the wreckage to the door beating flames out from his trousers and the back of his head as he went. He bumped into Keitel, who embraced him, weeping and crying out: 'My *Führer*, you are alive, you are alive!'[9] Keitel helped Hitler outside.

Hitler's singed hair stood on end, his trousers and long white underwear had been shredded and hung in strips like a raffia skirt, and his legs bled from hundreds of wooden splinters that had flown around the room like high velocity needles. His face was blackened and he was deaf in one ear, his eardrum ruptured by the blast. He also had bad bruising to his hands and a haemorrhaged elbow because he was leaning on the table when the bomb had exploded. His right arm was swollen and painful and he could barely lift it. He also had cuts to his forehead. But he was very much alive and none of his injuries was life threatening. As with so many things in Hitler's life, his survival had been purely by chance. After Stauffenberg had left the room to answer his telephone call, *Oberst* Brandt's boot had connected with the Count's briefcase. To clear some standing space Brandt, who was standing closest to Hitler, had leaned down and moved the briefcase to the other side of one of the very thick oak table supports, away from Hitler. If the bomb had remained where it was Hitler would almost certainly have been killed – as it was, the table support absorbed much of the bomb's blast leaving Hitler with only superficial injuries. Stauffenberg had also only been able to arm one of the two slabs of plastic explosives that he had carried into the Wolf's Lair after being disturbed when he and his aide had been priming the time pencil fuse. The other slab remained in von Haeften's possession as they drove away from the scene of the crime in the staff car.

Dr Morell soon arrived to begin treating Hitler's wounds. When the *Führer*'s valet, Heinz Linge, rushed to his master's side he was surprised to find Hitler composed and with a grim smile on his face. 'Linge, someone has tried to kill me,'[10] said Hitler. The identity of that 'someone' had yet to emerge.

Stauffenberg's car passed through the checkpoint out of *Sperrkreis I* without any problems, the Count bluffing the guards, muttering something about '*Führer* orders' of the highest priority. The guards should not have let the car pass, but they were still reeling with confusion after the nearby bomb blast. When Stauffenberg and von Haeften arrived at *Wache Süd*, the southern guardhouse in the perimeter fence, they found their path to freedom was blocked. The FBB manning the gates had dropped the barrier and placed obstacles across the road. The NCO in charge resolutely refused to let the plotters pass. Stauffenberg, feigning anger at such an insufferable delay, got out of the Mercedes and paced into the guardroom where he telephoned his breakfast companion, *Rittmeister* Leonhard von Möllendorf who worked in the HQ Commandant. Repeating his story about *'Führer's* orders' von Möllendorf interceded on Stauffenberg's behalf and ordered the guard commander to open the gates. Speeding through, Stauffenberg and von Haeften headed for the airfield where *General* Wagner had placed a Heinkel He 111 transport at his disposal. Within a few minutes they were on their way to Berlin, confident that Hitler was no more and ready to take charge of the coup.

At the Wolf's Lair Hitler continued to receive treatment from his personal physician, Dr Morell. When Hitler had been dragged from the burning and ruined conference hut Fellgiebel had been watching from in front of the Guest Bunker, trying to ascertain whether Hitler was alive or dead. Later, Fellgiebel fell into conversation with *Generaloberst* Jodl, remarking about the attack: 'You see, this comes from being so close to the front lines.' Jodl retorted sharply: 'No, this comes from the HQ being a construction site.'[11] It appeared that at this stage most of Hitler's entourage believed that the bomb had been planted by one of the several hundred *Organisation Todt* workers who were labouring at the Wolf's Lair. But suspicion would soon fall on Stauffenberg when it was noticed that he was missing from the headquarters and he had been seen leaving by the switchboard operator without his briefcase.

Hitler, rather than being downhearted or depressed by his latest close call with death, was ecstatic. As Morell patched him up he kept repeating 'I am invulnerable, I am immortal!'[12] It was indeed some sort of miracle that Hitler survived such a powerful explosion only feet from him. Many would attribute Hitler's survival once again to having his own 'guardian devil'.

The RSD immediately sealed off the ruined conference hut and began a forensic investigation of the scene in order to gather evidence. The *Führerbunker* was also sealed off and very carefully searched for explosives. The entire Wolf's Lair complex was placed on high alert.

Over the coming days security was considerably tightened, meaning that Stauffenberg's failure would actually make it even harder to kill the *Führer*.

Stauffenberg's coup attempt began to unravel very quickly. While he was aboard the plane taking him to Tempelhof Airport in Berlin, a two-hour flight from Rastenburg, he was identified as the assassin. *General* Fellgiebel had severed all communications to and from *Führer* Headquarters, or at least thought that he had. Fellgiebel had sent off one short message to *Generalmajor* Fritz Thiele, Communications Officer at Army High Command in Berlin, stating that Hitler was still alive. No further details were given. Later, further messages came through that something had happened at the Wolf's Lair, but that Hitler had survived.[13] Hitler had summoned Himmler and Göring to the *Führerbunker* and he had placed Himmler in command of the Replacement Army. At the Bendlerblock, Replacement Army Head-quarters in Berlin, Olbricht concluded that to take action before having definitive news would be to court disaster, and his resulting inaction caused a lot of time to be lost.[14]

At the Bendlerblock *Generaloberst* Fromm had been growing increasingly concerned about what was happening at the Wolf's Lair. Fromm got through to Keitel at 4.00pm, thirty minutes before Stauffenberg landed at Tempelhof Airport. Keitel informed Fromm that there had been a bomb but that Hitler had suffered only minor injuries. Keitel also asked him about Stauffenberg's whereabouts.[15] Then Stauffenberg phoned from the airport insisting that Hitler was dead. When Stauffenberg and von Haeften had landed they had discovered that there was nobody to meet them, not even a car and driver. It was a bad sign. The Count was forced to make his own way to headquarters, where he found the mood to be cautious and hesitant.

Stauffenberg managed to pull the plotters together for a while, sending out a flurry of orders. He gave his colleagues an account of Hitler's death, admitting that he had planted the bomb. 'No one who was in that room can still be alive,'[16] he asserted. Olbricht demanded that Fromm sign the alert order for Operation Valkyrie, but Fromm, having spoken to Keitel, knew that a coup was being attempted and he refused. *Oberst* Ritter Mertz von Quirnheim, one of Stauffenberg's plotters, grew impatient at the delay and faked the alert order himself. When Fromm tried to have von Quirnheim arrested Stauffenberg instead placed Fromm under arrest and had him locked in his apartment in the building.[17]

Operation Valkyrie was activated with units of the Replacement Army surrounding or occupying all offices of the Nazi state and SS, including in the regions and foreign capitals under German occupation. In Paris, *General der Infanterie* Karl Heinrich von Stülpnagel and his subordinate officers firmly backed the coup. But the Supreme Commander in the West, *Generalfeldmarschall* Gunther von Kluge, vacillated. *Generaloberst* Ludwig Beck, who had arrived at the Bendlerblock, tried to persuade Kluge on the telephone to back the coup, but failed.

The plotters also failed to order the troops to seize the Nazi broadcast and communications network, or to arrest senior SS and Party leaders. Keitel and Jodl at the Wolf's Lair began to issue a stream of counter-orders along with *Reichsführer-SS* Himmler, all firmly scotching rumours of a coup against Hitler by the Party and the SS. Most began with the chilling sentence: 'The *Führer* is alive! In perfect health!'[18]

Regardless of Stauffenberg's assurances that Hitler was dead, the stream of messages to the contrary from the Wolf's Lair caused confusion and vacillation at the Bendlerblock. *Generalmajor* Stieff started informing on his fellow plotters, while Olbricht had clearly lost heart. By mid-evening the coup was faltering. When Kluge received word that Hitler was still alive he immediately overrode von Stülpnagel's orders in Paris to arrest all SS, SD and Gestapo officials, dismissed von Stülpnagel from his post and denounced him to Keitel at the Wolf's Lair.

Dr Goebbels' Propaganda Ministry was surrounded by Replacement Army troops who genuinely thought that the Nazi Party was attempting a coup against Hitler. Goebbels had first become aware that something was very wrong at between 2.00 and 3.00pm that afternoon when he had been awakened from his usual afternoon nap by a telephone call from Wilfried von Oven, head of the press office. Oven had just finished a call from an agitated Heinz Lorenz, deputy to Hitler's press secretary Dr Otto Dietrich, informing him of the events at the Wolf's Lair and issuing the text for a radio announcement from Hitler to the German people denouncing the coup. It was clear to Goebbels that the army was involved in some kind of uprising. Goebbels frantically telephoned around, trying to make sense of what was happening. Eventually he got through to Hitler who told him that the army was launching a putsch against him.[19]

Goebbels later called Hitler's Armaments Minister Albert Speer over to his office and told him that a full-scale putsch was underway. Speer immediately offered Goebbels his help. It was then that Goebbels and Speer noticed Replacement Army troops were moving to cordon off the Propaganda Ministry building. Goebbels was also concerned that he could not locate Himmler, and also slightly suspicious that perhaps Himmler might be a part of the coup.

Goebbels summoned the commander of the troops surrounding the ministry, *Major* Otto Remer, a 32-year-old committed Nazi. He had taken the precaution of placing a small box of cyanide capsules into his tunic pocket before the meeting in case the plotters arrested him. When Remer explained that he had been ordered by the City Commandant, *Generalleutnant* Paul von Hase, to cordon off the government district because Hitler was dead, Goebbels retorted: 'The *Führer* is alive! I spoke with him a few minutes ago.'[20] Remer began to realise that he and his men had been duped. Goebbels got Hitler on the phone and handed the receiver to Remer. 'Do you hear me? So I'm alive! The attempt has failed,' said Hitler in a chilling voice. 'A tiny clique of ambitious officers wanted to do away with me. But now we have the saboteurs of the front. We'll make short shrift of this plague. You are commanded by me the task of immediately restoring calm and security in the Reich capital, if necessary by force. You are under my personal command for this purpose until the *Reichsführer-SS* arrives in the Reich capital!'[21] Remer understood perfectly and went straight to work, moving his troops over to surround the Bendlerblock instead of the Propaganda Ministry after Goebbels had personally addressed the men in the Ministry garden. Nazi officials were released and order restored throughout Europe.[22]

At 6.30pm, Goebbels delivered a radio broadcast announcing that Hitler was alive and well. Between 8.00 and 9.00pm the army cordon around the government district was lifted. Later in the evening the coup was finished, with just a handful of the original plotters holed up in the Bendlerblock. Arguments began to break out among the plotters and those officers who had found themselves inside the building but were not connected with the plot. A group of staff officers led by *Oberstleutnant* Franz Herber who had not been party to the plot armed themselves and marched to Olbricht's room. As they were talking to Olbricht shots were fired in the corridor outside and during the resulting melee Stauffenberg was shot in the shoulder. Herber and his men pressed into Fromm's office where Stauffenberg and *Generaloberst*

Erich Hoepner, former commander of the Fourth Panzer Army on the Eastern Front until dismissed and retired by Hitler in 1942, had retreated. Herber demanded to speak to Fromm who had been placed under guard in his apartment after his refusal to enact Operation Valkyrie. A rebellious officer went and told Fromm what had happened. Liberated, Fromm had the arrested plotters brought before him. 'Well gentlemen, now I am going to do to you what you wanted to do to me this afternoon.'[23]

Fromm charged the plotters with high treason. Found guilty, they were sentenced to death. It was later discovered by the Gestapo that Fromm acted with such haste because he wanted to distance himself from the fact that he knew all about Stauffenberg's plot but had chosen to remain silent, waiting to see which way the chips fell. Now Fromm decided to eliminate the witnesses to this fact and ingratiate himself with Hitler. He had also been informed that Himmler was on his way to take command.

Ludwig Beck attempted to commit suicide with a pistol that Fromm permitted him to retain for this purpose. Beck only managed to graze his forehead with the first shot. Trying again, Beck shot himself in the head, but he did not die. Instead, he writhed in agony on the floor of the office until Fromm had an army sergeant unceremoniously drag the grievously wounded general by his legs into an adjoining room where the NCO finished him off himself. Around midnight Fromm gave the following order to a subordinate: 'Take a few men and execute the sentence downstairs in the yard at once.'[24] Stauffenberg, von Haeften, Olbricht and *Oberst* von Quirnheim, Fromm's former chief of staff, were taken out into the Bendlerblock's courtyard and summarily shot by firing squad in front of a large pile of building sand. Stauffenberg's last words before he was killed have gone down in history: 'Long live sacred Germany!'[25]

Resistance to Hitler was ruthlessly purged, with most of those involved in the July Plot exposed, arrested, tried and executed. *Generalfeldmarschall* Erwin von Witzleben, who was to have become head of state if the coup had succeeded, was slowly strangled at Plötenzee Prison with piano wire wound around a meat hook. Dr Carl Goerdeler and Erich Fellgiebel suffered the same fate, the hangings being filmed for Hitler to watch. Henning von Treskow decided upon suicide, going to the front in Russia and exploding a hand grenade beneath his chin. Eduard Wagner also committed suicide, shooting himself in the head three days after the plot failed, before the Gestapo arrested him. Among the many thousands who were arrested and murdered was Friedrich Fromm. His quick execution of Stauffenberg, Olbricht, Haeften and Quirnheim could not save him from arrest. The Gestapo failed to find enough proof linking him directly to the plot so he was instead charged with 'cowardice in the face of the enemy.' Fromm was shot on 12 March 1945.

Following the attack on Hitler, security at his headquarters was considerably strengthened. On the night of 20/21 July elements of the *Leibstandarte SS Adolf Hitler* (LSSAH) arrived at the Wolf's Lair and occupied all important areas, completely sealing off *Sperrkreis I*. LSSAH guards were also added to the FBB posts both inside and outside the complex, creating quite a bit of tension and argument between the SS and the *Wehrmacht* over jurisdictional issues. The LSSAH were finally withdrawn two weeks after Stauffenberg's attack. On 13 November 1944, *I* and *II SS-Panzer-Grenadier-Führer-Begleit-Kompanie LSSAH* were added to Hitler's escort detachment, marking a considerable increase in manpower and firepower.[26] One noticeable result of the July Bomb Plot was Hitler's increasing reliance upon the SS to guard him. The Army's good name had been considerably tarnished at *Führer* Headquarters by the incident and even the FBB was held in some suspicion – after all the FBB's founder and first commander, Erwin Rommel, was also revealed to have been part of the July Plot and was forced to commit suicide for the sake of his good name and that of his family.

At the Wolf's Lair, administrative changes were immediately made by splitting the Commandant HQ, which had operated under direct orders from Keitel, into two separate parts. The first was the *Lagerkommandant* (Camp Commandant) who would be responsible for the administration of the site. The second post was *Kampfkommandant* (Battle Commandant), a post that was initially held by the newly promoted *Oberst* Remer, a reward for his successful crushing of the coup in the government district of Berlin. It is believed that a few weeks after the July Plot the old system was quietly reintroduced and Remer was sent off to the front.[27]

New security procedures were also introduced for all those who were to be in the *Führer*'s presence. For the first time all briefcases were to be carefully checked and military officers were forbidden from wearing any weapons in Hitler's presence, a new rule that extended to ceremonial daggers and swords.

One day soon after the new regulations came into force the arrival of Foreign Minister von Ribbentrop's adjutant at Wolfsschanze created a major incident. *Hauptmann* Otting carried a briefcase that contained secret and sensitive Reich documents, and a rule stated that the holder of the briefcase had to also keep the means to hand to destroy those documents immediately if the need arose. In adherence to this regulation, when the RSD opened Otting's briefcase for examination they discovered a number of secret files and tucked in beside them was a hand grenade and a small flask of petrol.[28] Needless to say, the regulation was quietly ignored, but from then on such articles were never brought into the Wolf's Lair again.

The security staff at the Wolf's Lair expected more attacks in the wake of 20 July. *Hauptmann* Gaum, a company commander in the FBB, makes the hitherto unheard of claim that in Autumn 1944 'several Soviet sabotage bands were picked up ... One party which was captured had intended to drop by parachute on the site of the FHQ [*Führer* Headquarters] but had been scared off by the intense Flak, which the Russian pilot imagined came from what he thought was an airfield.' Gaum insisted that the wireless sets that the FBB captured from these sabotage bands were 'turned round and used to maintain communications with the Russian home stations.'[29]

Gaum and his colleagues were most concerned by an Allied assault on the Wolf's Lair by glider-borne troops. 'Tactical exercises always bore this in mind.' But, in Gaum's opinion, 'such an operation might have led to severe casualties among the guard troops at Rastenburg, but was not likely to have succeeded.'[30] He believed that the RSD and the *SS-Begleitkommando* would have easily spirited Hitler to safety while the FBB tackled the enemy troops.

Following Stauffenberg's bomb, visitors were now required to turn out the contents of their trouser and tunic pockets for inspection by the RSD, and, in a final humiliation, visitors were frisked. This new rule went down very badly with professional army officers but in the climate of fear that followed the bombing attempt no one was likely to publicly complain. The RSD even considered using an X-ray machine to examine briefcases and other packages more closely.

Although security around Hitler was considerably tightened, lapses still occurred. For example, at the end of July Hitler suddenly decided to visit those who had been injured in the conference hut bombing and who were being treated at Rastenburg Reserve Hospital in Karlshof, a treatment centre for wounded soldiers. *Hauptmann* Gaum actually encountered Hitler's motorcade on the road during the day of the visit and noted that Hitler was travelling, as was his usual custom, in the passenger seat of the first open-topped black Mercedes next to his driver, while several SS adjutants rode in the back. In a departure from usual practice, on both running boards and standing on the back of the car were *SS-Begleitkommando* armed with machine pistols. Two more black cars followed Hitler's; each filled with armed SS. Gaum estimated that the motorcade drove at 55 km/h.[31]

Hitler arrived at the hospital completely unannounced and was mobbed by convalescing soldiers the moment he stepped down from his Mercedes. Many of these crippled veterans had good reason to wish for harm to come to the man who had caused their injuries, but even at this late stage of the war most German soldiers remained loyal to their *Führer* and Hitler was only bothered for photographs. Hitler's valet, Heinz Linge, was horrified by the risks his boss took. 'Any of them could have killed him had they been so inclined. Although still suffering from wounds to his head and legs from the bomb he was so unmoved by it all that I became anxious for his safety and only relaxed when we finally drove off.'[32]

On 19 September Hitler was himself admitted to the same hospital for an X-ray. This time RSD and *SS-Begleitkommando* bodyguards descended upon the hospital an hour before Hitler arrived, carefully searched all of the rooms that the *Führer* would use, and posted guards at all of the entrances. The *Führer* arrived at the head of a three-car motorcade accompanied by his aides and adjutants.

According to one of *Hauptmann* Gaum's fellow officers, who was received by the *Führer* after the July Bomb Plot, Hitler did not look well. 'His face was pale and covered with loosely hanging flesh. Hitler himself complained that his doctors were a bad lot and that matter was still dripping internally from his ear [Hitler had suffered a burst eardrum in the bombing] on to his tongue.'[33] Gaum saw Hitler quite regularly as part of his duties and noticed Hitler's physical deterioration following the bombing. 'It was noticeable ... that one of the *Führer*'s hips was causing him pain.'[34]

One of Hitler's doctors noticed something strange at the Wolf's Lair when he was summoned to the *Führerbunker* on 1 October 1944 to examine the *Führer*. Hitler would complain of various medical problems caused by Stauffenberg's bomb and required regular examinations and visits by doctors. On this occasion the doctor noticed that there was an automatic pistol on the night table beside Hitler's bed.

When Heinz Linge, Hitler's valet, noticed the doctor staring at it he quickly put it out of sight inside a cupboard.[35] Perhaps Linge thought that the doctor was tempted to snatch up the weapon and finish what Stauffenberg had begun.

Following the bombing there was a fair amount of recrimination amongst the senior officers around Hitler. Von Kluge had been relieved of his command and replaced by Walther Model on 17 August. Recalled to Berlin for a meeting with Hitler, von Kluge rightly suspected that he would be arrested and punished over his links to the Stauffenberg plot in Paris so during the journey by car to Germany he had his driver pull over near Metz. Claiming that he was going to relieve himself, von Kluge took a cyanide pill. He was 61. Rommel, the Desert Fox and a national hero, required careful handling. Knowing that a public trial would damage Hitler's standing with his people, the *Führer* decided that the 52-year-old Rommel would be quietly disposed of. Burgdorf was one of the two generals sent to persuade Rommel to kill himself. The field marshal took cyanide after being assured that his family would not be persecuted. He was given a state funeral and a statement was issued to the public explaining that Rommel had succumbed to injuries sustained by a car crash after his staff vehicle had been strafed in Normandy.

When Hitler left the Wolf's Lair for the last time on 20 November 1944 for Berlin security was tight. A general ban on private correspondence and private telephone calls was instituted. FBB *Hauptmann* Gaum was of the opinion that censorship of mail and the monitoring of telephone calls was regularly carried out as part of the security clampdown following Stauffenberg's bombing. Gaum believed that this spying was done by the *Führer Nachrichten Abteilung* (*Führer* Intelligence Unit) under the command of *Hauptmann* Wolf.[36]

The best opportunity to kill Hitler had been missed with the failure of Stauffenberg's bomb. The resulting round ups, show trials and executions deeply alarmed the German officer corps and ensured their almost complete loyalty for the rest of the war. Hitler was on the move again, headed to the West where he would attempt to change the outcome of the war with one last desperate roll of the dice.

Chapter 10

Storm of the Century

*'Berlin stays German, Vienna will be German again, and Europe will
never be Russian.'*

Führer Proclamation, 15 April 1945

The thunder of Soviet guns could be heard along the line of the Rivers
Oder and Neisse. It was 16 April 1945 and the final act in the drama
of Hitler's Germany had begun. Soviet Marshals Georgi Zhukov and
Ivan Konev unleashed over 1.1 million men and thousands of tanks
against the depleted German 9th Army and 4th Panzer Army that
could muster barely 400,000 men.[1] The final barrier to Berlin was the
Seelow Heights, a line of steep hills behind the Oder. If the Red Army
managed to smash its way through the defence lines that had been
hastily constructed over the preceding panicked weeks, then there was
virtually nothing to stop them from reaching the Berlin suburbs. Stalin
had set his sights on the Reich capital and was determined to capture it
before the British or Americans. He had also set his sights on capturing
Adolf Hitler, who was now deep underground inside his last field
headquarters of the war – the *Führerbunker*.

Hitler had arrived in Berlin on 20 November 1944 from East Prussia.
He would not go east again – in fact the Eastern Front was fast
approaching his devastated capital. Hitler's departure from the Wolf's
Lair was not taken as final at the time. *Generalfeldmarschall* Wilhelm
Keitel issued orders that 'in view of the present situation on the
Eastern Front'[2] all preparations be made so that the Wolf's Lair would
not fall into Soviet hands intact. A detonation calendar for all the
bunkers and huts was drawn up. Within twenty-four hours of the
order, the Wolf's Lair complex would be destroyed. The password was
'Inselsprung'. On 4 December Keitel issued an order to keep the Wolf's
Lair and the *Mauerwald* army headquarters intact and ready for instant
use, until further notice. In January 1945, as the Soviets swept into East
Prussia, the code word was sent and engineers began to blow up the
Wolf's Lair. When the Red Army arrived they found that all of the

significant parts of the structure, including the *Führerbunker*, had been wrecked.

Berlin was a considerably more dangerous billet for Hitler than his quiet forest HQ. He entered the reality of war. Bombed day and night by the USAAF and RAF, the city had suffered extensive damage. Although power and utilities were still functioning, Berliners were forced to take shelter constantly as the Allies rained down high explosives and incendiaries. All across Germany, aerial bombing was systematically levelling city after city as well as devastating road and rail links.

On 11 December Hitler and his entourage transferred by train and car to his western field headquarters, the *Adlerhorst* (Eagle's Eyrie), near Ziegenburg, so he could direct the forthcoming Battle of the Bulge (see Chapter 4). Although managing to take the Allies by surprise and make some gains, by 25 January 1945 the German offensive had run out of steam and the Germans were forced onto the defensive with heavy losses in men and materiel.

Acknowledging the inevitable failure of the last German offensive in the West, a dispirited Hitler returned to Berlin on 16 January aboard his private train, the *Führersonderzug*. As the long train wound its way through the devastated capital Hitler reportedly looked out at the ruins from his Pullman carriage, both surprised and depressed by the grim sights that greeted him.[3] He needed no more than to look out the window to see the reality of his military failure. Arriving at Grunewald Station at 9.40am, Hitler climbed down from the *Führersonderzug* for the last time and was driven in a convoy of armoured Mercedes to the Reich Chancellery, passing through bomb-damaged streets whose gutted and roofless apartment buildings and shops bore silent witness to the final collapse of the Third Reich.

Arriving at the New Reich Chancellery at 10.00am, an hour later he received *Generaloberst* Heinz Guderian who delivered a gloomy situation report concerning the predicted Soviet offensive. At midday he presented *SS-Gruppenführer* Kruger with a decoration, had a forty-minute lunch and then presented *Generaloberst* Ferdinand Schörner, Commander of Army Group North, with the Diamonds to his Knight's Cross. In the afternoon Hitler watched the weekly newsreel.[4]

A huge Soviet winter offensive began just two days later. By the end of the month the Soviets were only 100km from Berlin. Hitler continued to live in his apartments in the Old Reich Chancellery until mid-February before moving into the *Führerbunker* to sleep. Until mid-

March 1945 Hitler also continued to take his meals in the New Reich Chancellery and to hold his military situation conferences there inside his enormous study. The grand hallway outside was still intact, though the artworks and priceless tapestries had been removed to protect them from the bombing. Although Hitler continued to come up from the *Führerbunker* into both Chancelleries to work in his study, and used some of the building's other rooms, he did not see the vast amount of damage that had been caused to both buildings by British and American aerial bombing. Staff officers visiting the Reich Chancellery for meetings had to take long and circuitous routes to reach Hitler's study, as corridors had been reduced to rubble by direct hits.[5] Soon the Reich Chancellery would start to come under artillery and rocket fire from the advancing Red Army.

The Western Allies thought that Hitler was still at the *Adlerhorst*, his headquarters beneath Kransberg Castle, and they determined to try and kill him. Although Hitler had already been gone for two months, a squadron of P-51 Mustangs launched a precision attack on Kransberg Castle and its environs on 19 March, dropping high explosive and incendiary bombs that killed ten civilians and did huge damage to both the Castle and surrounding buildings. The *Adlerhorst* was still functioning as a headquarters at the time of the raid. On 11 March, one week before the raid, the newly appointed Commander-in-Chief West, *Generalfeldmarschall* Albert Kesselring, had moved into the Castle with his large staff. He immediately ordered that all sensitive documentation and cipher machines be removed from the Castle, after which he moved with his staff into *Haus III*, the purpose-built OKW command bunker at the *Adlerhorst*. Kesselring and his staff escaped harm during the 45-minute American air raid.

By 28 March, with US forces only 19km from the *Adlerhorst*, Kesselring ordered the evacuation, by means of all the remaining motor transport, of civilian employees and the families of soldiers who were serving at the headquarters. He then ordered that the *Adlerhorst* complex should be blown up. This was only partially successful. When the US Army arrived they discovered that the *Führerbunker* and several other structures had been reduced to burned-out shells, but two buildings were captured intact. The first was *Haus V* or 'Pressehaus', used by Goebbels' Propaganda Ministry. The second was the largest building on the site, *Haus VII*, the 'Wachhaus' with its long concrete tunnel that connected directly with the Castle.

In Berlin, guarding the Reich Chancellery complex proved to be increasingly challenging as bomb damage had destroyed perimeter walls and fences. It was impossible to guard everywhere, and military stragglers and civilians often entered the complex, especially as the chaos grew worse with the approach of the Red Army. But military officers attending conferences in Hitler's office were still forced to pass through stringent security checkpoints from where their cars deposited them.

SS-Begleitkommando and RSD checked the names of visiting generals and their adjutants against log book entries. *SS-Begleitkommando* guards were posted in all of the ground floor corridors and passageways that led to Hitler's office, and all visitors were constantly stopped and their identity documents perused by these sentries, irrespective of rank. Approaching Hitler's office down the long gallery visitors would have been checked again outside the anteroom. All visitors were then required to hand over their side arms to the SS guards, who logged them. Their briefcases were then carefully searched for bombs or other weapons. But the visitors were not physically frisked as had been done at the Wolf's Lair, which, with hindsight, was a glaring security omission as a potential assassin could have concealed a small gun, knife or explosive charge on his person, as several young officers had in fact done during previous assassination attempts.[6]

Once suitably searched and cleared, visitors then entered the heavily guarded anteroom to Hitler's study where SS orderlies would serve them with refreshments while they waited. Hitler's orderly *SS-Sturmbannführer* Otto Günsche would appear and invite the senior officers' adjutants to come in to the *Führer*'s study and set out maps and reports on Hitler's large marble-topped table ready for the conference. The adjutants would then go back into the anteroom to wait with their superiors, the rule that these younger officers were not permitted in the *Führer*'s conferences still firmly in force.

Generalleutnant Wilhelm Burgdorf, Hitler's 50-year-old Chief of the Army Personnel Department since the demise of *General der Infanterie* Rudolf Schmundt from injuries sustained in the Wolf's Lair bombing, would then appear and invite the conference attendees into Hitler's study where the *Führer* would shortly appear. Burgdorf, one of Hitler's more unquestioning military officers, had played a central role in convincing Erwin Rommel to kill himself rather than face a treason trial for his part in the July Bomb Plot. He was seen as ultra-loyal by the Nazis but held in contempt by many in the army.

On their departure from the Reich Chancellery the generals and their staffs would go through the same series of security checkpoints, and have their documents repeatedly checked by sentries, until they left the premises.

Because of the constant bombing raids and air raid alerts Hitler decided to move his headquarters underground into the *Führerbunker* beneath the Old Reich Chancellery gardens in mid-March 1945. Although now safe from aerial attack, the *Führerbunker* was completely inadequate for use as a military headquarters as it was too small to accommodate sufficient staff or visiting generals attending conferences. It came to be described by many who visited it during the last weeks of the war as a fetid hole in the ground or a 'concrete coffin'.

Hot and stuffy, and furnished with only the bare essentials, the *Führerbunker* was a far cry from the vast complex at the Wolf's Lair, or Hitler's main Western Front HQ at the *Adlerhorst*. The reason was that the bunker was never designed to be anything other than an air raid shelter for use by Hitler and his inner circle, a temporary refuge from the real business of government conducted in the Reich Chancellery above.

Most in Hitler's inner circle expected the *Führer* to flee Berlin before the Soviets managed to encircle the ruined city. As the Red Army closed in on Berlin, Hitler's personal pilot Hans Baur, promoted by Hitler on 30 January 1945 to *SS-Gruppenführer*, frantically tried to preserve the F.d.F aircraft for the expected escape south to Berchtesgaden. Standing by in Pöcking, near Passau in Lower Bavaria, was a brand new aircraft for Hitler's exclusive use that would be the perfect getaway vehicle from the ruins of the Thousand Year Reich.

On 26 November 1943 Hitler had attended a demonstration of new *Luftwaffe* aircraft types at Insterburg in East Prussia. One aircraft in particular had caught his eye. The giant Junkers Ju 290 was a long-range transport, maritime patrol aircraft and heavy bomber first introduced into *Luftwaffe* service in August 1942 to replace the slower and smaller *Condor*. With a crew of nine, the Ju 290 was 28.64m long with a wingspan of 42m. Capable of a maximum speed of 440km/h it had a range of 6,150km and a maximum service ceiling of 6,000m. Hitler asked Göring for one to be assigned to the F.d.F. for his personal use. The Ju 290 had made several successful trips to Japan via the Arctic Ocean and Manchuria and proved to be an excellent maritime patrol aircraft and transport, seeing service at Stalingrad and in Tunisia.

The aircraft destined for Hitler's squadron was a former maritime reconnaissance aircraft that had been extensively refitted. A Ju 290A-7, it was given the code KR + LW. Hitler's passenger cabin was protected by 12mm of armour plating and 50mm thick bulletproof glass. As on his main *Condor*, a special parachute seat and escape hatch was fitted.

The plane was ready for Hitler's use from February 1945, just as the situation around Berlin was turning very bad. Baur was able to visit Pöcking and test-flew the new plane once. If Hitler, Eva Braun and the inner circle were going to escape death or capture in Berlin, the Ju 290 was going to be their salvation. It had the range to carry them to a neutral country like Spain and Baur prepared for what he thought would be an inevitable final rescue mission. Even if Hitler did not leave Germany at this point, most felt certain that he would nonetheless flee Berlin for Berchtesgaden and continue to direct the war from his mountaintop hideout in Bavaria. But Hitler had no intention of leaving the capital and instead continued to use both the partially wrecked Reich Chancellery and the *Führerbunker* to direct the resistance to Stalin's encroaching Soviet juggernaut. Baur was left frustrated and increasingly concerned for the safety of the remaining aircraft that made up the F.d.F.

The *Führerbunker* had its genesis in air raid shelters built under and adjoined to buildings on Wilhelmstrasse and Vossstrasse in 1935. When the New Reich Chancellery complex was completed in January 1939 it included more air raid shelters. One was the *Vorbunker*, or Upper Bunker. Architect Leonhard Gall submitted plans in 1935 for a large reception hall-cum-ballroom to be added to the Old Reich Chancellery. Completed in 1936, the *Vorbunker* had a roof that was 1.6m thick, the bunker's thick walls partially supporting the weight of the large reception hall overhead.[7]

There were two entrances into the *Vorbunker*; one from the Foreign Ministry garden and the other from the New Reich Chancellery. Both led to a reinforced steel gas-proof door leading to a set of small rooms. On the left was the Water Supplies/Boiler Room, to the right the Airfilters Room. Moving forward there was a middle Dining Area with a Kitchen to the left, which was where Hitler's cook/dietician Frau Constanze Manziarly prepared the *Führer*'s meals. There was also a well-stocked Wine Store. To the right of the Dining Area was the Personnel/Guard Quarters. Moving forward again, there was a Conference Room in the middle and on the left two rooms that originally housed Hitler's physician Dr Theodor Morell and, following his departure in April 1945, Dr Goebbels' wife Magda and her six young children. To the right of the Conference Room was a room used for guest quarters, two storerooms and then a stairway set at right angles connecting to the *Führerbunker* that was 2.5m lower than the *Vorbunker* and west-southwest of it. Steel doors could close off the *Vorbunker* and *Führerbunker* from one another and the SS closely guarded all entrances and exits.

Hitler's *Führerbunker*, or Lower Bunker, was built in 1942–43, 8.5m beneath the Old Reich Chancellery Garden 120m north of the New Chancellery at a cost of 1.4 million *Reichsmarks*. It was deep enough to withstand the largest bombs that were being dropped by the British and Americans over the city.

Designed by the architectural firm Hochtief under Albert Speer's supervision, the *Führerbunker* was one of about twenty bunkers and air raid shelters used by Hitler's inner circle, bodyguards and military commanders in the region of the Reich Chancellery. Many cellars in the surrounding buildings were also utilised as auxiliary bunkers during the Battle of Berlin.

The *Führerbunker* suffered from noise caused by the steady running of aeration ventilators twenty-four hours a day and also had a problem with cool moisture on the walls, as Berlin has a high ground water level.

Entry into the *Führerbunker* was via the *Vorbunker*, passing down the dogleg staircase, which led to a guarded door giving access to a long Hall/Lounge, where RSD and *SS-Begleitkommando* sentries checked identity papers before permitting entry to the *Führerbunker* proper. This was through double steel gas-proof doors set into the bunker's 2.2m thick protective wall. The *Führerbunker* was divided along a central corridor that gave access to an emergency exit staircase at the far end that led up to the surface in the Reich Chancellery Garden. This corridor was divided into two long rooms. The first of these on entering the *Führerbunker* was the Corridor/Lounge. A door on the left led to the Toilets and Electricity Switch Room. From the Toilets a connecting door led to the Bathroom/Dressing Room with Eva Braun's Bedroom on the right of the Bathroom. A door connected the Bathroom with Hitler's Sitting Room. To the right of this room was Hitler's Study, dominated by a large painting of King Frederick the Great that Hitler would spend much time staring at as the Soviets fought their way into Berlin's suburbs, hoping that he could emulate Frederick and turn back the Bolshevik horde with some final grand military gesture. A door connected Hitler's Sitting Room with Hitler's Bedroom. A door on the right of Hitler's Study led back into the central corridor, this section called the Conference Room. The last three rooms on the left of the *Führerbunker* were not connected to Hitler's suite and consisted of the Map Room where Hitler held most of his military situation conferences during the last weeks of the war, the Cloakroom and a Ventilation Room.

The left side of the *Führerbunker* consisted, moving from the staircase connecting it with the *Vorbunker* to the emergency exit to the Reich Chancellery Gardens, of a series of rooms. First was the Generator/ Ventilation Plant Room. This was connected to the Telephone Switchboard Room where *SS-Oberscharführer* Rochus Misch of the *SS-Begleitkommando* worked, Martin Bormann's Office and the Guard Room. Hitler's loyal valet *SS-Obersturmbannführer* Heinz Linge lived here. Next were two rooms: Goebbels' Office and the Doctor's Room. The last two rooms on the right of the central Conference Room were Goebbels' Bedroom and the Doctor's Quarters. Parts of the two bunkers were carpeted and one section of this material was recently discovered in a British regimental archive. It reveals that the carpet had a pattern of yellow flowers and blue leaves on a fawn background.[8] The rooms were furnished with expensive pieces taken from the Reich Chancellery above and there were several framed oil paintings on the walls. But the interior, in keeping with Hitler's other field headquarters, could not be described as anything other than Spartan and functional.[9]

By mid-April the end was fast approaching on all fronts for Hitler's Germany. On 11 April US forces had crossed the River Elbe placing them only 100km west of Berlin. British and Canadian forces had crossed the Rhine and were pushing into the Ruhr, the industrial heartland of Germany. On 18 April Army Group B, the last major German formation west of Berlin, was surrounded and surrendered with the loss of 325,000 men. In Italy, the Allies' Spring Offensive had seen their forces cross the River Po and push German forces into the foothills of the Alps. But the greatest threat came from the east where Stalin was poised to unleash hell.

On 16 April the Red Army commenced the operation to capture Berlin, assaulting the Seelow Heights, the last significant German defence line east of the city.[10] The fighting was fierce, the Soviets suffering heavy casualties, but by the 19th they had broken through and there was now no longer a proper defence position left to protect the city.[11]

On 20 April, Hitler's 56th birthday, Soviet artillery came in range of the Berlin suburbs and opened fire.[12] By the next evening T-34 tanks had arrived on the outskirts. As the Red Army began to close a ring around Berlin and started to fight through the city suburbs in several directions aiming for the nearby Reichstag building, efforts were taken to increase the protection afforded to the Reich Chancellery and the *Führerbunker*. On 22 April 1945 *Kampfgruppe Mohnke* (Battle Group Mohnke) was formed out of all available elite guard units from across Berlin and sent to defend the government quarter, Sector Z (Citadel), from the Soviets.[13] Its commander, 34-year-old *SS-Brigadeführer* Wilhelm Mohnke had been one of the founding members of the *SS-Stabswache* (Staff Guard) in Berlin in 1934. A highly decorated *Waffen-SS* field commander, by 1945 Mohnke commanded the *Leibstandarte SS Adolf Hitler Division* (LSSAH). He had been wounded in Hungary and whilst recovering in Berlin was appointed by Hitler to command the defence of Sector Z.[14]

Kampfgruppe Mohnke consisted of several units. *SS-Wachbataillon I*, the section of the LSSAH that was retained in Berlin on ceremonial guard and security duties when the rest of the LSSAH was sent to the Western Front, numbered about 800 men. On 15 April, one regiment of two battalions had been formed out of the remaining *Wachbataillon* troops, reinforced by other SS and *Wehrmacht* stragglers. It was placed under the command of *SS-Standartenführer* Anhalt until he was killed-in-action on 24 April. *SS-Sturmbannführer* Herbert Kaschula then assumed command. *SS-Hauptsturmführer* Mrugalla commanded its I Battalion while *SS-Hauptsturmführer* Fritz Schäfer led the II Battalion.

Another unit, *SS-Panzer-Grenadier-Ausbildungs-und Ersatz Bataillon I* under 32-year-old *SS-Sturmbannführer* Arthur Klingermeyer, was brought in from Spreenhagen. In January 1945 this unit consisted of twelve companies. On 15 April two battalions under Klingermeyer had been transferred to Berlin. Both battalions were later merged together and given some reservist reinforcements. There was the *LSSAH Flak Kompanie* and the 800-man *SS-Begleitkommando* under *SS-Sturmbannführer* Franz Schädle and the usual RSD close-protection detachment.

Finally, there were 600 men from the *Begleit-Bataillon Reichsführer-SS*. This special unit had been formed in May 1941 as Himmler's personal escort and most had remained in Berlin after Himmler left the capital. They were part of the larger *16th SS Panzergrenadier Division Reichsführer-SS* then currently fighting in Austria.

Further troops within the Citadel sector included the remains of the *33rd Waffen Grenadier Division der SS Charlemagne*, consisting of approximately sixty French SS under the command of *SS-Brigadeführer* Gustav Krukenberg, who would fall back on the sector and take command of the remnants of the *11th SS Volunteer Panzer Grenadier Division Nordland* on 27 April.[15] There were also stragglers and small units from various *Wehrmacht*, SS, *Volkssturm* (Home Guard), Hitler Youth and *Kriegsmarine* units that were also pushed or fell back into Defence Sector Z.

By 22 April the Germans defending Berlin were outnumbered virtually 10-1. German units had been severely degraded and worn down by almost continuous fighting since the start of the Soviet spring offensive. Some 100,000 *Volkssturm*, mostly consisting of older men above military age, plus some Hitler Youth and foreign SS volunteers, were backing up the regular troops in the hopeless defence. With virtually no tanks, limited artillery and no viable *Luftwaffe* over the capital, the defence of Berlin would not last for long.

Hitler grasped at anything that he thought might turn the tide. When he observed the vulnerability of one of the Soviet flanks he gave orders for *SS-Obergruppenführer* Felix Steiner's Army Detachment to counterattack, refusing to accept that Steiner's forces were severely depleted and simply not up to the task. When Hitler discovered at the afternoon situation conference on 22 April that Steiner had failed to attack he suffered a complete mental collapse,[16] and once he stopped screaming declared to his shocked audience that the war was lost.[17] Later that day Hitler consulted *SS-Obersturmbannführer* Prof. Dr Werner Haase on the best method to kill oneself. Haase suggested that he bite down on a cyanide capsule whilst simultaneously shooting himself in the head.

Hitler's pilot, *SS-Gruppenführer* Baur, spent most of his days organising last-minute flights out of the doomed city for certain VIPs aboard the handful of serviceable transport aircraft.

This movement of key personnel was codenamed Operation 'Seraglio'. *Konteadmiral* Hans von Puttkammer, Hitler's naval aide, was ordered to destroy all of Hitler's personal papers at the Berghof.

Hitler's personal *Condor*, CE + IB, carried the Puttkamer party south from Berlin's Gatow Airport to Neubiberg near Munich.[18] Among the passengers was Hitler's personal doctor, Theodor Morell, who carried an army footlocker containing all of Hitler's medical records.[19]

On 21 April *Grossadmiral* Karl Dönitz's personal *Condor*, GC + SJ, was pressed into service on a secret mission. The aircraft had just returned from a hazardous sortie to evacuate Spanish diplomats and some important German passengers from Berlin to Munich. Hitler had decided to send more non-essential staff out of Berlin to Berchtesgaden. GC + SJ touched down at Tempelhof, which was by then under fire, and met three black cars. Leading the group was *NSKK-Gruppenführer* Albert Bormann, brother of Hitler's much-feared secretary Martin Bormann. Accompanying him were his family, servants and twenty-five former occupants of the Berlin *Führerbunker*.

The plane was soon airborne and the pilot ducked into thick cloud cover to avoid Soviet fighters and flak. Near Dresden the *Condor* again came under Soviet anti-aircraft fire. Shell fragments struck the cockpit, shattering some of the instrument displays. One engine was knocked out but they made it intact to Neubiberg Airfield near Munich.

Albert Speer's *Condor*, TA + MR, had been destroyed in a bombing raid and on 21 April his personal pilot, *Major* Erich Adam, had flown Heinkel He 111 transport TQ + MU to Neubiberg. As the flak-damaged *Condor* GC + SJ carrying Albert Bormann and party came in to land at Neubiberg's blacked out airfield the pilot, *Hauptmann* Husslein, suddenly saw *Major* Adam's Heinkel 111 sitting on the runway directly ahead. The *Condor*'s brakes were engaged so hard that all four landing gear tires blew out, but a terrible ground collision was narrowly avoided.[20]

Throughout the war the British and Americans never seriously targeted Hitler's numerous military headquarters for destruction; that was, somewhat ironically, until the final days of the war. The reason was not that they did not know where these complexes were located – on the contrary, the British, Americans and the Soviets had detailed information about the Obersalzberg, the Reich Chancellery in Berlin and the Wolf's Lair in East Prussia. The reason was that such a strike was viewed to be counter-productive to the Allied cause. The same reason was given for cancelling Operation Foxley, the British plan to use a sniper to shoot Hitler during one of his daily walks at the Obersalzberg. The reasoning was that if the Allies had bombed Hitler out of his home, they would simply have bound him further to the German people, who were suffering greatly under the Allied aerial onslaught. If Hitler was killed in an air raid the Allies feared that they would have made him a martyr. The same outcome would have been likely from shooting him using a concealed sniper. 'Hitler and his like can only be irrevocably discredited if he is at the helm when the final collapse comes,'[21] read one American report on the subject. There was also the compelling argument put forward by many Allied assessments that Hitler's bungling attempts at grand strategy were actually aiding the Allied cause and shortening the war. If Hitler was removed, the German General Staff may have run the war considerably more competently and managed to hold off the Allies long enough for a negotiated peace when Churchill, Roosevelt and Stalin were determined upon nothing short of unconditional surrender.

The Allies finally decided to attack the Obersalzberg, though the purpose of the raid remains unclear. Hitler was in Berlin – and this information was known through Ultra signals decrypts – but there was a genuine fear among the Allies that he might yet fly south to the Berghof and direct the war from there. This is indeed what many of his inner circle and generals continued to urge him to do when it became clear that the Battle of Berlin was a lost cause.

The reason for the bombing may have had a lot to do with a clever German deception plan that managed to fool the Allies into believing in something called the *Alpin Festung* (Alpine Redoubt). It was believed that remaining fanatical SS units would retreat into the mountains on the Bavarian/Austrian border where they could have blocked any Allied advance for months or even years, dominating the high mountain passes into the region and churning out weapons from secret underground factories. Central to the Alpine Redoubt plan was Hitler's house and its surrounding complex. Hitler had already used the Obersalzberg as a military headquarters and the entire site was littered with bunkers, air raid shelters and formidable anti-aircraft defences. Perhaps by targeting the Obersalzberg the Allies intended to destroy Hitler's command facility, effectively forcing the *Führer* into inferior or ad hoc headquarters.

Whatever the true reason, and some historians have suspected that the motive for the attack was more symbolic than tactical, the assault necessitated a huge diversion of resources. On 25 April 1945, just twelve days before the German surrender, sixteen RAF Mosquito pathfinder planes guided in 359 Lancaster bombers. By way of comparison, this is the same number of planes that the RAF had used ten days previously to devastate the large German city of Kiel. They were now targeting what was effectively a small alpine village in a high mountain valley.

As the British aircraft approached the Obersalzberg the remaining anti-aircraft batteries opened fire. Two Lancasters were shot down, with four crewmen perishing and the rest taken prisoner. But hundreds of tons of bombs rained down over the Obersalzberg area, causing extensive damage to the site. German casualties were kept to a minimum because of the large number of air raid shelters and bunkers. Göring and Bormann's villas were both hit and wrecked, as well as the SS Barracks, the Platterhof Hotel and the Gästhaus zum Türken (RSD headquarters). Huge impact craters turned the Obersalzberg into a moonscape, with blasted and burned trees and smashed wooden buildings.

Hitler's house took two British bomb hits. One bomb made a direct hit on the central part of the north side of the west wing, collapsing the roof. Another bomb landed on the east side of the building, causing some blast damage.[22] If Hitler had been in residence he would have taken shelter beneath his house in his personal bunker and survived the bombing, so the attack would not have succeeded in its aims. Only six Germans perished in the air raid, all of them civilians.

By the last week of April 1945, Hitler's world had shrunk to a few grey concrete rooms deep beneath the Reich Chancellery Garden in Berlin. Up above, Soviet artillery shells and rockets blasted the once immaculate Chancellery buildings into ruins. Huge sections of roof and walls had collapsed, while the remaining structures were shell- and shrapnel-scarred, fire-scorched, or windowless. The Reich Chancellery Garden, its trees blasted and stripped of their foliage and the lawn churned up by shell craters, was only passable between bombardments and Hitler's RSD and *SS-Begleitkommando* guards were largely withdrawn from exposed sentry posts on the Chancellery roof and outside the bunker entrances. Each time another Soviet barrage went up the guards fled inside the bunker entrances, slamming the thick steel doors closed behind them. Hitler forbade smoking in the *Führerbunker*, so smokers had to go up to the *Vorbunker* to enjoy a cigarette. With their nerves on edge, many of the bunker inhabitants were smoking and drinking heavily. Some hardier souls would emerge into the shattered gardens to smoke or catch a few minutes of fresh air before Soviet shelling forced them once more into the dank subterranean bunkers, while Hitler's dog Blondi was still walked in the garden by his handler.

Senior officers and their staff continued to brave the maelstrom outside to get to the bunker for Hitler's increasingly stressful and pointless military conferences. Hitler was becoming more and more unreasonable, refusing to believe that the units he ordered around on his maps were in reality only shadows of their former selves, completely worn out by constant combat and lack of replacements and equipment. He would not listen to reason and still appeared to believe that he could somehow save the situation.

Hitler had by now decided to stay in Berlin and die in the *Führerbunker*, so the *Führer*'s personal squadron and its aircraft had essentially become surplus to requirements. The huge Junkers Ju 290 that was to have replaced the *Condor* as Hitler's personal transport was never used by the *Führer*. On 24 March 1945 Hans Baur had flown the Ju 290 to Munich-Riem Airport. It was parked inside a large hanger while Baur visited his home nearby. He was informed that American bombers had destroyed the hanger and the plane, killing several of his men. Baur was flown back to Berlin in a smaller aircraft – an extremely dangerous flight as Soviet fighters had gained air superiority over the capital.

More F.d.F aircraft were destroyed during the final weeks of the war. Baur had stashed some aircraft and crews at the airfield at Schoenwalde outside Berlin. In late March Baur visited the base during a large scale American air raid on the capital. Two P-51 Mustang fighters, escorting the attacking B-17s, broke off and engaged ground targets at Schoenwalde. As the silver Mustangs screamed down onto the airfield for a strafing run Baur and his crews took cover in a bunker while *Luftwaffe* anti-aircraft guns opened up. American cannon shells set fire to a *Condor* and a Junkers 52, both aircraft blowing up in massive fireballs. Berlin was now virtually untenable, so Baur transferred the remaining F.d.F aircraft and spare engines to Pöcking in Bavaria and to Bad Reichenhall Airfield, also in southern Germany.

At this time, Baur turned over operational control of the F.d.F to a highly decorated Luftwaffe officer, 28-year-old *Oberstleutnant* Werner Baumbach. A holder of the Knight's Cross with Oakleaves and Swords,

Baumbach had previously commanded the Luftwaffe's special operations squadron, the top secret *Kampfgeschwader 200*. Baur, it seems, had decided to stay with his *Führer* inside the bunker.

As Hitler continued to try and salvage the battle raging in the capital, and with Soviet forces smashing their way into eastern Berlin, *Grossadmiral* Karl Dönitz had been ordered to take command of what was left of the Reich in northern Europe, establishing a rump state and *ad hoc* government at Flensburg on the Danish border. This was where the F.d.F still had a job to perform. Baumbach ordered several F.d.F aircraft north to Flensburg to assist with the new government.

Once Hitler announced that he would definitely not fly south to Bavaria, but instead remain in Berlin and commit suicide when the government quarter was about to fall, the remaining F.d.F aircraft were no longer held on standby and instead could be sent away. Condor TK+CV, flown by Hitler's co-pilot, *Oberleutnant* Hans Münsterer, left Gatow with twelve passengers and delivered them to Wittstock in northern Germany, then flew back into Berlin, landing safely at Schoenwalde Airfield.

As Soviet ground forces threatened Schoenwalde, most of the remaining F.d.F. aircraft there flew out in one group. It consisted of three aircraft: a Siebel Fh 104, Junkers Ju 52/3m SF+IF and Junkers Ju 352 KT+VJ. They powered away from the burning capital, managing successfully to dodge Soviet fighters. Hitler's *Condor*, TK+CV, was flown to Staaken, outside Berlin. All aircraft moved again when Staaken, and also Tempelhof Airport, came under Soviet ground attack. The planes were now placed at the disposal of the OKW.

Hitler's support aircraft, *Condor* CE+IC, piloted by *Hauptmann* Joachim Hübner, was shot down by Soviet flak as it attempted to bring a party of *Kriegsmarine* sailors into Gatow who had been sent by Dönitz to try and bolster Berlin's defences. The *Condor* crash-landed in a forest killing eight of those aboard. But by now most people were trying to get out of Berlin rather than enter the maelstrom of a lost battle.

Like rats on a sinking ship, so the people around the *Führer* had a choice – go down with Hitler or escape. Many were starting to look to escaping, but in spite of the chaos and the ultimate futility of resistance, Hitler's bodyguard units continued with a dogged defence of the increasingly threatened government quarter. In doing so, they bought precious time for the final act to be played out.

Chapter 11

The Eagles Have Flown

*'Adolf Hitler looked composed. Even I, who'd known him for 13 years,
could not tell that he'd already decided to end his life. Dressed in his
usual field-grey tunic with black trousers, he held a map of Berlin in his
right hand. His left trembled. It was April 29, 1945 and Soviet troops
were closing in on the city centre and the Führer-bunker.'*

SS-*Obersturmbannführer* Erich Kempka

Hitler, standing in the elegant Old Reich Chancellery on 30 January 1933, the day he was appointed Chancellor, had declared to his guests: 'No power on earth will get me out of here alive!'[1] Twelve years later and Hitler and his intimates could hear the dull thump of heavy artillery shells impacting on the garden above them from their position deep inside the *Führerbunker* below the Reich Chancellery garden. It was a sobering reminder of how close the Soviets were getting. The occasional whiff of cordite or the dust from pummelled masonry drifted into the bunker from any open door or air vent. Hitler's 1933 declaration now appeared on the verge of becoming a self-fulfilling prophecy.

By 27 April 1945 Berlin was completely surrounded. The bunker had lost secure radio communications with the main German units fighting desperately in the ruins and had to rely on the telephone network for news. To all intents and purposes the last *Führer* Headquarters was blind and incapable of really commanding anything. Soviet troops were on the Alexanderplatz and would soon reach the Potsdamer Platz, where the bunker was located. Efforts were still being made to affect a linkup between the remnants of the 9th Army defending the city and General Wenck's 12th Army that was attempting to fight its way into Potsdam. As this last desperate attempt was being made *SS-Brigadeführer* Mohnke reported that enemy tanks had penetrated the nearby Wilhelmsplatz – they had been repulsed this time, but time was running out.[2]

The following day news of Heinrich Himmler's entreaties to the Western Allies reached the bunker.[3] Hitler was incensed and ordered

Himmler's arrest for treason. He demanded to see *SS-Gruppenführer* Hermann Fegelein, Himmler's representative in the bunker, but he was nowhere to be found. An RSD snatch squad was dispatched that discovered Fegelein in his apartment with his mistress, drunk and with a suitcase of civilian clothes packed. He was escorted back to the bunker, summarily sentenced to death by a court martial and shot in the Reich Chancellery garden. By now, the Red Army was at the Potsdammer Platz and was evidently preparing to storm the Reich Chancellery.

Topside, the remaining men of *Kampfgruppe Mohnke* fought the Soviets around the Chancellery site from prepared positions and a multitude of other bunkers and cellars, as well as utilizing the remaining portions of the underground railway system that were still in German hands. The French SS of the *Charlemagne Division* in particular distinguished themselves as tank destroyers, knocking out dozens of Soviet T-34s with handheld *Panzerfaust* rocket launchers. Ironically, it was two Frenchmen who were the last soldiers to be decorated with Nazi Germany's highest bravery award, the Knight's Cross. Ammunition supplies were dwindling rapidly alongside the mounting casualties. The main Reich Chancellery bunker had been transformed into an emergency casualty clearing station and refuge.

In late April 1945 Hitler's oldest ally Benito Mussolini had been captured and executed by Italian partisans in the foothills of the Alps. Mussolini had been trying to reach Germany with his mistress Clara Petacci and several of his ministers from the Italian Social Republic, the rump-state created for him after the German occupation of northern Italy following Italy's capitulation in 1943. Disguised as a German soldier, Mussolini was easily recognised. Along with his mistress and several fascist followers, the *Duce* was shot. Then, in a final indignity, the partisans took the bodies to Milan where they were hung upside down on meat hooks from an Esso petrol station forecourt where a huge crowd spat at them and shot and beat the corpses. Hitler had no intention of suffering such a degrading end and he instructed his servants to make sure that after his death his body was destroyed to avoid its capture and public display by the Soviets.

Knowing that the end was near seemed to make up Hitler's mind concerning a personal matter. Just after midnight on 29 April, Hitler married his longtime girlfriend Eva Braun in a simple ceremony inside the bunker.[4] It was her reward for her years of loyalty to him. She was under no illusions – she had come to Berlin to die with Hitler.

At 1.00am on 30 May *Generalfeldmarschall* Keitel reported to Hitler that all German forces that had been ordered to relieve the capital were either surrounded or had been forced on to the defensive.[5] No relief of the government quarter could be expected. Later that morning the attacking Soviets managed to penetrate to within 500 metres of the *Führerbunker*, despite the fanatical resistance being put up by Hitler's guard detachments. Hitler met with *General der Artillerie* Helmuth Weidling, the commander of the Berlin Defence Area. He informed the *Führer* that there was enough ammunition to sustain the defence for a maximum of twenty-four hours. Weidling asked permission for the remaining troops to attempt a breakout, but Hitler did not reply. Weidling returned to his headquarters at the Bendlerblock. At 1.00pm he received permission from Hitler for a breakout.[6]

Hitler had lunch with two of his secretaries and his cook and then he bade farewell to his staff and the remaining bunker occupants, including Bormann and Goebbels. With his wife, Hitler went into his study and closed the door at 2.30pm. Differing accounts of what happened next have surfaced over the years. The officially accepted story is that at shortly after 3.30pm Heinz Linge, with Bormann right behind him, opened the study door and was met with the strong smell of burnt almonds, a signature of hydrogen cyanide.[7] Again accounts differ in the details but according to Linge, Eva Hitler was slumped to the left of the *Führer* on a sofa, her legs drawn up. Hitler 'sat ... sunken over, with blood dripping out of his right temple,' wrote Linge. 'He had shot himself with his own pistol, a Walther PPK 7.65.'[8]

Hitler's adjutant Günsche then entered the room, surveyed the scene and left shortly afterwards to declare to those waiting outside that the *Führer* was dead. Preparations had already been made to dispose of the bodies of Hitler and his wife, as Hitler had made sure that Günsche understood that on no account was his body to be found intact by the Soviets. A few hours before Hitler killed himself Günsche had telephoned the Reich Chancellery garage and spoken to Hitler's principal driver, Erich Kempka. Günsche ordered Kempka to bring over a large quantity of petrol. 'I was ... to ensure that five cans of gasoline, that is to say 200 litres, were brought along,' recalled Kempka. 'I at once took along two or three men carrying cans. More were following, because it took time to collect 200 litres of gasoline.'[9] The cans were left near the bunker's emergency exit.

Hitler's body was wrapped in a blanket and carried up the stairs to the bunker's emergency exit by Linge[10], *SS-Hauptsturmführer* Ewald Lindloff and *SS-Obersturmführer* Hans Reisser of the *SS-Begleitkommando*, and *SS-Obersturmbannführer* Peter Högl, deputy commander of the RSD. Bormann carried Eva Hitler's body upstairs. Once outside, the SS officers placed both of the bodies, still wrapped in grey blankets, into a shell crater and then doused them liberally with petrol.[11] An attempt was made to light the petrol, but it was unsuccessful. Linge went back into the bunker and returned with a thick roll of papers. Bormann lit the papers and threw them into the hole, the petrol igniting with a whoosh. Others had joined them. Standing just inside the emergency exit door Günsche, Bormann, Högl, Linge, Lindloff, Reisser, Kempka and Goebbels raised their arms in the Nazi salute.[12] But the party was soon driven inside as Soviet shells began to land in the Reich Chancellery garden.[13]

For Heinz Linge it was a peculiar and emotional event. He had been Hitler's valet for ten years, and knew him perhaps more intimately than anyone. He was reminded of how much had changed in that decade of service. 'The man who had asked my name in Obersalzberg in the summer of 1934 had been a domineering personality exuding a spellbinding charisma to which few were not prey. He embodied sovereign power, total power. The man whom I burnt and interred under a hail of Red Army shells near the Reich Chancellery was a terribly old man, a spent force, feeble, a failure.'[14] Linge was struck by the parallels between the destruction of Hitler and the ruin of the nation he had led. 'Like the Reich which he had said would bring in an era of unparalleled brilliance and opulence and had become a heap of rubble, he was the disfigured embodiment of his earlier self.'[15]

Thirty minutes after the cremation of Hitler and his wife was begun, Günsche ordered Lindloff to go out and see how it was progressing. Lindloff reported that both bodies were charred and had burst open. He also said that they had been damaged by shellfire. During the afternoon, *SS-Begleitkommando* guards continued to add jerry cans of fuel to the burning hole in between the Soviet barrages.[16]

At 4.15pm Linge ordered *SS-Untersturmführer* Heinz Krüger and *SS-Oberscharführer* Werner Schwiedel to roll up the bloodstained rug from Hitler's study, carry it up to the Reich Chancellery garden and burn it.[17] At 6.30pm Lindloff reported to Günsche that he and Reisser had disposed of the remains.[18] It appears that from the remains later found by the Soviets some days later that the bodies of Hitler and his wife were burned beyond recognition and possibly damaged by shellfire, if indeed they were the mortal remains of the tyrant and his spouse.

Although Hitler was dead, the business of government continued, as well as the defence of the remaining areas of the government quarter by Hitler's bodyguard units and associated troops. Hitler's Last Will and Testament had broken up the position of '*Führer*' into three separate offices. Goebbels was named Reich Chancellor, with *Grossadmiral* Dönitz appointed Reich President and Bormann made Party Minister.[19] But at this stage, only Dönitz could exercise any limited control from Flensburg in the north. Goebbels made it very clear that he and his wife Magda would emulate their beloved *Führer* and commit suicide when the time came.

On 1 May Chancellor Goebbels drafted a letter to the Soviets and ordered 47-year-old *General der Infanterie* Hans Krebs, Chief of the Army General Staff (OKH), to deliver it under a white flag of truce to General Vasili Chuikov, commander of the 8th Guards Army which was occupying central Berlin.[20] The letter informed the Soviet High Command of Hitler's death, the appointment of Goebbels as Reich Chancellor and his offer of a cease-fire. When Krebs was sent packing with the clear instruction that the Soviets would only accept unconditional surrender, Goebbels knew that it was futile to continue. Later that day *Vizeadmiral* Hans-Erich Voss and almost a dozen other military officers arrived at the *Führerbunker* to say farewell to Goebbels as their supreme commander.

At 8.00pm that evening Goebbels instructed dentist *SS-Sturmbann-führer* Helmut Kunz to drug his six children with morphine. Then Hitler's personal physician, *SS-Obersturmbannführer* Dr Ludwig Stumpfegger, crushed a vial of cyanide in each of their jaws, killing them. A little while later a subdued Goebbels pulled on his gloves and hat, and arm-in-arm with his wife, climbed the stairs to the bunker's emergency exit and emerged into the Reich Chancellery garden. His adjutant, 29-year-old *SS-Hauptsturmführer* Gunther Schwägermann, followed him.

Schwägermann went to collect more petrol to burn the Goebbels' bodies while Goebbels and his wife went around the corner out of sight. Schwägermann said that he heard a pistol shot and came upon his master and Magda Goebbels dead. She had taken poison while Goebbels had shot himself in the head. Schwägermann ordered the *SS-Begleitkommando* sentry at the bunker emergency exit to shoot Goebbels again in the head to make sure – Schwägermann could not face doing so himself. The two men then poured petrol over the bodies and set fire to them. Unfortunately, there was insufficient petrol remaining to burn the bodies and the fire-blackened corpses remained easily recognizable to Voss when he was forced by the Soviets to identify them the following day. The shape of Goebbels' head and jaw as well as his leg brace were unmistakable, along with the remains of his brown Nazi uniform and Golden Party Badge.

There was another suicide on 1 May. *SS-Obersturmbannführer* Franz Schädle, the 38-year-old commander of the *SS-Begleitkommando*, shot himself through the mouth with a pistol inside the bunker.

Before he killed himself on 30 April, Hitler had signed an order permitting the remaining members of the bunker to attempt to break out of Berlin. 'It was planned for ten groups to break out from the *Führer-*bunker on the night of 1 May 1945 and penetrate the encirclement by force of arms,'[21] recalled Hitler's driver Erich Kempka. In the event three groups eventually departed from the *Führerbunker* during the night of 1–2 May.

Group 1, led by *SS-Brigadeführer* Mohnke, included Hitler's three remaining secretaries, Traudl Junge, Gerda Christian and Else Krüger, his cook Constanze Manziarly, one of Hitler's doctors *SS-Standarten-führer* Dr Ernst-Gunther Schenk, diplomat Walter Hewel, Otto Günsche and *SS-Sturmbannführer* Arthur Klingermeyer plus fifteen other mostly SS officers and men. The group was armed to the teeth and Mohnke planned to link up with German forces still fighting on the Prinzeallee. Mohnke's group initially made good progress and eluded Soviet detection before reaching the underground railway station at Wilhelmplatz. From there the group walked down the tunnel towards Stadtmitte Station. They had no contact with the other two groups as they had no radios with them. Eventually they arrived at a closed steel door that sealed the tunnel. Two uniformed officials were guarding it and refused to open the door. Mohnke's group returned to the surface and eventually reached the Schulteiss-Patjenhofer Brewery on Prinzeallee where they surrendered to the Soviets on 2 May.

Hitler's secretaries were all raped by Soviet troops but did eventually manage to get through to American lines, while Hitler's cook Manziarly was most probably murdered by Soviet troops. The last of Hitler's secretaries, Traudl Junge, died in 2002 aged 81. Dr Schenk was released from Soviet captivity in 1953 and returned to West Germany.

He died there in 1998 aged 94. Mohnke and other senior SS commanders were imprisoned in the dreaded Lubjanka Prison in Moscow. Mohnke was released in 1955 and became a truck dealer in West Germany. He died in 2001 aged 90. Walter Hewel committed suicide when Soviet forces arrived to take their surrender, crunching down on a cyanide capsule the same moment that he shot himself in the head. *SS-Sturmbannführer* Otto Günsche, Hitler's ever-loyal servant, survived NKVD captivity and brutal interrogation before returning to West Germany in 1956. He died in 2003 aged 86.

Group 2 was under the command of Hitler's RSD commander Johann Rattenhuber, but was captured by the Soviets the same day it left the bunker. Rattenhuber shared Mohnke's fate and died shortly after his release from Soviet captivity in 1957 aged 60.

Group 3 was led by Werner Naumann, the State Secretary in the Propaganda Ministry who had been created Propaganda Minister in Hitler's Last Will and Testament. Naumann's group included Martin Bormann, Hitler Youth Leader Artur Axmann, Hitler's pilot Hans Baur[22], Kempka, and another of Hitler's doctors, Dr Stumpfegger plus some other prominent bunker characters. This group managed to cross the River Spree at the Weidendammer Bridge on their third attempt. During the first attempt one of the last remaining Tiger tanks in Berlin had attempted to force back the Soviets at the other end of the bridge but had been knocked out. 'After the tank had gone about 30 or 40m it received a direct hit,' recalled Kempka. 'The tank flew apart. I saw a short flash of lightning and fell to the ground where I remained lying unconscious. My last impression was that Dr Naumann, Bormann and Dr Stumpfegger fell together and remained lying.'[23] Eventually, sheer weight of numbers, as thousands of military personnel and civilians charged across the bridge, forced the Soviets to retreat, though they indiscriminately mowed down hundreds including Heinrich Himmler's brother, during the stampede. Kempka was not among them. He came round to find that Bormann, Stumpfegger and the others had gone on. Kempka was slightly wounded by shrapnel in his thigh and upper arm but otherwise was in one piece. He saw another German attack go on, 'but I decided not to go along any more because of its futility. I returned to the Admiralsplatz, assembled my men and told them that they were dismissed. Each one could go on his own, to join a combat group or go home. I also advised them to procure for themselves civilian clothes.'[24]

Hans Baur carried in his backpack one of Hitler's most prized possessions, the portrait of Frederick the Great that had adorned the wall of his bunker study. Baur was seriously wounded by machine gun fire in the leg, face and chest as he attempted to reach cover in a wrecked train station after crossing the Weidendammer Bridge. A Soviet soldier who found him robbed Hitler's pilot of his possessions, including the rolled up painting. Baur carried no identity documents and had changed into a nondescript uniform, as had most of those escaping from the bunker. But, in great pain and fearing that he would die if he didn't receive proper medical treatment, he identified himself to his Soviet captors. Soviet NKVD officers interrogated him in detail, desperate to know as much about Hitler's supposed suicide as possible, before he was given an operation in a field hospital. His leg had become infected and required amputation below the knee. He was to endure a decade in Soviet hands, held in Moscow along with other members of Hitler's personal staff, as the Soviets probed the circumstances of the *Führer*'s demise.[25] The Soviets later released him to France in 1955. There he was imprisoned until 1957, before being returned to West Germany where he wrote his memoirs. Baur died in Bavaria in 1993 aged 95.

Dr Goebbels' adjutant Gunther Schwägermann managed to escape Berlin and was eventually arrested by the US Army. He was released in 1947 and lived in West Germany until his death. The SS dentist who had drugged the Goebbels' children in preparation for their murder, Helmut Kunz, returned to work in the Reich Chancellery casualty clearing station and was captured on 2 May. He spent ten years in Soviet captivity before moving to Munster where he operated a dental practice, German courts refusing to prosecute him for his part in the deaths of the Goebbels' children. Kunz died in 1976 aged 65.

Two of Hitler's bodyguards were killed as they attempted to cross the Weidendammer Bridge. *SS-Obersturmbannführer* Peter Högl, second-in-command of the RSD, was shot through the head and fatally wounded. He was 47-years-old. Thirty-six-year-old *SS-Hauptsturmführer* Ewald Lindloff, the officer who had burned Hitler and Eva Braun's bodies, was also killed alongside Högl. Erich Kempka, Hitler's driver, had left the bunker in company with *SS-Hauptscharführer* Heinrich Doose, one of the other drivers, and *SS-Obersturmbannführer* Heinz Linge, Hitler's valet. During the escape they came across Georg Betz, Hitler's second pilot, 'who had been wounded crossing the Weidendammer Bridge, he had a serious head injury'[26] recalled

Kempka. Betz was left in the care of Hitler's dental assistant Kaethe Hausermann, but he later died.

Kempka returned to Friedrichstrasse Station with seven of his SS drivers. They then crossed the Spree on a footbridge and reached a house on its northern bank without being fired at.[27] Pushing on to Albrechtstrasse, they were captured in a rail yard but Kempka, with the help of a civilian overcoat, managed to escape and get through Soviet lines. He was eventually captured by the US Army on 20 June at Berchtesgaden. Released in 1947, Kempka later wrote his memoirs. He died in 1975 aged 64. Linge was not so lucky. He was cornered and captured by the Soviets and hauled off to the Lubjanka for ten years. Released in 1955, he died in Bremen in 1980 aged 66.

Once across the Weidendammer Bridge Axmann, Bormann and Stumpfegger left the main group and started walking along the railway tracks to the Lehrter Station. Bormann and Stumpfegger then continued along tracks towards Stettiner Station. Axmann went on alone in the opposite direction but was forced to backtrack by a Soviet patrol. He later claimed to have seen Bormann and Stumpfegger's bodies lying near the railway-switching yard at Stettiner Station, though he did not pause to check them.[28] Axmann was one of several members of Naumann's group who managed to break through the encirclement of Berlin and escape the Soviets. He went to ground in the Bavarian Alps under the alias 'Erich Siewert' until captured by the US Army's Counter Intelligence Corps in December 1945 when he was trying to establish a Nazi underground movement. In 1949 Axmann was sentenced to three years and three months in prison. He died in 1996 aged 83, the last of Hitler's ministers.

The search for Martin Bormann, considered to have been the most senior Nazi to have escaped capture and/or trial in 1945, continued for decades despite Axmann's insistence that Bormann and Dr Stumpfegger had died during the escape from the *Führerbunker*. Digs were made for Bormann's body in Paraguay in March 1964 and Berlin in July 1964 without result. The same year the West German government offered a 100,000 Mark reward for information leading to Bormann's capture, but it remained unclaimed. In 1965 a retired postal worker named Albert Krumnow came forward to claim that on 8 May 1945, or thereabouts, he and his colleagues had been ordered by the Soviets to bury two bodies near the Lehrter Station in the exact same location as that reported by Artur Axmann. Krumnow claimed that one body was dressed in a *Wehrmacht* uniform – indeed Bormann had changed into nondescript dress for the breakout – while the other was an SS doctor. Krumnow stated that they found a paybook on the SS officer's body identifying it as Ludwig Stumpfegger's. When they gave the document to the Soviets, they destroyed it.

Then, in 1972 workmen found two skeletons only 12 metres from where Krumnow stated that he had buried two bodies in May 1945. Using dental records reconstructed in Soviet captivity from memory in 1945 by *SS-Brigadeführer* Dr Hugo Blaschke, Hitler's dentist, the smaller skeleton was identified as Bormann's. The skeleton also had a damaged collarbone consistent with a 1939 riding accident suffered by Bormann. The second skeleton was identified as Stumpfegger's based largely on the body's great height. Fragments of glass found in the jaws of both skeletons seemed to suggest that Bormann and Stumpfegger had crunched down on cyanide capsules to avoid capture. The British press labelled the investigation a 'whitewash' perpetrated by the German government to finally lay its Nazi past to rest. In 1998 DNA tests proved that the skeleton identified as Bormann's was indeed the 'Lord of the Obersalzberg'. His remains were cremated and scattered in the sea. However, several authors and researchers have pointed out inconsistencies with the official German investigation's findings, notably that Bormann's skeleton was covered in flecks of red clay when the Berlin soil is yellow sand. It is the kind of clay found in Paraguay, where Bormann was reported several times to have been living after the war. Perhaps Bormann did escape and after he died in freedom his skeleton was 'planted' in Berlin near to where Axmann and Krumnow claimed to have seen it. It remains an intriguing historical mystery and like that of Rudolf Hess, will continue to generate conspiracy theories for decades to come.[29]

One man who had been at Hitler's side since the old days was missing from the last act of the Nazi opera – the *SS-Begleitkommando* chief Bruno Gesche. Gesche, who had already been dismissed and reinstated following episodes of heavy drinking, managed to really foul things up for himself in December 1944. Once again, drunken shenanigans with a service pistol ended his career with Hitler. This time the *Führer* did not intervene on his behalf. Heinrich Himmler had Gesche demoted an astonishing nine ranks, dropping from a lieutenant-colonel all the way down to the junior rank of *SS-Unterscharführer* (corporal) and assigned to a penal unit, the infamous *Dirlewanger Brigade* on the Eastern Front.

The problem for Himmler was the very fact that the *Dirlewanger Brigade* was fighting the Soviets. Hitler had expressly forbidden any of his bodyguards to serve on the Eastern Front, a fact pointed out by two of Gesche's powerful friends, Hermann Fegelein and *SS-Obergruppenführer* Maximilian von Herff. Instead, Gesche was assigned to the *16th SS Panzer Grenadier Division Reichsführer-SS* where, in spite of everything that had happened to him, Gesche fought valiantly until surrendering to the US Army in Italy in May 1945.

One prominent bunker occupant who simply vanished without trace was the feared Gestapo chief, *SS-Gruppenführer* Heinrich Müller. He was last seen in the bunker on 1 May 1945 and no trace has ever been found of the third most powerful man in the SS after Himmler and Reich Security Main Office chief Dr Ernst Kaltenbrunner. Forty-five-year-old 'Gestapo Müller', as he was called by colleagues to differentiate him from another SS general with the exact same name, disappeared into thin air. There are four possible theories for the fate of Müller, all explored by historians and security services. Firstly, that he may have successfully escaped from Berlin and disappeared down one of the many ratlines to safety in South America or the Middle East. As head of the Gestapo, Müller certainly had access to the necessary people and documentation. Secondly, that he was killed in Berlin in May 1945 and his body was never found, one of thousands of decomposing corpses that were thrown into mass graves after the fighting ended. Thirdly, that he was captured by the Soviets and used as an intelligence asset. Or, fourthly, that he was captured by the Americans and secretly went to work for them. The Americans, British and Soviets all used Gestapo and SD officials during the early stages of the Cold War. We will probably never know.

Dr Werner Naumann made it into Western Germany before fleeing to Argentina where he worked as the editor of a Nazi newspaper. He returned to Germany in 1947 and became an apprentice bricklayer. Arrested by the British Army in 1953, Naumann was released after seven months detention and later became a director in a metal firm owned by his old boss Dr Goebbels' stepson Harald Quandt. Naumann died in West Germany in 1982 aged 73.

SS-Oberscharführer Rochus Misch, the bunker telephone operator, was one of the last to flee on 2 May 1945. He was captured by the Soviets, released in 1954 and for many years was the last living witness to what happened in the bunker. He lived in Berlin for the rest of his life, just 3km from the ruined *Führerbunker*. Misch died in September 2013 aged 96.

Some members of Hitler's personal squadron were able to fare better than those left behind in the *Führerbunker*. One group of pilots and ground crew gathered their families together just before the end, commandeered a Junkers 52/3m and flew it to neutral Sweden. Many other F.d.F crewmen were taken prisoner by the Soviets, British or Americans, the latter two nations processing and then releasing them soon after. No former members of the F.d.F., even though many of them were SS, were prosecuted for war crimes.

On 4 May 1945 SS troops at the Obersalzberg set fire to the bomb-damaged Berghof before they evacuated the complex. By now, Allied forces were close by. A few hours after the last SS had left, the first Allied soldiers reached Berchtesgaden: elements from the US 2nd Infantry Division and the French 2nd Armoured Division. The Americans were confused – they appeared to think that Berchtesgaden was the Obersalzberg. However, a French captain and his driver soon located Hitler's still smouldering house. Pulling up outside in a jeep, they were joined shortly afterwards by a French tank crew and then by some American troops. Over the following few days the house was extensively looted, along with many of the other properties that made up the Obersalzberg complex.

On 8 May more American troops arrived at Berchtesgaden, namely Company C, 1st Battalion, 506th Parachute Infantry Regiment. They had had to fight their way in, knocking out two German 88mm guns in the high mountains. These GIs soon joined in with the looting. Many of Hitler's furnishings and other personal items ended up being hauled back to America as the spoils of war and continue to emerge today.

Hitler's personal train was no longer needed after it had delivered the *Führer* to Berlin for the final time on 16 January 1945. The *Führer-sonderzug* was moved from Berlin before the Soviets encircled the city and was then sent south to Brück near Zell am See in Austria. Here the luxurious carriages were used by some of Hitler's staff who had been flown south to prepare an 'Alpine Redoubt' headquarters, should Hitler have decided to join them. Later *General der Gebirgstruppe* August Winter and his staff, commanding mountain troops in the area, joined them at Hofgastein. The train was then moved into a mountain tunnel near Mallnitz to protect it from air attack.

Following the German surrender on 8 May 1945 the *Führersonderzug* was still in German hands. Hitler's personal Pullman coach was blown up and destroyed by Nazi loyalists. The rest of the train then went to Saalfelden and remained there until the end of the month. It was then moved to Pullach near Munich and finally commandeered by the US Army.

The *Führersonderzug*, minus Hitler's Pullman coach, was used by the US and British military occupation authorities for several years after the war, with different coaches being sent to different parts of West Germany. These carriages were returned to West German ownership between 1950 and 1953. One of the carriages from Hitler's train was returned by the British Army in 1953 and was used by the first West German chancellor, Konrad Adenaur, ironically for a visit to Moscow two years later. The carriage also visited East Germany in 1970, carrying Chancellor Willy Brandt. Hitler's dining carriage was finally taken out of German service in 1990 and is now in a museum in Neuenmarkt in Bavaria.

Those F.d.F. aircraft that had survived the fighting now also fell into Allied hands. When the British captured Flensburg airfield on the German-Danish border in May 1945 shortly after the final capitulation of Karl Dönitz's government, they found four intact *Condors*. Fw 200C-4/U1 (TK+CV) had been used as one of Hitler's support aircraft, but was unserviceable when seized. Another, Fw 200C-4/U2 (GC+SJ) *'Albatros III'* had been assigned to Dönitz as his personal transport aircraft since 1943. He had used it to fly to Flensburg and set up a government as the last Reich President. The nose of the aircraft was emblazoned with a U-Boat war badge, though its crew was drawn from the *Luftwaffe*. Seized as a war prize by the RAF it was flown to Farnborough, making three round trips between England and Germany in July and August 1945. Handed over to the Danish airline DDL it was wrecked following a takeoff accident at Schleswig on 28 February 1946 and subsequently scrapped. The British also captured Fw 200C-4 *'Thuringen'*, an aircraft belonging to *Lufthansa*. This plane was also flown to Farnborough, was given to DDL and eventually cannibalised for spares in August 1947. The final *Condor* captured at Flensburg was Fw 200C-4/U1 GC+AE, *Reichsführer-SS* Heinrich Himmler's personal aircraft. Flown to Farnborough for evaluation in

July 1945, it was subsequently placed on public display during October and November. The RAF scrapped Himmler's aircraft on 15 December 1946. Unbelievably, none of these very significant planes was given to a museum as a war prize.

The Battle for Berlin lasted for twelve days. When Berlin surrendered on 2 May 1945 it 'was a corpse of a city. All that was left were ruins, craters, burned-out tanks, smashed guns, tramcars riddled with holes, half-demolished trenches, litters of spent shells, fresh graves, corpses still awaiting burial, masses of white flags and crowds of glum and hungry inhabitants.'[30] A hunt had already begun for one corpse in particular. Adolf Hitler, the man so many tried to guard and protect for decades, and who survived so many assassination attempts, was missing. To many it seemed as if Hitler had simply vanished in ruined and battered Berlin in 1945. Certainly his most loyal guards accorded him what they could by way of a funeral in the garden of the Reich Chancellery before they themselves attempted to flee his concrete bolthole beneath the city. But many unanswered questions remain to this day, and perhaps the most important is what actually happened to Hitler's body?

Lindloff and Reisser reported to Otto Günsche that they had covered over the thoroughly burnt remains of Hitler and his wife in the shallow shell crater at around 6.30pm on 30 April 1945. The German people were informed of Hitler's death in a radio broadcast by Reich President Dönitz on 1 May. Although fighting would continue in other parts of Europe for a further seven days, the Reich Chancellery and the *Führerbunker* were captured in the early hours of 2 May. At this point *Generals der Infanterie* Burgdorf and Krebs shot themselves deep in the bunker to avoid capture.[31] The only people who were still alive in the bunker when the Soviets stormed in were *Feldwebel* Fritz Tornow, Hitler's army dog handler, and Johannes Hentschel, the bunker's master electro-mechanic.

A Red Army SMERSH intelligence unit that was under orders to discover what had happened to Hitler was able to interrogate several members of Hitler's staff who had been captured trying to flee Berlin. They soon excavated the area where Hitler and his wife had been cremated, discovering two unrecognizable bodies, as well as the body of Hitler's dog Blondi and her puppy Wulf. These remains were placed inside two ammunition crates and taken to a pathology lab on the outskirts of Berlin, along with the bodies of Krebs, Goebbels and his wife and their six children. The body believed to be Hitler's was identified as such from a dental chart drawn from memory by his captured dental assistant Kaethe Heussermann, as Dr Morell had taken all of Hitler's medical records with him when he had flown south to Berchtesgaden several days before.

SMERSH decided to relocate to a large house in Magdeburg and took the remains with them, packed into five wooden boxes. Each time they stopped they buried them, and then exhumed them the next morning. The remains were finally interred beneath a paved front courtyard at the house on 21 February 1946. Some body parts were kept as trophies and taken back to Moscow, including Hitler's supposed lower jaw and part of his skull with a bullet hole through it. These would rest undisturbed in an archive until the breakup of the Soviet Union.

In 1970 it was decided that the house in Magdeburg, now used by the KGB, would be turned over to the East German government. Yuri Andropov, head of the KGB, decreed that the human remains must be exhumed and destroyed to prevent the building becoming a neo-Nazi shrine.[32] Accordingly, in great secrecy on 4 April 1970 the five boxes were dug up and examined. They contained the badly decomposed remains of ten or eleven people. They were put through a local crematorium oven and the bones were then carefully crushed. Then the entire quantity of ash was unceremoniously dumped into the Biederitz River, a tributary of the Elbe.

That may have been the end of the story of Adolf Hitler had it not been for the fall of communism in 1991. In 2009 scientists were able to conduct DNA tests on the piece of Hitler's skull that SMERSH had kept in 1945. It was discovered that it was that of a woman less than forty years old.[33] In a final historical twist, perhaps the *Führer*'s loyal bodyguards had succeeded in concealing their master's body from the Soviets after all?

German Commissioned Ranks

SS	Wehrmacht	British Army
Reichsführer-SS	Generalfeldmarschall	Field Marshal
SS-Oberstgruppenführer	Generaloberst	General
SS-Obergruppenführer	General[1]	Lieutenant General
SS-Gruppenführer	Generalleutnant	Major General
SS-Brigadeführer	Generalmajor	Brigadier
SS-Oberführer	*No equivalent*	*No equivalent*
SS-Standartenführer	Oberst	Colonel
SS-Obersturmbannführer	Oberstleutnant	Lieutenant Colonel
SS-Sturmbannführer	Major	Major
SS-Hauptsturmführer	Hauptmann/Rittmeister[2]	Captain
SS-Obersturmführer	Oberleutnant	Lieutenant
SS-Untersturmführer	Leutnant	Second Lieutenant

1. This rank would also carry a branch of service designation, e.g. *General der Infanterie* (General of Infantry). The branches were: Cavalry, Armoured Troops, Infantry, Mountain Troops, Artillery, Engineers, Signals.
2. *Rittmeister* ('Riding Master') was the equivalent rank for Cavalry officers.

Present in the *Führerbunker* 30 April 1945

Personal Protection
RSD
- *SS-Gruppenführer* Johann Rattenhuber (Commander)
- *SS-Obersturmbannführer* Peter Högl (Deputy Commander)

SS-Begleitkommando
- *SS-Obersturmbannführer* Franz Schädle (Commander)
- *SS-Obersturmbannführer* Heinz Linge (Hitler's valet)
- *SS-Obersturmbannführer* Erich Kempka (Hitler's chief driver)
- *SS-Untersturmführer* Heinz Krüger
- *SS-Hauptscharführer* Heinrich Doose (driver)
- *SS-Oberscharführer* Rochus Misch (Telephonist)
- *SS-Oberscharführer* Werner Schwiedel

Führer Squadron
- *SS-Gruppenführer* Hans Baur (Commander)
- *SS-Obersturmbannführer* Karl Betz (Deputy Commander)

Senior Military Officers
- *General der Infanterie* Hans Krebs (Chief of the Army General Staff (OKH))
- *General der Artillerie* Helmuth Weidling (Commander Berlin Defence Area)
- *Generalleutnant* Wilhelm Burgdorf (Chief of the Army Personnel Office and Chief Army Adjutant to the *Führer*)
- *SS-Brigadeführer* Wilhelm Mohnke (Commander of Defence Sector 'Z')

Adjutants
- *Oberst* Theodor von Dufving (Weidling's 'Military' Chief of Staff)
- *Oberst* Hans Refior (Weidling's 'Civil' Chief of Staff)
- *Major* Siegfried Knappe (Army Staff Officer)
- *Major* Willi Johannmeyer (*Wehrmacht* Adjutant)

- *SS-Gruppenführer* Hermann Fegelein (Senior SS Adjutant)
- *SS-Sturmbannführer* Otto Gunsche (Personal SS Adjutant)
- *NSKK-Oberführer* Alwin-Broder Albrecht (Adjutant)
- *Oberst* Nicolaus von Below (*Luftwaffe* Adjutant)
- *Vizeadmiral* Hans-Erich Voss (*Kriegsmarine* Liaison Officer)

Secretarial
- *Reichsleiter* Martin Bormann (Private Secretary to the Führer)
- *SS-Standartenführer* Wilhelm Zander (Bormann's Adjutant)
- Else Krüger (Bormann's Secretary)
- Gertraud "Traudl" Junge (Hitler's Secretary)
- Gerda Christian (Hitler's Secretary)

Medical
- *SS-Standartenführer* Dr Ernst-Gunther Schenk (Physician)
- *SS-Obersturmbannführer* Prof. Dr Werner Haase (Physician)
- *SS-Obersturmbannführer* Dr Ludwig Stumpfegger (Physician)
- *SS-Sturmbannführer* Helmut Kunz (Dentist)
- Erna Flegel (Red Cross nurse)

Others
- Eva Braun
- *Reichsminister* Dr Josef Goebbels (Propaganda Minister)
- Magda Goebbels and her six children
- *SS-Hauptsturmführer* Gunther Schwägermann (Goebbels' Adjutant)
- Gerhard Schach (Chief of Goebbels' *Gauleiter* Staff & Propaganda Ministry liaison)
- *SS-Gruppenführer* Heinrich Müller (Head of the Gestapo)
- *SS-Brigadeführer* Werner Naumann (State Secretary in the Propaganda Ministry)
- Walter Hewel (Foreign Minister von Ribbentrop's representative)
- Artur Axmann (Leader of the Hitler Youth)
- *SS-Obersturmführer* Josef Ochs (*Kriminalpolizei*)
- Constanze Manziarly (Hitler's cook and dietician)
- *Feldwebel* Fritz Tornow (Hitler's dog handler)
- Johannes Hentschel (Master Electro-engineer)
- Armin Lehmann (Hitler Youth courier)

Notes

Chapter 1: Time of Struggle

1. Ian Kershaw, *Hitler: A Biography* (New York: W.W. Norton & Company, 2008), pp. 59–60.
2. Peter Hoffmann, *Hitler's Personal Security: Protecting the Führer, 1921–1945* (New York: Da Capo Press, 2000), p. 1.
3. Roger Moorhouse, *Killing Hitler: The Third Reich and the Plots to Kill the Führer* (London: Vintage, 2007), p. 15.
4. Peter Hoffmann, *op. cit.*, p. 2.
5. *Ibid*, p. 3.
6. Richard Evans, *The Third Reich at War* (New York: Penguin Books, 2008), p. 508.
7. Peter Hoffmann, *op. cit.*, p. 16.
8. Bruce Campbell, *The SA Generals and the Rise of Nazism* (Lexington: Kentucky University Press, 1998), pp. 19–20.
9. *Murdering Hitler: The Failed Attacks on Hitler's Life*, www.valkyrie. greyfalcon.us (accessed 1 August 2013).
10. *Ibid*.
11. Ian Kershaw, *op. cit.*, p. 313.
12. *Third Reich in Ruins*, www.thirdreichruins.com (accessed 18 May 2013).

Chapter 2: *Ein Reich, Ein Volk, Ein Führer!*

1. *Murdering Hitler: The Failed Attacks on Hitler's Life*, www.valkyrie. greyfalcon.us (accessed 4 August 2013).
2. Ronald Pawly, *Hitler's Chancellery: A Palace to Last a Thousand Years* (Ramsbury: The Crowood Press Ltd, 2009), p. 9.
3. *Murdering Hitler, op. cit.*
4. Peter Hoffmann, *Hitler's Personal Security: Protecting the Führer, 1921–1945* (New York: Da Capo Press, 2000), p. 32.
5. Ronald Pawly, *op. cit.*, p. 162.
6. Peter Hoffmann, *op. cit.*, p. 162.
7. *Ibid*, p. 162.
8. *Murdering Hitler, op. cit.*

9. Peter Hoffmann, *op. cit.*, p. 163.
10. Roger Moorhouse, *Killing Hitler: The Third Reich and the Plots to Kill the Führer* (London: Vintage, 2007), pp. 43–58.

Chapter 3: Trains and Automobiles
1. Otto Dietrich, *The Hitler I Knew: Memoir of the Third Reich's Press Chief* (New York: Skyhorse Publishing, 2010), Kindle edition.
2. Peter Hoffmann, *Hitler's Personal Security: Protecting the Führer, 1921–1945* (New York: Da Capo Press, 2000), p. 66.
3. *Ibid*, p. 71.
4. Heinz Linge, *With Hitler to the End: The Memoirs of Hitler's Valet* (New York: Frontline Books, 2009), p. 11.
5. *Ibid*, p. 13.
6. Peter Hoffmann, *op. cit.*, p. 127.
7. *Ibid*, p. 127.
8. Roger Moorhouse, *Killing Hitler: The Third Reich and the Plots to Kill the Führer* (London: Vintage, 2007), pp. 145–6.
9. Peter Hoffmann, *op. cit.*, p. 128.
10. *Ibid*, p. 135.
11. *Ibid*, p. 202.
12. *Ibid*, p. 136.
13. *Ibid*, p. 136.
14. *Ibid*, p. 202.
15. Roger Moorhouse, *op. cit.*, p. 162.
16. Peter Hoffmann, *op. cit.*, p. 145.

Chapter 4: Eagle's Eyrie
1. Sir Ian Kershaw, *Hitler: 1936–1945 Nemesis* (London: Penguin Books, 2001), p. 742.
2. 'Hitler's Ultra-Secret Adlerhorst' by Irwin J. Kappes, militaryhistoryonline.com (accessed 14 June 2013).
3. 'Guide to Hitler's Headquarters' by Richard Rieber, *After the Battle*, No. 19 (London: Battle of Britain International, 1977), pp. 48–51.
4. *Ibid*, p. 51.
5. Sir Ian Kershaw, *op. cit.*, p. 294.
6. Richard Rieber, *op. cit.*, p. 4.
7. Peter Hoffmann, *Hitler's Personal Security: Protecting the Führer, 1921–1945* (New York: Da Capo Press, 2000), p. 208.
8. *Ibid*, p. 214.
9. Richard Rieber, *op. cit.*, p. 18.

10. Peter Hoffmann, *op. cit.*, p. 214.
11. Richard Rieber, *op. cit.*, p. 1.
12. Irwin J. Kappes, *op. cit.*
13. *Ibid.*
14. *Ibid.*
15. *Ibid.*
16. Sir Ian Kershaw, *op. cit.*, p. 756.
17. *Ibid*, p. 757.
18. *Ibid*, p. 768.

Chapter 5: The Führer's Squadron
 1. Peter Hoffmann, *Hitler's Personal Security: Protecting the Führer, 1921–1945* (New York: Da Capo Press, 2000), p. 75.
 2. C.G. Sweeting, *Hitler's Squadron: The Führer's Personal Aircraft and Transport Unit, 1933–1945* (London: Brassey's, 2001), p. 70.
 3. *Ibid*, p. 72.
 4. *Ibid*, p. 64.
 5. *Ibid*, p. 70.
 6. Peter Hoffmann, *op. cit.*, pp. 76–7.
 7. *Ibid*, p. 78.
 8. *Ibid*, p. 76.
 9. Roger Moorhouse, *Killing Hitler: The Third Reich and the Plots to Kill the Führer* (London: Vintage, 2007), p. 190.
10. *Ibid*, p. 191.
11. C.G. Sweeting, *op. cit.*, p. 80.
12. *Ibid*, p. 83.

Chapter 6: Eagle's Nest
 1. Roger Moorhouse, *Killing Hitler: The Third Reich and the Plots to Kill the Führer* (London: Vintage, 2007), p. 167.
 2. James Wilson, *Hitler's Alpine Retreat* (Barnsley: Pen & Sword Books Limited, 2005), p. 7.
 3. *Ibid*, p. 8.
 4. Hoffmann, Peter, *Hitler's Personal Security: Protecting the Führer, 1921–1945* (New York: Da Capo Press), 2000, p. 157.
 5. *Report on information obtained from PW KP/29750 SS Schutze Obernigg*, FO/1020,3471 (The National Archives (Public Record Office)), Kew.
 6. *Ibid.*
 7. *Ibid.*

8. *Third Reich in Ruins*, www.thirdreichruins.com (accessed 12 July 2013).
9. Sir Ian Kershaw, *Hitler: 1936–1945 Nemesis* (London: Penguin Books, 2001), p. 34.
10. *Ibid*, p. 34.
11. *Obernigg, op. cit.*
12. *Third Reich in Ruins, op. cit.*
13. *Ibid.*
14. *Ibid.*
15. *Ibid.*
16. *Obernigg, op. cit.*
17. *Ibid.*
18. *Ibid.*
19. *Ibid.*
20. *Third Reich in Ruins, op. cit.*
21. Peter Hoffmann, *op. cit.*, p. 190.
22. *Obernigg, op. cit.*
23. *Ibid.*
24. *Ibid.*
25. *Ibid.*
26. *Third Reich in Ruins, op. cit.*
27. Sir Ian Kershaw, *op. cit.*, p. 202.
28. *Obernigg, op. cit.*
29. Peter Hoffmann, *op. cit.*, p. 196.
30. Roger Moorhouse, *op. cit.*, p. 167.
31. *Ibid*, p. 167.
32. *Ibid*, p. 168.
33. *Ibid*, p. 169.

Chapter 7: Wolf's Lair

1. *Third Reich in Ruins*, www.thirdreichruins.com (accessed 20 July 2013).
2. 'Guide to Hitler's Headquarters' by Richard Rieber, *After the Battle*, No. 19 (London: Battle of Britain International, 1977), pp. 48–51.
3. Peter Hoffmann, *Hitler's Personal Security: Protecting the Führer, 1921–1945* (New York: Da Capo Press, 2000), p. 225.
4. *Ibid*, p. 226.
5. *Interrogation report: Hauptmann Gaum, 3rd Panzer Grenadier Battalion, Führer Begleit Brigade*, FO/1020/3471, The National Archives (Public Record Office), Kew.

6. Traudl Junge, *To the Final Hour* (Phoenix, 2004), p. 116.
7. Peter Hoffmann, *op. cit.*, p. 229.
8. *Ibid*, p. 232.
9. *Ibid*, p. 232.
10. *Ibid*, p. 232.
11. *Interrogation report: Hauptmann Gaum, op. cit.*
12. Kershaw, Sir Ian, *Hitler: Nemesis, 1936–1945* (London: Penguin Books, 2001), p. 396.
13. *Ibid*, p. 396.
14. *Ibid*, p. 396.
15. *Ibid*, p. 397.
16. *Ibid*, p. 397.
17. *Ibid*, p. 397.
18. *Interrogation report: Hauptmann Gaum, op. cit.*
19. Peter Hoffmann, *op. cit.*, p. 238.
20. *Interrogation report: Hauptmann Gaum, op. cit.*
21. Antony Beevor, *Stalingrad* (London: Penguin Books, 2007), p. 80.
22. *Ibid*, p. 80.
23. Peter Hoffmann, *op. cit.*, p. 240.
24. Matthias Uhl & Henrik Eberle, *The Hitler Book: The Secret Report by his Two Closest Aides* (London: John Murray, 1978), p. 400.
25. *Ibid*, p. 400.
26. Peter Hoffmann, *op. cit.*, p. 242.
27. *Ibid*, p. 242.

Chapter 8: Enemies Within
1. Sir Ian Kershaw, *Hitler: 1936–1945 Nemesis* (London: Penguin Books, 2001), pp. 662–3.
2. Philip von Boeselager, *Valkyrie: The Plot to Kill Hitler* (London: Phoenix, 2009), p. 99.
3. Sir Ian Kershaw, *op. cit.*, p. 663.
4. Peter Hoffmann, *Hitler's Personal Security: Protecting the Führer, 1921–1945* (New York: Da Capo Press, 2000), p. 192.
5. *Ibid*, p. 152.
6. Roger Moorhouse, *Killing Hitler: The Third Reich and the Plots to Kill the Führer* (London: Vintage, 2007), p. 197.
7. *Ibid*, p. 197.
8. *Ibid*, p. 198.
9. Sir Ian Kershaw, *op. cit.*, p. 656.
10. Roger Moorhouse, *op. cit.*, p. 191.

11. Joachim Fest, *Plotting Hitler's Death: The German Resistance to Hitler, 1933–1945* (London: Phoenix, 1996), p. 219.
12. *Ibid*, p. 220.
13. Sir Ian Kershaw, *op. cit.*, p. 663.
14. Roger Moorhouse, *op. cit.*, pp. 192–3.
15. Philip von Boeselager, *op. cit.*, pp. 99–105.
16. Roger Moorhouse, *op. cit.*, p. 193.
17. *Ibid*, 195.
18. Sir Ian Kershaw, *op. cit.*, p. 657.
19. Joachim Fest, *op. cit.*, p. 219.
20. Roger Moorhouse, *op. cit.*, p. 199.

Chapter 9: Valkyrie
1. Sir Ian Kershaw, *Hitler: 1936–1945 Nemesis* (London: Penguin Books, 2001), p. 657.
2. *Murdering Hitler: The Failed Attacks on Hitler's Life*, www.valkyrie.greyfalcon.us.
3. Peter Hoffmann, *Hitler's Personal Security: Protecting the Führer, 1921–1945* (New York: Da Capo Press, 2000), p. 247.
4. *Ibid*, p. 247.
5. *Ibid*, p. 248.
6. *Murdering Hitler, op. cit.*
7. Sir Ian Kershaw, *Hitler: 1936–1945 Nemesis* (London: Penguin Books, 2001), p. 672.
8. *Murdering Hitler, op. cit.*
9. Sir Ian Kershaw, *op. cit.*, p. 674.
10. *Ibid*, p. 674.
11. Peter Hoffmann, *op. cit.*, p. 252.
12. *Ibid*, p. 252.
13. *Murdering Hitler, op. cit.*
14. Sir Ian Kershaw, *op. cit.*, p. 675.
15. Pierre Galante, *Operation Valkyrie* (London: Harper and Row, 1981), pp. 11–12.
16. *Ibid*, p. 205.
17. *Murdering Hitler, op. cit.*
18. Roger Moorhouse, *Killing Hitler: The Third Reich and the Plots to Kill the Führer* (London: Vintage, 2007), p. 205.
19. Pierre Galante, *op. cit.*, p. 209.
20. *Ibid*, p. 210.
21. Sir Ian Kershaw, *op. cit.*, p. 680.

22. Pierre Galante, *op. cit.*, p. 209.

23. Sir Ian Kershaw, *op. cit.*, p. 206.

24. *Ibid*, p. 682.

25. *Ibid*, p. 207.

26. Peter Hoffmann, *op. cit.*, p. 252.

27. *Interrogation report: Hauptmann Gaum, 3rd Panzer Grenadier Battalion, Führer Begleit Brigade*, FO/1020/3471, The National Archives (Public Record Office), Kew.

28. Peter Hoffmann, *op. cit.*, p. 253.

29. *Interrogation report: Hauptmann Gaum, op. cit.*

30. *Ibid.*

31. *Ibid.*

32. Heinz Linge, *With Hitler to the End: The Memoir of Hitler's Valet* (New York: Frontline Books, 2009), pp. 12–13.

33. *Interrogation report: Hauptmann Gaum, op. cit.*

34. *Ibid.*

35. Peter Hoffmann, *op. cit.*, p. 255.

36. *Ibid.*

Chapter 10: Storm of the Century

1. Earl F. Ziemke, *Battle for Berlin: End of the Third Reich* (New York: Ballantine Books, 1969), p. 71.

2. Peter Hoffmann, *Hitler's Personal Security: Protecting the Führer, 1921–1945* (New York: Da Capo Press, 2000), p. 257.

3. C.G. Sweeting, *Hitler's Squadron: The Führer's Personal Aircraft and Transport Unit, 1933–1945* (London: Brassey's, 2001), p. 72.

4. Peter Hoffmann, *op. cit.*, p. 258.

5. Ronald Pawly, *Hitler's Chancellery: A Palace to Last a Thousand Years* (Ramsbury: The Crowood Press Ltd, 2009), p. 151.

6. Peter Hoffmann, *op. cit.*, p. 261.

7. Steven Lehrer, *The Reich Chancellery and Führerbunker Complex: An Illustrated History of the Seat of the Nazi* Regime (New York: McFarland & Company, Inc., 2006), p. 122.

8. *'Wartime relic found in archives of Green Howards Regimental Museum'* by Mark Foster, *The Northern Echo*, 1 February 2010.

9. See: Steven Lehrer, *The Reich Chancellery and Führerbunker Complex: An Illustrated History of the Seat of the Nazi Regime* (New York: McFarland & Company, Inc., 2006).

10. Antony Beevor, *Berlin: The Downfall 1945* (London: Penguin Books, 2003), p. 255.

11. *Ibid*, p. 255.
12. *Ibid*, p. 262.
13. Thomas Fischer, *Soldiers of the Leibstandarte* (J.J. Fedorowicz Publishing, 2008), pp. 42–3.
14. Antony Beevor, *op. cit.*, pp. 310–12.
15. *Ibid*, p. 297.
16. *Ibid*, p. 275.
17. Kershaw, Sir Ian, *Hitler: Nemesis, 1936–1945* (London: Penguin Books, 2001), p. 803.
18. Ronald Pawly, *op. cit.*, p. 173.
19. Antony Beevor, *op. cit.*, pp. 276–7.
20. C.G. Sweeting, *op. cit.*, p. 91.
21. Peter Hoffmann, *op. cit.*, p. 195.
22. Roger Moorhouse, *Killing Hitler: The Third Reich and the Plots to Kill the Führer* (London: Vintage, 2007), p. 172.

Chapter 11: The Eagles Have Flown

1. Ronald Pawly, *Hitler's Chancellery: A Palace to Last a Thousand Years* (Ramsbury: The Crowood Press Ltd, 2009), p. 1.
2. Sir Ian Kershaw, *Hitler: Nemesis, 1936–1945* (London: Penguin Books, 2001), p. 813.
3. *Ibid*, p. 817.
4. Antony Beevor, *Berlin: The Downfall 1945* (London: Penguin Books, 2003), p. 343.
5. John Erickson, *The Road to Berlin: Continuing the History of Stalin's War with Germany* (Boulder: Westview Press, 1983), pp. 603–4.
6. Antony Beevor, *op. cit.*, p. 358.
7. Heinz, Linge, *With Hitler to the End: The Memoirs of Hitler's Valet* (London: Frontline Books, 2009), p. 199.
8. *Ibid*, p. 199.
9. Ronald Pawly, *op. cit.*, p. 174.
10. Heinz Linge, *op. cit.*, p. 1.
11. *Ibid*, p. 200.
12. Sir Ian Kershaw, *op. cit.*, pp. 829–31.
13. Heinz Linge, *op. cit.*, p. 200.
14. *Ibid*, p. 1.
15. *Ibid*, pp. 1–2.
16. Anton Joachimsthaler, *The Last Days of Hitler: The Legends, The Evidence, The Truth* (London: Brockhampton Press, 1999), p. 210.
17. *Ibid*, p. 175.

18. *Ibid*, p. 210–11.
19. Antony Beevor, *op. cit.*, p. 381.
20. *Ibid*, p. 367.
21. Erich Kempka, *Die letzten Tag mit Adolf Hitler* (Oldendorf: Preussisch, 1981), p. 281.
22. Antony Beevor, *op. cit.*, pp. 381–3.
23. Ronald Pawly, *op. cit.*, p. 177.
24. *Ibid*, p. 177.
25. C.G. Sweeting, *Hitler's Squadron: The Führer's Personal Aircraft and Transport Unit, 1933–1945* (London: Brassey's, 2001), p. 93.
26. Ronald Pawly, *op. cit.*, p. 174.
27. *Ibid*, p. 177.
28. Antony Beevor, *op. cit.*, p. 383.
29. *'DNA test closes book on mystery of Martin Bormann'* by Imre Karacs, *The Independent*, Bonn, 4 May 1998.
30. Ronald Pawly, *op. cit.*, p. 152.
31. Antony Beevor, *op. cit.*, p. 383.
32. *'Russian who 'cremated' Adolf Hitler refuses to reveal where he scattered his ashes'* by Will Stewart, *Daily Mail*, 30 April 2010.
33. *'Tests on skull fragment cast doubt on Adolf Hitler suicide story'* by Uki Goñi, *Guardian*, 27 September 2009.

Bibliography

Archives

The National Archives (Public Record Office) Kew, London.

Führergebiet and its buildings, 1944–1945, FO/1020/3471.

Notes on the Führer HQ (Nov. 44), FO/1020/3471.

Report on information obtained from PW KP/29750 SS Schutze Obernigg, FO/1020/3471.

Interrogation report: Hauptmann Gaum, 3rd Panzer Grenadier Battalion, Führer Begleit Brigade, FO/1020/3471.

Books

Beevor, Antony, *Stalingrad*, London: Penguin Books, 2007.

Beevor, Antony, *Berlin: The Downfall 1945*, London: Penguin Books, 2003.

Boeselager, Philip von, *Valkyrie: The Plot to Kill Hitler*, London: Phoenix, 2009.

Campbell, Bruce, *The SA Generals and the Rise of Nazism*, Lexington: Kentucky University Press, 1998.

Dietrich, Otto, *The Hitler I Knew: Memoir of the Third Reich's Press Chief*, New York: Skyhorse Publishing, 2010.

Dunstan, Simon & Williams, Gerrard, *Grey Wolf: The Escape of Adolf Hitler*, New York: Sterling, 2011.

Erickson, John, *The Road to Berlin: Continuing the History of Stalin's War with Germany*, Boulder: Westview Press, 1983.

Evans, Richard, *The Third Reich at War*, New York: Penguin Books, 2008.

Fest, Joachim, *Plotting Hitler's Death: The German Resistance to Hitler, 1933–1945*, London: Phoenix, 1996.

Fischer, Thomas, *Soldiers of the Leibstandarte*, J.J. Fedorowicz Publishing, 2008.

Galante, Pierre, *Operation Valkyrie*, London: Harper and Row, 1981.

Hoffmann, Peter, *Hitler's Personal Security: Protecting the Führer, 1921–1945*, New York: Da Capo Press, 2000.

Joachimsthaler, Anton, *The Last Days of Hitler: The Legends, The Evidence, The Truth*, London: Brockhampton Press, 1999.

Junge, Traudl, *Until the Final Hour: Hitler's Last Secretary*, Phoenix, 2004.

Kershaw, Sir Ian, *Hitler: Nemesis, 1936–1945*, London: Penguin Books, 2001.

Kershaw, Sir Ian, *Hitler: A Biography*, New York: W.W. Norton & Company, 2008.

Kempka, Erich, *I Was Hitler's Chauffeur: The Memoir of Erich Kempka*, Frontline Books, 2010.

Lehrer, Steven, *The Reich Chancellery and Führerbunker Complex: An Illustrated History of the Seat of the Nazi Regime*, New York: McFarland & Company, Inc., 2006.

Linge, Heinz, *With Hitler to the End: The Memoirs of Hitler's Valet*, Frontline Books, 2009.

Moorhouse, Roger, *Killing Hitler: The Third Reich and the Plots to Kill the Führer*, London: Vintage, 2007.

Pawly, Ronald, *Hitler's Chancellery: A Palace to Last a Thousand Years*, Ramsbury: The Crowood Press Ltd, 2009.

Schroeder, Christa, *He Was My Chief: The Memoirs of Adolf Hitler's Secretary*, Frontline Books, 2009.

Sweeting, C.G., *Hitler's Squadron: The Führer's Personal Aircraft and Transportation Unit, 1933–45*, London: Brassey's, 2001.

Thomas, Hugh, *SS-1: The Unlikely Death of Heinrich Himmler*, London: Fourth Estate, 2002.

Uhl, Matthias & Henrik Eberle, *The Hitler Book: The Secret Report by his Two Closest Aides*, London: John Murray, 1978.

Weale, Adrian, *Renegades: Hitler's Englishmen*, London: Warner Books, 1995.

Wilson, James, *Hitler's Alpine Retreat*, Barnsley: Pen & Sword Books Limited, 2005.

Ziemke, Earl F., *Battle for Berlin: End of the Third Reich*, New York: Ballantine Books, 1969.

Newspapers and Magazines

After the Battle
Daily Mail
Guardian
Northern Echo
The Independent

Internet Sources
'Hitler's Ultra-Secret Adlerhorst' by Irwin J. Kappes
   (militaryhistoryonline.com)
Murdering Hitler: The Failed Attacks on Hitler's Life
   (www.valkyrie.greyfalcon.us)
Third Reich in Ruins (www.thirdreichruins.com)

Index

186   *Guarding Hitler*